METROPOLITAN AMERICA

METROPOLITAN AMERICA

URBAN LIFE AND URBAN POLICY IN THE
UNITED STATES 1940–1980

Kenneth Fox

University Press of Mississippi
Jackson

© Kenneth Fox

First published in 1986 in the United States of America by the University Press of Mississippi

Printed in Hong Kong

Library of Congress Cataloging in Publication Data
Fox, Kenneth.
    Metropolitan America.
    Bibliography: p.
    Includes index.
    1. Metropolitan areas—United States—History—20th century.   2. Cities and towns—United States—History—20th century.   3. Urban policy—United States.
4. United States—Race relations—History—20th century.
5. Middle classes—United States—History—20th century.
I. Title.
HT334.U5F66   1986   307.7′64′0973   85–15057
ISBN 0–87805–283–6

Contents

List of Plates

Preface

This book grew out of efforts to communicate a point of view to students in my classes. I was teaching contemporary urban development and policy every academic year, and at the end of each year I found myself dissatisfied with the books and articles I had asked the students to read, and with the strategy I had employed to teach the material. The following year I would assign new books and initiate a new strategy. Just as the third go-around was ending, Bill Issel approached me about writing a comprehensive, compact history and analysis of urban development and policy since the Depression. I had thought of trying to write my own book, but not seriously enough to put other projects aside. His invitation was the incentive I needed.

I had two important purposes in those classes and I have pursued the same two purposes here. The first is to show, by the example of recent US urban history, that official government data, social science research, and sound logical argument can shape and change government policy. While some political scientists and policy experts believe this, they are a minority; most experts believe that policy-making is overwhelmingly political. Social scientific theories, research and skilful polemicising have their role, unquestionably, but in the main analysts of policy-making believe that policies evolve from the interplay of powerful interests, leaders, institutions and constituencies. The history of urban policy since the Depression of the 1930s argues otherwise, in my view, and I have striven to convince readers I am right. Those who espouse the 'politics of policy-making' are forewarned.

My second purpose, aimed specifically at *urban* policy, is to argue that good national policy for cities depends upon coordinating government action with what I have called the 'forces of settlement'. The most important of these forces arise from people's preferences about the kind of community they want to live in. Their desires are fulfilled to some extent through the formation of new communities and to some extent by efforts to change existing communities. The most direct way people satisfy their preferences about the kind of community they want to live in, however, is by picking themselves up from where they are and moving to a place that better resembles the ideal in their mind's eye.

In order to coordinate with these settlement forces, urban policy must anticipate not only how people would like existing urban communities to change, but also which kinds of existing urban communities they will move away from, which kinds they will prefer moving to, and which kinds of new communities will appear and flourish. Two monumental migrations dominate US urban history since the Depression: the 'Second Great Migration' of black people from the rural South to metropolitan central cities in the North, Middle West and Far West, beginning with the onset of the Second World War and continuing into the 1960s; and the 'suburban exodus' of young working-class and white-collar couples and families from central cities to suburbs, the beginning immediately after the Second World War and extending into the 1970s. Federal urban policy anticipated neither of these migrations accurately, and did not alter its strategy as their significance became more and more apparent.

My purposes are not disinterested ones; I believe better research and argument can foster better urban policy. I have described the years from the late 1930s to 1980 as a distinct era of American urban development, the metropolitan era. If I am right, the metropolitan era is closing and a new era of urban development is beginning. My hope for this book is that it will contribute to better policy-making as the new era unfolds.

In addition to my two purposes, an important influence on the way I wrote the book was the prospect that it would be read both in England and in the United States. I tried my best to look at cities and suburbs I knew well with a foreigner's eyes, and to consider the history of the era from an ocean's distance away. One overwhelming impression emerges from such an exercise: the tremendous similarity of development in metropolitan cities and suburbs everywhere in the country, North to South, Atlantic to Pacific. To the foreigner, Los Angeles' San Fernando valley and New York's Nassau county are not identical, but they are both characteristically 'American suburban'.

What the 140 metropolitan areas delineated by the Census Bureau in 1940 had in common, and the 318 areas of 1980 as well, was an American metropolitan *culture*. Foreign visitors do not find this surprising, but to Americans it borders on the heretical. Their protestations express the intense competitiveness Americans feel about culture, the sense that accepting any fixed style of living would be equivalent to abandoning the American dream of progress and opportunity. I have tried to present a synthesis that incorporates both the foreigner's perception of a common metropolitan culture and the Americans' belief that their cultural options remain perpetually open, even after buying a split-level suburban house, a wide-track V-8 station wagon, a thirty-inch colour television, a side-by-side refrigerator-freezer with automatic ice maker, and an electric in-sink garbage disposal unit.

In the end, the aspect of metropolitan culture that foreigners find most characteristically American may be this refusal to accept the products and life style of the moment as in any way permanent. Few Americans are aware of the great increase in British interest in the US and its culture during the 1970s, of the waning of British snobbery about the 'former colonies' and the rise of sincere admiration for Americans. Not only do British teenagers wear jeans and dream of visiting Nashville, Tennessee, the Mecca of country and western music, but American Studies has acquired the aura and popularity among British university and polytechnic college students that British literature and history had for American undergraduates for more than a century. Perhaps for corresponding reasons, British history went into disastrous decline in US colleges in the 1970s.

As Americans realise that their culture is held in esteem in England and Europe, their collective reluctance to embrace a cultural tradition may abate. Suburbanites may begin to admit that the typical American community is a complex metropolitan area of more than 1 million population, and not the self-governing descendant of a colonial New England village that they imagine their unincorporated school, sewer and water district to be. I have no doubt that research and reasoned argument can produce better urban policy. Whether historical analysis can produce 'better' culture, or rather better understanding of the culture common to more than 150 million metropolitan residents, is less clear. At a minimum, judging from response to my presentations of the book's ideas in classes and at conferences, the notion of a national metropolitan culture in the post-war period is controversial. Out of controversy can come new characterisations of the 1940–80 period and new insights into the cultural factors in urban development.

I am indebted to many for their ideas and assistance. For ideas, first and foremost, to Charles Levenstein, Peter Meyer and Ira Katznelson, each of whom has asserted that the social class structure of the US is as much a function of community and culture as it is of the ownership of capital and control of the workplace. Manuel Castells, by way of his book *The Urban Question*, provided the rudiments of my analytic framework relating urban policy to 'forces of settlement'. He of course bears no responsibility for how I have used his conceptualisation. Nor do Robert and Helen Lynd, whose classic anthropology of the class structure of the 1920s, *Middletown*, was very important to the book's development. Ferruccio Gambino helped me to recognise the importance of migration as a form of racial, class and group activism. Battista Borio originated the diffuse economy analysis in chapter 8. Evan Stark provided crucial encouragement and invaluable criticism at every stage. Robert Wood shared his insights on policy with me and gave the first draft a tremendously helpful critical reading. Seymour Mandelbaum also helped greatly with a sympathetic commentary and his friendly support. William Issel's role was quintessential, without him the book never would have been written. He also served as a marvellously constructive and supportive editor.

Others who were crucial to the book's evolution include my students at two State University of New York campuses, Binghamton and Old Westbury, and at the University of New Haven, especially Brenda Brown, who asked a simple question that even the entire book answers only in part, and Kathy Wimer, who understood at an early stage what I was trying to argue about policy. Friends and colleagues who also assisted include Matthew Edel, Ann Markusen, William Barnes, who got me to San Francisco at the right moment, Mark Gelfand, Richard Burton, who argued with me about the urban crisis, Phillip Singerman and Henry Fisher, who helped me understand policy's impact on city governments, and Christopher Brookeman, William Issel's partner as series editor. I am grateful to Marshall Kaplan for his comments. Cole Harrop at United Press International Photo Library and Lucinda Burkepile at the New Haven Colony Historical Society provided invaluable assistance in locating real photographs resembling the imaginary ones I hoped to find. Thanks to Terry Dintenfass, and also Chris Wohler, for permission and assistance in reproducing *The Ironers* by Jacob Lawrence. Thanks to Richard French for assistance in obtaining permission to photograph Village Creek and for sharing his insights and experiences with me.

I am especially grateful to my excellent and sympathetic editor at Macmillan, Vanessa Peerless, for her work on the book and for her helpfulness and patience. The typing, and later word processing, I did myself; however, much gratitude is due to IBM for the PC and to MicroPro International for WordStar. To my wife, Susan Logston, very special appreciation, particularly for the day I deleted half a chapter and for persuading me not to work on the manuscript at the beach.

Introduction

The years between the Depression of the 1930s and the 1980s form a distinct era of the urban history of the United States, the *metropolitan era*. Metropolitan areas were the prevailing type of urban community in those years and the characteristic form of a metropolitan area, the large central city and its surrounding suburban fringe, shaped the interaction of urban forces, institutions and ideas. Three great events dominate the period's political and social landscape: the development of the suburbs and the forging of a suburban middle class beginning in the late 1940s, the riots of the 1960s, and the urban crisis of the late 1960s and early 1970s. The three events and their significance will absorb much of our attention. Equally important will be the metropolitan context in which suburban development, the riots, and the urban crisis occurred.

In defining a beginning, an end, and a particular character to a historical period, we attempt to provide a meaningful perspective on what transpired. Describing the 1940–80 period as 'metropolitan' establishes one framework for interpreting the major events, as well as the less spectacular occurrences and the short- and long-term trends. Another characterisation would frame the major events differently. Their significance, and their relationship to other developments of the period, might change considerably. The value of the analysis of events and trends presented here depends upon the validity of the metropolitan perspective, and vice versa. Let us begin with an overview in Section I, followed by a plan of the book in Section II.

I

In 1965, and more dramatically in 1967, Americans were shocked by several of the most extraordinary incidents in the nation's history. The black communities of Watts, California, a neighbourhood of Los Angeles (August 1965), Newark, New Jersey (July 1967), and Detroit, Michigan (August 1967) erupted spontaneously and

1

unexpectedly in rioting on a scale that even the participants could scarcely comprehend. Throughout the country and around the globe, people watched the television coverage in disbelief. They wondered how such outbreaks could occur in the world's wealthiest, most democratic and most open society. The full proportions of the rioting only became apparent several years later. Between 1964 and 1970 more than a hundred cities experienced major violent disturbances. Watts, Newark and Detroit began to seem part of something very like a revolution.

Another quieter revolution had been in progress twenty years when the riots erupted. Between the end of the Second World War and the mid 1960s, the rapidly expanding white-collar category of workers took the lead in forging a new social class: the middle class. Two classes divided American urban society before the Great Depression of the 1930s. The upper one-third of city dwellers constituted the business class. The remaining two-thirds belonged to a sharply delineated working class, distinct from the business class in its speech, style of dress, attitudes, and patterns of day-to-day living. In the post-war era a broad middle class eclipsed both the business and working classes. By the 1970s, three Americans out of every four considered themselves middle class. The 1960s riots disturbed the middle class intensely, in part because the middle-class revolution had not required anger and violence.

METROPOLITAN REVOLUTIONS IN A METROPOLITAN SOCIETY

Both post-war social revolutions were distinctly metropolitan events. The major trends of national political, social, economic and cultural change since the Great Depression and the Second World War do not explain why a racial and a class transformation of American society should have occurred. No intimations preceded the riots; even the big city black communities that mounted them were amazed by the level and duration of the violence year upon year, city after city. Nor was it immediately apparent, in the case of the middle class, why people in urban white-collar occupations would want to separate themselves so deliberately from the working class of their parents, childhood friends and fellow employees. The core of the new middle class worked for the same monopoly corporations that employed millions of factory workers in basic industries, yet the white-collar workers chose to pursue their destiny independently.

The two revolutions had such a dramatic national impact because metropolitan areas, central cities and their suburban fringes, have been the prevailing type of American community in the post-Depression, post-war period. Metropolitan area residents constituted two-thirds of the national population by the 1960s and metropolitan influences strongly affected most of the remaining third. We can justly call the 1940–80 period the 'metropolitan' era of United States history. To understand the two revolutions, we must examine them in relation to metropolitan area economic, social and political structure, and the forces acting within and upon metropolitan communities. Also a better understanding of the two revolutions will help us chart the implications of America's becoming a metropolitan society.

Accurate interpretation of the riots is possibly only through an appreciation of their metropolitan context. After the Newark riot, President Lyndon Johnson appointed a prestigious commission to investigate all the riots and draw conclusions that would indicate appropriate responses to the violence. The commission took to heart the President's request for a clear statement. 'Our nation', they proclaimed, on the basis of massive investigations and analyses, 'is moving toward two societies, one black, one white – separate and unequal.'

The report supporting this remarkable assertion wrapped up the riots and their causes in a tidy package. White America controlled the nation's economy and its social structure, and was enjoying the fruits of economic expansion and social mobility. Black America confronted exclusion and repression, restricted to second-class opportunities and confined to central city ghettoes. Eventually, black anger bred of righteous indignation and pride in their humanity could be contained no longer. The riots were neither irrational nor unexpected, in the commission's opinion. Rather, the report argued, rioting was the irrepressible consequence of social developments since the Second World War, and of three preceding centuries of slavery and oppression since black people were first brought to American shores.

The reality of the riots and their origins was profoundly different from the commission's portrayal. Up to the Watts incident, the common assessment of both blacks and whites was that a Second Reconstruction had been evolving since the early war years. More progress toward racial equality had been made in the twenty-five years leading up to 1965 than in any period since the premature termination of the first Reconstruction in 1877. In addition, a second major migration out of the rural South to northern and western cities, similar to the Great Migration of the First World War period, had greatly enhanced blacks' access to economic and social opportunities. The black people rioting in metropolitan central city ghettoes in the mid 1960s were better educated, better employed, and achieving greater social advancement than any generation of blacks in American history.

Most importantly, the specific nature of riot activity was not consistent with the riot commission's assertion that white oppression of blacks had precipitated the rioting. Unlike racial rioting in the nineteenth and early twentieth centuries, in which whites invaded black neighbourhoods and perpetrated violence upon black victims, it was blacks who conducted the 1960s riots. Rioting was confined entirely to black neighbourhoods; riot crowds virtually never ventured outside their own community. Riot crowds did not attack whites, with the exception of occasional beatings of whites who happened by chance to be walking or driving their cars in riot areas. Far more frequently, black rioters paid no attention to whites or yelled at them to go away. In a number of cities, whites participated in riot activity. Blacks and whites cooperated harmoniously in many of the crowd mobilisations and looting incidents during the Detroit riot.

No riots included major assaults on white institutions such as city halls, hospitals or even police headquarters. Although whites owned and ran most stores in the black neighbourhoods where the rioting occurred, post-riot analysis showed that looting and setting fire to stores occurred indiscriminately. Rioters did not target their anger exclusively at white merchants and property owners. Proportionate to their numbers, stores owned by blacks were just as likely to have been looted and burned as stores owned by whites. Even popular riot terms and rallying cries, such as 'shopping for free' and 'burn, baby, burn', revealed little concern for whites or white oppression of black people.

As more and more metropolitan area central cities experienced rioting, the metropolitan character of the riots should have been more apparent. By 1967 it was clear that blacks in cities not yet affected were working to create riots in order to add their city to the growing national list. *Every* metropolitan central city with a sizeable black community experienced a significant disturbance between 1964 and

1970, with the exception of some old Southern cities. On the other hand, rural and small town blacks made few attempts to mobilise riot activity. The national civil rights organisations did everything they could to dissociate themselves from the rioting. Black leaders kept their distance, fearing they would be castigated by riot participants. Either overtly or intuitively, black organisations and leaders perceived that the rioters were engaged in something more complex than merely giving a violent form to the civil rights campaign against racist beliefs and discriminatory practices.

The metropolitan character of the middle-class revolution received better recognition. Anxious to differentiate themselves from the working class, white-collar workers seized the opportunity presented by large suburban housing developments of the late 1940s and 1950s to lead a new style of life. At first, new suburbanites sought primarily to escape, to distance themselves from parents, from childhood friends, from working class neighbourhoods. As suburban communities asserted their social superiority and exclusiveness, buying a suburban house and adopting suburban mores and attitudes became a dependable path to middle-class status. The principal factors determining one's social class shifted from education and occupation to income, life style and community of residence. Suburban communities aided and encouraged the middle-class revolution by planning land uses, public facilities, school systems and commercial and residential development along recognisably middle-class lines. 'Suburban' and 'middle class' became synonymous.

A family structure and life style focused upon advancing the husband and father's career, and increasing his income, emerged as the suburban cultural norm. Middle-class membership, and social standing within the middle class, came to be measured in the context of home life. Distance of residence from the central city, house and lot size, costliness of furnishings, number and variety of appliances and automobiles, all served as crucial variables. The ideal number of children declined to three, and later to two, as the expense of rearing a child according to middle-class standards escalated. Propelling children into middle-class status as adults became virtually the sole objective of suburban child-rearing.

Popular commentary frequently portrayed the suburban way of life as the reward for success in middle-class occupations. More correctly, it was the invention and promulgation of a middle-class way of life in metropolitan suburban communities that constituted the essence of the middle-class revolution. The expense of the newly invented middle-class life style then became the basis for salary and promotion demands at work. Suburban family life served as the rationale for middle-class ambitions, rather than as the prize for diligent efforts. Building the foundations of the new class on family, life style and community made it possible to avoid having to organise collective struggles in white-collar workplaces or along occupational lines. This is how the 'man in the grey flannel suit' could form the vanguard of a social revolution and yet be the quintessence of 'conformity' to the corporate bureaucracy employing him.

INTERPRETING METROPOLITAN AMERICA

Americans have not heartily embraced the notion that they live in a metropolitan society. They may never accept it fully. Adjusting to the industrial city in the previous era was also a slow, uncertain process. In the last third of the nineteenth century, industrialisation, farm-to-city migration, and European and Asian immigration, turned American cities into cauldrons of turmoil. The great railroad strike of 1877 sparked rioting in many cities. The President sent the army to restore order, but the troops provoked more violence. In 1894, a strike by workers at the Pullman Palace Car Company, producer of railroad sleeping cars, escalated into a national railroad strike accompanied by sympathy strikes in many industries. It was the closest the United States has come to a general strike. Again the President called out the army, initially to deliver the mail. Again there was rioting in many cities.

But despite three decades of crisis over industrial cities, a resolution eventually emerged. The turn of the century saw an urban political reform movement and the birth of professionalised city planning amidst a 'City Beautiful' campaign for clean, open cities of monumental public buildings, broad boulevards and romantic wooded parks. City governments and public utility companies sank billions of dollars into water systems, sanitary sewers, electric streetcar networks, and electricity, gas and telephone systems. Health regulation and building codes revolutionised working-class housing. The public did more than accept industrial urbanisation: Americans took pride in their reformed, rebuilt cities.

By comparison, the metropolis has had an ambivalent reception. At first, in the late 1940s and early 1950s, suburban development created excitement. The brief but severe Depression of 1919–21 had struck within months of the First World War Armistice and many expected the Second World War boom to collapse in similar fashion. The Depression of the 1930s might resume in the late 1940s, if not something worse. Instead, the boom persisted and swelled, and the suburbs received much of the credit. Sustained prosperity was still possible under industrial capitalism.

Yet by the mid 1950s existential gloom already clouded the suburban prospect. America had purportedly become a mass society and the emptiness of suburban living was the consequence. In escaping the city, the emerging suburban middle class had left the nation's civic culture to wither and dissipate. Among the tract houses, superhighways and shopping centres, no alternative culture was flourishing. The quest for *togetherness*, the quintessence of suburban existence in the 1950s, was an outright admission of suburbia's failings. All too often, togetherness came down to parents and children huddled in front of their television set because they lacked social conventions for interacting with their neighbours.

At the centre of the booming suburban expansion, the metropolitan cities were not faring well economically. War production temporarily reopened city factories closed by the Depression, but after the war industry favoured cheap suburban land for new plants and warehouses. Prime city locations for office buildings or middle- and upper-income apartment houses went undeveloped because the cost of relocating slum residents and demolishing decrepit tenements or abandoned factories was prohibitive. Department store chains discovered that as they built new stores in suburban shopping centres, sales volume declined in their central city stores. Consumer demand was a metropolitan-wide quantity apparently. By the 1960s, chains were closing downtown stores in increasing numbers.

Sympathy for the aging industrial cities ran strong however. At the height of the war, Congress was already debating post-war revitalisation strategies. In housing legislation passed in 1949, they committed the federal government to a policy for saving metropolitan central cities. The initial urban redevelopment programme worked badly, but 1954 revisions transformed it into 'urban renewal', a more flexible adaptation to city needs and aspirations. Congress authorised more than \$10 billion in urban renewal spending over the programme's twenty-year life and almost every central city participated.

Urban renewal generated optimism about the future of the central cities and no one responded more enthusiastically to the prospect of new opportunities than black people in the towns and countryside of the old South. Migration sparked by the production boom of the Second World War grew larger in the 1950s in expectation of metropolitan central city revitalisation and development. Quietly but steadily, the black communities of northern and western metropolitan central cities swelled with new arrivals. The architects of federal 'save the central city' policy did not anticipate that the cities they planned to renew would experience tremendous growth of their black populations in the course of the redevelopment process. Much of the tension that exploded in the riots derived from failure to acknowledge the growing and changing central city black communities. In part, black communities opposed specific objectives of urban renewal in their cities, especially the destruction of significant proportions of the housing in black neighbourhoods under the mandate to 'eliminate slums and blight'. But more significant was their angry cry that urban renewal denied their very existence as a central city constituency.

The riots awakened everyone to the evolving racial and class structure of the metropolitan area. Nor was it only suburban middle-class whites who needed to have their eyes opened to the realities of black central city life. Black leaders and black professional people found themselves equally at a loss. 'We must hold ourselves responsible for not reaching them', Bayard Rustin, a prominent civil rights leader, lamented. He was referring to the failure of the civil rights movement to encompass the problems and the aspirations of working-class and poor blacks in big cities. Many middle-class blacks joined Rustin in painfully acknowledging that they had not realised the frustration and rage black ghetto youth had been suppressing within themselves.[1]

Looking forward from 1967, it appeared that the mature metropolitan community would be permanently segregated along class and race lines. The predominantly white, predominantly middle-class suburban fringe would never include more than scattered enclaves of working-class whites, middle-class blacks and working-class blacks. Multiracial and multiclass suburban communities seemed inherently unstable, eventually becoming mostly black or mostly working class. Central cities might continue to have aggressively protective upper-class and upper-middle-class neighbourhoods, but the white middle class threatened to desert the central city *en masse*. The black middle class clearly preferred the central city to the suburbs, but was separating itself increasingly from black working-class and ghetto neighbourhoods.

White and black central city working class and poor people dwelt in uneasy proximity to each other, struggling over who would control each public housing project, school or neighbourhood. Year by year, the blacks were winning these struggles because their numbers continued to increase. City working-class white populations were declining because many whites were elderly and because young white families were having fewer children than black families. When the opportunity arose, working-class whites were quick to move to the suburbs. Many working-class blacks were expending great effort commuting from the city to suburban jobs. Few were moving to the suburbs, however. Discrimination against them in the sale and rental of suburban housing was extreme, and in any case many simply preferred central city living.

It was at this juncture that the riot commission suggested America was becoming two societies, one black and one white. A more accurate interpretation would have been that the riots brought both races face to face with what metropolitan society was going to be like if the trends of the preceding twenty-five years continued. Was it possible to view a metropolitan future with enthusiasm? What could be done to rekindle optimism about life in big cities and suburbs?

CHOICE OR INEVITABILITY: THE URBAN CRISIS

The riots gave way to debate about an urban crisis. Metropolitan central city mayors clamoured to prove that first and foremost the crisis was a fiscal crisis of city governments. Urban renewal had removed severe impediments to new physical development, especially in central business districts, but now deterioration of the social climate threatened to make big cities ungovernable. Increasingly, the middle-class whites working and shopping in the central city were living in the suburbs and no longer contributing to city tax revenues by way of the property tax. City property values were declining. Raising the property tax rate tended to produce delinquency, mortgage foreclosures and abandonment. Absentee landlords of aging apartment buildings were delaying repairs, deferring their property taxes, and then forfeiting ownership when the tax collector demanded payment.

Meanwhile, on the expenditure side, the rising proportion of working class and poor people meant increasing needs for services of all kinds. City schools found it necessary to solve the poverty problems of their students before they could even begin to teach them reading or arithmetic. Subsidised lunch programmes, extensive school health services, and professional counselling for students and their families, became essential prerequisites to the educational process. City welfare, housing and social service agencies experienced tremendous increases in the need for assistance and in the cost of administration. Cities that operated hospitals and health clinics saw demands and costs skyrocket during the 1960s. Demands for police services also increased astronomically, in part because more poverty seemed to mean more crime, but more significantly because poor black victims of crime were overcoming their fear of asking the police for assistance.

At the national level, the urban crisis was a crisis of conscience. Two-thirds of all Americans were living in metropolitan areas, but more than 90 per cent of all black Americans who had left the rural South were living in metropolitan areas, the great majority of them in the largest central cities. Nominally, there was a national commitment to equal rights and equal opportunities for them. Practically, no concessions had been granted concerning where blacks had a rightful place to live, to work, to go to school, and to demand political and social recognition and influence. The big city slums had become theirs by default, and the riots had shown that they could control their communities by sheer force of numbers against the police or even the army. The crisis of conscience involved defining a national urban future in which blacks would no longer be invisible or unrecognised.

This aspect of the urban crisis included vigorous debate about appropriate locations for black people and black communities within metropolitan areas. Proposals to improve black opportunities to eventually enter the middle class called for 'opening up the suburbs' with assaults on housing discrimination and other racially exclusionary suburban practices. Competing city-oriented strategies hoped to strengthen black political and social influence, and economic wellbeing in existing black neighbourhoods through city industrial development, enriched schooling, job training and community organising. Detractors denigrated this strategy as 'gilding the ghetto'. Both strategies relied implicitly on corporate enthusiasm for hiring black workers in industry, either in new suburban factories or in rehabilitated central city plants or specially designed city industrial parks.

To city and suburban residents, the urban crisis symbolised despair for metropolitan life and its prospects. Concern surfaced most often as anger, and fear, about crime. Although crime is impossible to measure and compare accurately from one period to another, rates of violent crime in public places such as streets, parks and mass transit probably reached an extreme in the late 1960s and early 1970s. The contrast with the 1950s, probably the 'safest' decade in recent urban history, was shocking. Fear of crime was the most disturbing aspect of a pervasive unease about cities as communities, and suburbs as well. Discussion of public housing construction in suburbs, a favourite proposal of the 'opening up the suburbs' strategy, raised visions of poverty and crime implanted in healthy suburban tissue to spread like cancer until the entire metropolitan area was sick with the urban malaise. Nowhere in the metropolis would it be possible to have a sense of being in control of everyday circumstances and encounters, to know who one might meet on the street, who one's children would go to school with, who might buy the house next door if it came up for sale.

Despair deepened at the prospect that the urban crisis might not be effectively confronted and resolved. Martin Meyerson, a prominent urban political scientist, spoke for almost everyone concerned about the crisis when he wrote in 1968: 'It is to be hoped that whoever is the next President will be persuaded that his role should be to lead the nation in dealing with urban problems and achieving urban potentialities.'[2] But behind these hopes lurked fears that the processes at work in the urban crisis were largely inevitable and unalterable. Opposite Meyerson's optimism stood the pessimism of his friend and fellow urban political scientist Edward Banfield, who ended *The Unheavenly City*, his book on the urban crisis, with the gloomy prediction that cities were in for about twenty more years of decline and turmoil before the forces dominant in the late 1960s worked themselves out. Attempting to 'solve' the problems of the urban crisis with government programmes was worse than doing nothing at all, Banfield argued, for remedial programmes heightened the tensions of the crisis without speeding its resolution.[3]

Debate about programmes for alleviating the urban crisis raised very starkly the possibility that no meaningful choices were available. Confronting urban problems one at a time, such as crime, or poverty, or chronic unemployment, or inadequate education and training, might fail to generate results because of the interconnectedness and complexity of the processes causing the problems. Launching coordinated assaults on many problems would not necessarily overcome this difficulty. The favourite Democratic strategy was massive economic and social reconstruction of the central cities by the federal government, an economic and social renaissance to complement the physical redevelopment initiated by urban renewal. But as debate continued it became increasingly apparent that a strong popular consensus favouring economic and social renewal was not emerging. Any choice for taking action to resolve the urban crisis had to be supported by what Robert Wood, Assistant Secretary of the federal Department of Housing and Urban Development under President Johnson, called the 'necessary majority' of political strength. Unhappily, Wood feared, none of the proposed responses to the crisis seemed capable of evoking sufficiently numerous and powerful backing.[4]

BREAKING THE STALEMATE: REINTERPRETING URBAN DEVELOPMENT

President Nixon proclaimed the end of the urban crisis in 1973.[5] His attempt to start his second term on a hopeful note was somewhat premature, but by the time the Democratic administration of President Carter announced its urban programme, early in 1978, controversy over the urban crisis had subsided. Not that the problems constituting the crisis had been resolved; if anything, central city poverty, unemployment and neighbourhood deterioration were more entrenched than at the onset of concern about the crisis ten years before. Without the constituency worried about the urban crisis, especially black voters in central cities, Carter would have lost the 1976 election to incumbent President Ford, who made no secret of his opposition to federal involvement in big city problems. Yet within only a few months of taking office, Carter began to dissociate himself from a crisis approach. He was not uninterested in a progressive urban policy, but he feared that orienting national policy around a crisis of the metropolitan central cities would lead to programmes that absorbed tens and hundreds of millions of dollars without generating positive developments.

After a year of embarrassing confusion and delay, Carter released an urban programme purporting to deal with 'the deterioration of urban life'.[6] A detailed policy report explained that the President's approach followed upon imperatives of the 'economic and social transformation' of American life currently in progress. This transformation, from an industrial to a 'new post-industrial' economy and social system, was altering greatly the role cities would play in national life. Metropolitan central cities, the report confided, 'perhaps economically restructured and less populous than in the past – are essential to the new post-industrial economy now emerging. . . . For as long into the future as it is practical to foresee, central cities are likely to – and should continue to – remain centers for the Nation's financial, cultural and creative life.'[7]

In short, Carter had opted for the inevitability of the urban crisis, rather than for optimism and choice. The cities were deteriorating because the nation itself was in transition. Federal urban policy could confront the crisis and attempt to reverse the deterioration only by opposing, or attempting to alter, a national economic and social transformation already well under way. In preparation for defending the President against criticism, the report rejected the urban crisis approach as a policy of the past and therefore not appropriate for the post-industrial course urban development was now following. Appropriate policies for the future, the report argued, 'have to be predicated upon what new patterns of urban settlement and living are becoming and what the country wants them to become; not what they used to be or even are today.'[8]

Carter's solution to the urban crisis stalemate, delimiting one era of urban development and announcing the dawn of a new era, had the virtue of shifting controversy onto new ground. Sample surveys during the 1970s hinted that major alterations in population growth and migration trends were occurring. Carter's urban policy report used these preliminary studies to justify its assertions that the national settlement pattern was undergoing transformation. When the complete population counts of the 1980 Census became available, some analysts argued that the numbers revealed the termination of metropolitan growth relative to the proportion of the population living outside metropolitan areas. Later, following the customary reclassification of smaller cities that had grown to metropolitan area status, the Census Bureau announced that officially there had been a 6 per cent *increase* in the proportion of the nation's population living in metropolitan areas, from 69 per cent in 1970 to 75 per cent in 1980. Those who had perceived the termination of metropolitan expansion were correct about the trend in relative *rates* of growth between metropolitan and non-metropolitan parts of the country, but not about the absolute changes from 1970 to 1980.

If the growth and migration trends of the 1970s persist, Carter's proclamation of the end of the era of metropolitan expansion will prove accurate. If the trends of the 1940s, 1950s and 1960s resume, the 1970s will quickly acquire a deviant status similar to that of the 1930s. The Great Depression of the 1930s supposedly explains the curious shifts in population and social trends observed in that decade and experts could easily redefine the 1970s as a decade of 'quasi-' or 'mini-' Depression. Regardless of where growth and migration lead in the 1980s and beyond, the late 1970s were an appropriate time to reassess the direction of urban development.

II

This section sketches the plan of the book. There are two themes, urban settlement and urban policy. The importance of following the unfolding of two kinds of developments, and analysing their interaction with each other, is explained below. Each chapter highlights one theme, either settlement or policy. The chapters proceed in chronological order as much as possible, overlapping when necessary to keep both themes up to date. This method of organisation is mildly unorthodox, but the relationship between urban settlement and urban policy in the metropolitan era demands that each be treated independently as well as in conjunction. I believe the two-theme structure provides the reader with a better understanding of urban affairs in this period.

POLICY AND SETTLEMENT IN THE METROPOLITAN ERA: AN ANALYSIS WITH TWO THEMES

The book describes and analyses urban settlement and urban policy in the contemporary United States, since the Depression of the 1930s. The two revolutions and the urban crisis sketched above in Section I are its major events. The argument of the book is that the coordination, divergence and, at times, conflict between settlement and policy have shaped the urban history of this contemporary period.

URBAN SETTLEMENT DEFINED

Let us define the themes, beginning with settlement. Urban settlement concerns the formation of urban communities and their growth and changes. Most important in community development are people's intentions and actions as they locate themselves in the natural and social landscape. I have emphasised three kinds of intentions: preferences for particular types of communities; preferences in family types and sizes, such as whether grandparents should live in the household or how many children to have; and ambitions for social status, including desires to reconstitute the national social class structure. Actions consist of what I have called *forces* of settlement: *migration*, including out-migration away from a place because of its negative attributes, as well as in-migration to a place for positive reasons; *family change*, such as marriage, childbirth, separation, divorce; and *changes in work and life style*, especially when large numbers of people make similar alterations in their clothing, behaviour, tastes, occupations or employment, leisure pursuits, housing styles and appearances, for a common purpose such as giving their community a patently middle-class character.

In short, urban settlement consists of individual and group aspirations and preferences about where, how and among whom to live, and individual and concerted efforts to realise those aspirations and preferences. Urban settlement encompasses how communities form and grow, and also *what kinds* of communities form and why.

We will consider urban settlement on a national scale, emphasising the spatial distribution of the population in a national *settlement pattern*. Dividing the population between *urban* and *rural* settlement is a first approximation of the settlement pattern. A similar, but more complex, differentiation distinguishes between *metropolitan* and *non-metropolitan* populations on the basis of residence inside or outside metropolitan areas. Urban versus rural and metropolitan versus non-metropolitan are not directly comparable distinctions. Although a metropolitan area is generally considered an *urban* community, about 10 per cent of the metropolitan population qualifies as *rural* according to urban/rural criteria. Non-metropolitan settlement is even less congruent with rural settlement than metropolitan is with urban. All small cities and sizeable towns outside of metropolitan areas are *non-metropolitan*, but as long as they are densely settled and have a total population of more than 2,500, they qualify as urban settlements.

The importance of official definitions of community types introduces complications right at the outset, for official definitions are matters of policy, our other theme. The federal Bureau of the Census began using the concept of a metropolis to define a particular class of communities in preparing the Census of 1910. Some cities were very pleased. Comparison of the population and growth trends of the 'metropolitan district' of New York with the 1911 British Census population figures for Greater London inspired the Bureau to announce that around 1915 New York Metropolitan District would surpass Greater London in size.

The managing editor of the Providence, Rhode Island *Journal* and *Evening Bulletin* objected vociferously to the comparison and to the whole idea of publicising 'metropolitan districts' for American cities. Greater London, he pointed out, was an administrative area for police, fire and water services. New York Metropolitan District was no more than a conceptual invention of the Census Bureau, combining 'a series of entirely separate communities not connected in any official way with one another'.

The Director of the Census Bureau defended his comparison by pointing out that Greater London was not politically organised as a city and that economically and socially New York Metropolitan District was no less unified than the Greater London area. 'Jersey City, Newark, and other adjacent towns in New Jersey are as much a part of the industrial and social life of New York metropolis as Brooklyn is. Moreover, Jersey City, for example, is hardly more independent politically from New York than the towns in the outer ring of London outside London county are independent of the

political organization of London.' Comparing Jersey City with
Brooklyn was significant in 1911, for Brooklyn had been an
independent city up to its consolidation into the City of New York in
1898.[9]

The Census Bureau went ahead with the publication of data for
forty-four metropolitan districts in the 1910 Census volumes. We will
examine the Bureau's conception of a metropolitan district, and other
metropolitan area concepts introduced later, in Chapter 1. Our
concern here, in regard to defining *urban settlement*, is that
governmental policy designating types of communities, and the
collection and publication of information about those community
types, affects the processes of urban settlement. Small-city political
leaders, businesses, newspapers and residents have united frequently
in campaigns to boost their city and suburban population above the
Census Bureau's minimums for metropolitan status. Whether or not
a community is officially a city according to state law, or a
metropolitan area according to Census Bureau standards, can affect
its ability to attract migration or to persuade large corporations to
locate branch plants and regional offices within its boundaries.

Efforts to change a community in order to alter its status are aspects
of urban settlement. Governmental actions to define and classify
community types and settlement patterns, I have excluded from
consideration under the settlement theme. The purpose is to
emphasise, through the structure of the book's argument, the
separate origins and evolution of urban settlement and urban policy.
How communities form and change is *settlement*, how communities are
officially classified and categorised is *policy*.

The intentions and actions constituting urban settlement are
primarily social and cultural. Social status in twentieth-century
American society has been associated extremely strongly with
community and with neighbourhoods within communities. We will
discuss the most prominent example of this connection, the role of
suburban towns in the forging of the middle class, in Chapter 2.
Another example is the importance of city 'ethnic neighbourhoods' in
preserving national origin as a basis for group identification and
unity. Recently, clustering in a neighbourhood has been a means of
creating a 'gay community', whose existence encourages others to
alter their life style and appearance to become recognisable members.
No one element came first in any indispensable sense; the group, the
culture, and the community have all been mutually reinforcing.

Once settlements of various types are formed, they serve to signify the cultural and social identity of their residents to each other and to the rest of society. This signifying function has been particularly important in the contemporary period in regard to income and social class. Residential neighbourhoods in metropolitan cities and suburbs have been stratified in terms of income, and neighbourhood of residence has functioned, in turn, as the principal outward sign of one's wealth and income. Similarly with social class, large numbers of people with traditionally working-class occupations gained acceptance in the middle class by purchasing a home in a recognised middle-class community and assuming the life style and appearance characteristic of its middle-class residents. By the 1970s community of residence and life style had largely supplanted occupation as the objective basis for distinguishing between the middle class and the working class.[10]

In all, urban settlement encompasses numerous complex processes and relationships. They have in common the use of places, and spatial relationships between places, for a purpose. Geographers employ the term *space* to denote both of these characteristics: location, and also the relation of one location to another. Space is *socially constructed* in geographic analysis, emphasising the primacy of social action in shaping our three-dimensional world.

Our discussion of urban settlement will also draw upon methods developed by the sociological subfield of *human ecology*, which argues by analogy to the biological ecology of swamps or deserts that human populations function within systems of social interaction structured by their own relative locations, characteristics and movements. Human ecology emphasises that the social character of a community is in large part a function of its location relative to other communities with either similar or contrasting social characteristics. These relative locations and differing social characteristics of communities are generally the most important factor in decisions individuals make about where to live, where to work, and how great or small the distance between home and work shall be.[11]

URBAN POLICY DEFINED

Our other theme will be urban policy, meaning *governmental choices having to do with urban settlement*. Here I follow Thomas Dye, a politically conservative political scientist who has done some of the best writing on policy in the United States. Dye defines policy as 'whatever governments choose to do or not to do'. Policy analysis therefore involves discovering how governments make choices. Analysis of urban policy should reveal how governments make choices about what is *urban*.[12]

This approach to defining policy emphasises a very active awareness on the part of governments, whether federal, state or local, that they are initiating and shaping policy of a particular kind. Urban policy is *not* the sum of all laws, regulations and governmental programmes affecting cities, for many government actions having powerful effects upon cities are associated with *other* policies such as economic policy or tax policy. Our definition requires a recognition that choices are being debated *under an urban heading*.

The federal government, or state or local governments, cannot begin to make choices about how to take action on *urban* affairs, or choices about action in any other area of governmental concern either, until they delineate the *realm* or *sphere* within which they intend to act. Considerable drama and fanfare often accompany this initial process of defining a policy realm or sphere. There will be debate about which governmental functions and programmes appropriately belong within the newly defined policy area. Because policy spheres are frequently redefined, especially where federal involvement in domestic affairs is at issue, functions and programmes are often shifted from one policy realm to another. A major realignment of policy spheres we will be discussing in Chapter 7 involved the Nixon administration's creation of *social* policy and the transfer of various issues and programmes from the urban policy realm to that of social policy.

All policies have a distinct beginning point, the time when government committed itself to consider acting within a policy area. Historians of foreign affairs are especially careful to date the initiation of a policy accurately and exactly, for *when* a policy began explains a great deal about why it was begun. Domestic policy analysis benefits enormously from similar attention to timing. The federal government initiated its urban policy in 1937 with an announcement of intention by a presidential committee. Two years previously the same committee had announced an intention to initiate regional policy. This initiative fell flat on its face and regional policy never developed. The 1937 urban policy was in part a replacement for the failed regional policy. We will be discussing these initiatives in Chapter 3.

Once established, a policy realm is like a debating society. Virtually anyone can become a participant in policy controversy. What policy will be, how government will choose to act, depends in large measure on the outcome of controversy. In this, policy differs greatly from *politics*, where powerful interests and groups exert their influence to obtain desired outcomes. While some analysts assert that policy is a function of a political process, a 'politics of policy', I prefer to keep politics and policy analytically separate. Following the tradition of Max Weber, I associate policy with 'rationality' in government. Policy can be good and bad, depending on its logical consistency. Policy controversy is crucial, because it is through controversy that implications of new proposals are tested against established elements and ongoing programmes. Failings in logic can defeat a proposal more devastatingly than the most aggressive politisising. The unhappy fate of the urban crisis initiative in the early 1970s, which we will be considering in Chapter 6, resulted primarily from logical failings. Proponents could not devise and defend the necessary justifying arguments to support a major federal assault on the urban crisis.

Policy can keep separate from politics because it deals with *how* government chooses to act rather than with what government does when it finally takes action. Policy preferences therefore need not differ between political parties. I have tried to show that throughout the metropolitan era we will be examining, the most important urban policy divisions did not open up along party lines or between liberals and conservatives. Strength of numbers mattered less, in resolving several major confrontations, than compelling logical argument and long-run administrative consistency.

The history of urban policy described in the chapters emphasising the policy theme will be familiar to readers involved in policy formulation, controversy or implementation, but may come as something of a revelation to others. For example, from the late 1940s to the early 1970s urban policy pursued one grand objective: 'saving the metropolitan central cities'. Urban redevelopment and renewal were the principal means of accomplishing this objective. In 1969 the Nixon administration concluded that urban renewal had reached its limits and abandoned the 'saving the central cities' objective in favour of a new orientation. What most people outside the urban policy arena do not know, including most residents of metropolitan central cities, is that by 1977 virtually complete consensus had developed among policy participants that this was the right thing to do. True, the central cities had not been 'saved' according to any commonsense meaning of the word, but policy is not an exercise in defining issues as problems and setting about solving them once and for all. Between the two parties, the Democrats have been more at fault than the Republicans for presenting urban policy initiatives as if they were comprehensive cures for the nation's urban ills.

URBAN POLICY AND URBAN SETTLEMENT: THE PLAN OF THE BOOK

The interaction between settlement and policy has determined the course of urban affairs in the contemporary period. My purpose in treating settlement and policy as two distinct themes is to emphasise their independent dynamics as well as their interrelations. In part, President Franklin Roosevelt's administration initiated urban policy because they were striving to place all federal involvement with domestic affairs on a policy basis. The New Deal generation of officeholders, administrators and social scientists was the first to attempt to govern by a policy approach. Many miscalculations and blunders of the 1940s, 1950s, and 1960s were due to inexperience, especially in making complex programmes work. Social Security has been the greatest success; public housing has suffered from some of the unhappy miscalculations.

Urban settlement has been on a completely new footing in this era as well. Only in the period since the Second World War have manufacturing, the home-building industry, and office building and commercial real estate developers commanded the capital and the sheer physical power to undertake nationwide location and construction strategies. Much of the similarity of development in several hundred metropolitan areas is the product of their new capabilities.

Because it is recent history, there has been much more descriptive writing on the metropolitan era than explanatory analysis. In treating the two themes, I have addressed some important questions. How did the metropolitan area become the prevailing form of urban community in the decades leading up to 1940? Between 1940 and the 1970s metropolitan areas were the fastest growing sector of the nation; the number of metropolitan areas more than doubled from 140 in 1940 to 318 in 1980. What forces contributed to metropolitan growth and how did new metropolitan areas form? Will the metropolitan area continue to be the prevailing community form in the future? (I have argued that it may not.)

Concerning urban policy, where did the commitment to saving metropolitan central cities come from in the mid 1940s? Why did policy decline to adopt an anti-urban crisis orientation in the early 1970s, despite the perilous condition of most older metropolitan central cities? And why did President Carter propose in 1978 to abandon declining cities to whatever fate awaits them at the hands of post-industrial settlement forces?

Individual chapters concentrate either on settlement or policy. The three great events of the era, the development of the suburbs and the middle class, the riots of the 1960s, and the urban crisis, structure the book as a whole. Chapters 1 and 2 are settlement chapters, covering metropolitan development before 1940, and the emergence of the suburbs and the middle class. Chapter 3 describes the origins of urban policy, the commitment to saving the metropolitan central cities in the mid 1940s, and the beginnings of urban renewal and other federal programmes.

Returning to the settlement theme, Chapter 4 describes city life before the riots, in the late 1950s and early 1960s. We will examine the pre-riot character and significance of three factors very much in evidence *after* the riots: race, ethnicity, and poverty. This will provide a basis for debating which of two processes was more responsible for the urban crisis of the late 1960s and early 1970s: policy-inspired evaluations of increasing urban distress, or forces of settlement generating worsening central city conditions.

Chapter 5 discusses the riots in terms of forces of settlement, particularly migration and community formation. Chapter 6 considers policy controversy over the urban crisis with reference to the examination of city conditions before the riots in Chapter 4. Chapter 7 follows policy into the mid 1970s as its orientation shifted to federalism and community development after declining confrontation with the urban crisis. Chapter 8 concludes the book with a focus on settlement, arguing that concentration of the population in metropolitan communities ceased during the 1970s. This brought to a close the metropolitan era of urban development. At the end of Chapter 8 I have speculated on where settlement trends and community preferences may be leading, and suggested how policy debate might overcome its current drift and orient itself more decisively toward the future.

1. Settling Metropolitan America

The metropolitan pattern of United States settlement in the contemporary period is unique. Slightly less than half the nation's population lived in metropolitan areas in 1940, and by 1980 the proportion had increased to three-quarters. Most of the remaining one-quarter lived within twenty-five miles of a metropolitan area. With minor exceptions, America became a completely metropolitan society.

In addition to the overwhelming proportion of the population living in metropolitan communities, the American settlement pattern is unique in the large number of metropolitan areas that have developed, and the degree of similarity of development from area to area. Most highly urbanised countries have several distinctly differing types of urban areas: one extremely large metropolis, usually the national capital; a number of moderate sized metropolitan areas; and a series of smaller independent cities. A considerable proportion of the population may live in small towns and villages dotting an agricultural countryside. In the United States, the metropolitan areas predominate, while the population in small towns, villages and countryside, away from metropolitan areas, is no greater than 5 per cent of the national total. Whether the largest metropolis, New York, differs enough from other metropolitan areas to be classed with London, Paris, Rome and Tokyo as a *world city* is a controversial question. From abroad, New York looks exceptional. At home, the tendency has been to deny it special status.

Today's typical American community is a metropolitan area of more than 1 million people. More than half the national population lives in these larger metropolitan areas. Yet as recently as 1918, half the national population was *rural*, which meant they lived in communities of less than 2,500 people. Metropolitanisation has been a very recent and a very rapid transformation. In this chapter we will follow the rise of metropolitan settlement, beginning in the 1890s. The settlement forces defined in the Introduction play the prominent roles, especially migration and community formation. Policy is involved in relation to federal definitions of metropolitan areas and their impact on settlement forces.

The settling of metropolitan America occurred in stages. First, the concept of the metropolitan area evolved and became popular. This occurred between 1890 and 1920. The metropolitan area originated as a statistical method of compensating for the failure, or inability, of large cities to expand their political boundaries when they grew. The metropolitan area provided a standardised means of measuring the full extent of a large city's development, so that cities could be compared accurately with each other. As the original version of the concept, the *metropolitan district*, became familiar, large cities began to formulate metropolitan strategies for their industrial and commercial growth.

Metropolitan development quickly proved desirable to both capital and labour. The turn of the century was the period of transition from the competitive to the oligopolistic or *monopoly* phase of industrial capitalism in the United States, highlighted by the great industrial merger movement of 1895–1904. The new monopoly industrial corporations tended to disperse production among *branch plants* in several regions of the country and by the 1910s a preference for locating branch plants in industrial suburbs of large cities had emerged. Also in the 1910s, labour migration began to intensify its focus upon metropolitan cities as desirable destinations. Very large cities had been the preferred target of domestic migration and foreign immigration since the 1880s. Between 1900 and 1920 the trend toward medium-sized cities began that eventually populated the more than three hundred metropolitan areas of today. The second section of the chapter describes the metropolitan strategies of capital and labour.

Metropolitan development spread to all regions of the country in the decades from 1910 to 1940. Regional differences in settlement diminished as metropolitan growth superimposed itself on existing patterns. Thus large proportions of the land area of the central and southern sections of the country continued to be agricultural, but the agricultural population was shrinking. Cities and towns were growing, primarily because of migration from the regions' agricultural areas. Growth of cities and towns was large enough to offset the rural decline. Monopoly corporations favoured the growing regional cities as locations for new factories, increasing their attractiveness to rural and small town out-migrants.

The fourth section describes the evolution of the internal structure of metropolitan areas. The two most prominent features of metropolitan structure, the central business district and the residential suburb, solidified their characteristic form in the 1920s. By the mid 1930s, it was possible to generalise about the common elements of more than one hundred metropolitan areas. The fifth section provides a tour of a prototypical metropolitan area, *c.* 1929.

The final section covers the Depression years of the 1930s. In the depths of the Depression, the metropolitan settlement pattern began to be interpreted as the *mature* form of national development. The prevailing view of the future foresaw a moderation of the Depression toward a steady economic and social equilibrium. Metropolitan areas appeared as the culmination of urban and industrial growth, as the appropriate form of urban area for a stabilised modern society.

In the late 1930s, as tensions heightened in Europe and Asia, prospects of a more exciting American future took shape. By the mid 1940s Keynesian economists were promoting an analysis of economic recovery from Depression that went on to become the primary basis for national economic policy-making in the 1950s and 1960s. Metropolitan areas were central to this Keynesian conception of the economic and social system. I have described the Keynesian approach briefly, with emphasis on the role metropolitan areas play in national development.

Americans were optimistic in the early 1940s, despite the Second World War. The view that metropolitan areas represented the maturity and stabilisation of industrial urban society was discarded. Dynamic growth and change within a metropolitan settlement pattern began to appear not just possible but probable. A new era was beginning and as soon as the war was won its shape would become clear.

CONCEPTUAL ORIGINS OF THE METROPOLITAN AREA

Separation of powers is a fundamental principle of American government. Executive, legislative and judical separation is the most familiar application of the principle. Separation of powers among federal, state and local governments has been equally important. Where urban affairs are concerned, separation has imposed fundamental structural divisions, especially between federal and local government. Unlike centralised systems of national government, federal, state and local separation denies the US federal government the power to design or alter the governing of cities. The forms and powers of city governments are controlled by state legislatures under the terms of state constitutions. What influence the national government exercises over cities must be largely persuasive.

Foreign observers have perceived best the difficulty separation of powers presents for American cities. When the British commentator James Bryce published his analysis of American government in 1888, he reported only one 'conspicuous failure': the governing of cities. Bryce meant by this not that city governments were bad, but that the structure of the national political system *as a whole* hindered national coordination of urban political, economic and social development. Three separated levels of government worked well in many ways, Bryce argued, but it was a poor structural arrangement for accommodating the urban growth of the late nineteenth century.[1]

Bryce's solution was to call upon influential people to start a national urban reform movement. His book struck a responsive chord among those already involved in reform and anti-corruption efforts in their own cities, and also among people involved in national governmental reform through professionalisation of the civil service and changes in the electoral system. During the 1890s, a nationwide *municipal reform* movement took shape, with Bryce among its prominent personalities. It was under the influence of the national municipal reform movement that the concept of the metropolitan area originated.[2]

The reform movement hit upon *municipal home rule*, strong city powers of self-government independent of the control of state governments, as the key to nationwide coordination of urban government. By persuading state legislatures throughout the country to grant their cities a set of universally recognised powers of urban government, the reformers hoped to elevate urban issues to national prominence. In so far as they succeeded, they would be able to bring nationwide influence to bear on local interests, factions and political machines in cities and implement structural changes in city government and politics.

The federal government's Bureau of the Census played a tremendously important part in the national urban reform movement by designing and publicising statistical definitions of urban areas and urban populations that emphasised the similarities of cities large and small. Government statistical offices in Germany, Britain and other European countries had demonstrated the power of standardised social data as an administrative and political tool. The Census Bureau was given permanent status in 1902 as a step toward introducing European statistical capabilities and practices into American national administration. The Bureau's chiefs were eager to prove the value of federal statistics. They chose to emphasise urban statistics in order to reap the benefits of cooperation with the urban reform movement.[3]

The Bureau planned its urban statistical programme to include all areas and populations characterised by *urban conditions*. Most of the data concerned conditions within the boundaries of established cities. But urban growth in the 1880s and 1890s had been very rapid and large cities had expanded considerably beyond their political boundaries. The Bureau's focus on urban conditions spurred the development of methods of including these areas and their populations in the national urban statistics. The first method they devised employed the concept of the *industrial district*:

> The development of the telephone, electric railway, and other means of transportation and intercommunication has to a great extent done away with the necessity of close physical association in industrial enterprises; therefore the increase in our urban population and industries is in many instances due to the development of the suburbs of the cities rather than to growth within corporate limits. Under these conditions the publication of statistics for population and industries included within the corporate limits of the city often conveys an erroneous idea of the importance of the district in which the city is located.

The report introducing the industrial district concept appeared in 1909. It presented data on thirteen cities and their suburbs collected during the 1905 census of manufactures.[4]

Two years later the Bureau prepared a report on *metropolitan districts* for the Census of 1910. Virtually identical to industrial districts, *metropolitan districts* consisted of cities of 100,000 and greater population, plus surrounding jurisdictions meeting two criteria: because they were within ten miles of the city, or because they were contiguous to the central city and other surrounding jurisdictions having a population density of greater than 150 persons per square mile. 'All of our great urban communities', the Bureau argued in justification of its new concept,

> extend far beyond the confines of the official city limits, and have suburban districts with a comparatively dense population adjacent to the boundary and so closely connected with the business center of the city by numerous electric and street car lines as to be practically a part of the city. The wage earners residing in these suburbs are employed in the city, but through the restrictions of the city boundary are not counted by the Census as part of its population.

The Bureau presented data for forty-four districts in the 1910 Census.[5]

The Bureau's emphasis on urban conditions, and its adoption of the metropolitan district as an official statistical concept, helped create national consensus about the metropolitan character of large urban areas. In the hands of real estate promoters, city boosters, chambers of commerce, banks, city officials and municipal reformers the metropolitan district concept sparked inter-city competition for metropolitan status. Some intense races resulted. When the Merchants' Association of San Francisco used Census figures to promote the size and grandeur 'Greater San Francisco' could achieve if the city of Oakland across the Bay were only annexed, Oakland merchants countered that a 'Greater Oakland' metropolis made up of Oakland and its suburbs could rival and outdistance San Francisco. Their claims became a basis for resisting annexation.

Creation of metropolitan communities by formal annexation of surrounding suburbs and close-lying cities was extremely difficult, however. New York City acquired its twentieth-century form in 1898 when a *Greater New York* movement persuaded the state legislature to consolidate the independent cities of New York and Brooklyn, plus other less densely settled territory. The prospect of a unified metropolitan New York helped the necessary popular referendum to pass narrowly in Brooklyn, but the opposition and subsequent bitterness were intense.

The Greater New York consolidation was the last time metropolitan unity was achieved with the willing cooperation of the cities and towns being absorbed. In 1906, Pittsburgh swallowed up the independent city of Alleghany in the face of strong opposition. This proved a turning point for metropolitan annexation movements; Alleghany's resistance stiffened resistance all over the country. Between 1909 and 1914 Los Angeles forced annexation on communities in a very large surrounding area under threat of denying them access to a new water supply system. After that, annexation became little more than a distasteful but possibly necessary evil for potential victims.

The metropolitan district was an ideal conceptual substitute for formal metropolitan consolidation. It allowed the people most enthusiastic about metropolitan unity, such as commercial, financial and real estate interests, to promote area-wide development without threatening the political independence of suburban cities and towns. By 1915, the idea that large cities and their developed suburban areas constituted *metropolitan communities* was an accepted notion. Political scientist Robert Brooks, a follower of Bryce, suggested freeing metropolitan areas from state government control and constituting them as 'free city commonwealths' similar to the free cities of Hamburg, Lubeck and Bremen in the German federal system. Brooks believed that free commonwealth status would encourage suburban towns to give up their resistance to metropolitan consolidation. While there were no practical attempts to implement Brooks' proposal, there were also no objections to his assertion that the metropolitan districts described by the Census Bureau were true urban communities.[6]

CAPITAL AND LABOUR IN METROPOLITAN DEVELOPMENT

The Census Bureau's emphasis on industrial development in its metropolitan district statistics encouraged both industrial capital and industrial workers to favour metropolitan settlement. Between 1910 and 1940 metropolitan areas became the foci of confrontation between manufacturing capital and the working class. For their own reasons, each found the metropolitan area a desirable community.

And their common interest in metropolitan development helped resolve confrontation in the direction of coordination and industrial growth.

Manufacturing capital was entering a new phase at the time metropolitan areas began to develop. The previous phase of industrial capitalism, the *competitive* phase, had culminated in a severe profitability crisis in the 1890s. The crisis was resolved through a great *trust* or *merger* movement in manufacturing. In the years from 1897 to 1904 one-third of all manufacturing companies disappeared into merged and consolidated firms. The five hundred largest corporations of 1904 held possession of more than half the nation's manufacturing assets. Single-product manufacturers selling to regional markets merged into monopolies dominating the entire national market and capable of launching effective international competition. The trust movement replaced competitive conditions among numerous firms in each specific line of manufactured products with monopolistic relations among very large firms producing complexes of products in major industries. The age of monopoly capitalism had dawned.

The new organisation of industry created possibilities that favoured metropolitan areas. The emergence of monopolies and monopolistic competition greatly diminished the importance of natural resources and raw materials as the rationale for industrial location. Manufacturing a product exclusively in one city, or one region, made sense when raw materials were expensive to transport and appropriately skilled workers could be found only in certain areas. The transportation and communications revolutions of the mid and late nineteenth century significantly lessened these two obstacles, and the new consolidated manufacturing firms had capabilities to exploit the resulting opportunities.

Another reason most firms in any given industry had concentrated in the same part of the country in the competitive era was to obtain the benefits of technological innovation and freelance expertise. Economists refer to these advantages as *agglomeration economies*. The paper industry had concentrated in upper New England, as had textiles; chemical production had centred in Delaware and New Jersey; steel had clustered around Pittsburgh; agricultural machinery in Illinois, Wisconsin and Minnesota. The new consolidated corporations found they could keep abreast of technological innovation without such close physical proximity to potential competitors. Agglomeration economies were no longer a compelling reason for concentrating production in one region of the country.

The monopoly manufacturers gained powerful control over raw materials and technology; physical production of goods posed few difficulties for them. Instead, the crux of profit-making shifted to minimising labour costs per unit, expanding markets, and developing new products. Metropolitan urbanisation provided a favourable environment for confronting the new challenges. Rather than expand capacity at the old centre of an industry in its competitive phase, monopoly firms began to construct branch plants within each marketing region. Preferred regional locations included metropolitan districts identified by the Census Bureau, and, in less urbanised regions of the country, cities with the potential to become metropolitan in scale.

The success of the monopoly strategy depended upon labour's enthusiasm for metropolitan living. Monopoly manufacturers needed metropolitan industrial workers for their branch plants who would also be enthusiastic consumers of manufactured products. The branch plant strategy looked to strong rural-to-urban migration for an adequate supply of wage workers, especially in less urbanised parts of the country. Successful marketing of manufactured products depended on assumption of an expanded standard of living by the migrants and their new metropolitan families. Henry Ford linked the new work and the new consumption precisely; he paid his assembly line workers the unheard-of sum of $5 a day, but he also expected them to spend their wages buying the Model T's they made.

For long-term metropolitan settlement and growth, coordination between working-class consumption patterns and manufacturer's development of new products was crucial. Monopolisation in the major product lines of 1900 did not in any way lessen the competitiveness of product development and marketing. Competition among numerous manufacturers of the same product gave way to competition among monopoly producers of different products and product lines: competition for shares of total family expenditures. Advertising provided the arena and the weapons for this competition. The objective was to shift consumption patterns by altering the style of living to which families aspired. For their part, working-class families could realise their desires for a better living standard only through changes in housing, available products and services, or the kind of community they lived in. Consumers would favour one variety of new products rather than another depending upon their usefulness as components in evolving patterns of family and community life. Again, Henry Ford's Model T illustrates the accommodation that had to occur. Ford conceived the Model T as a *rural* vehicle designed to travel well on unpaved roads and to be adaptable as a power source for stationary machines used on farms. Instead, due to metropolitan urbanisation and rural-to-urban working-class migration, the Model T succeeded primarily as an affordable urban working-class car. Ford failed to understand the implications of his success, however. General Motors completely outdistanced him in the 1920s by catering to urban tastes with increased comfort, fashionable colours and status distinctions among brands and models.

Both capital and labour could benefit from metropolitan urbanisation. If branch manufacturing plants were built in an emerging metropolitan area, rural and small-town workers could increase their incomes by migrating there. Similarly, monopoly manufacturers could benefit from dispersing production among branch plants if migration from agricultural areas and small towns brought a sufficient labour supply to the emerging metropolitan areas selected as branch plant locations. Obtaining an adequate supply of workers in less urbanised parts of the country was a more serious problem than whether lower wages could be paid compared with existing plants in established metropolitan industrial centres.

On the consumption side, metropolitan living would prove superior to rural and small-town life for working-class families only if appropriate housing, community institutions, products and services were sufficiently cheap and available. For monopoly manufacturing to benefit from producing and marketing the elements of a new metropolitan life style, however, consumer demand would have to crystallise around an established selection of metropolitan consumer goods.

Coordination of capital and labour had to come as the resolution of confrontation. Working-class enthusiasm for migration to cities and metropolitan areas ultimately proved the crucial factor. A large proportion of the new city residents were immigrants deserting rural life in Europe and Asia. Immigration largely ceased in 1917, due to the First World War and then to legislative restrictions, but black migration from the rural South began in earnest around 1910 and accelerated when the First World War began. Effects of migration were particularly striking on the Pacific Coast, where Los Angeles, San Diego, Seattle and other cities grew as if by magic in the eyes of those who believed that natural resources and transportation advantages were the only important causes of urban growth.

METROPOLITAN DEVELOPMENT IN ALL REGIONS

The scale of metropolitan growth between 1910 and 1940 was remarkable. For the US as a whole, the proportion of the population residing in metropolitan areas increased from 31 per cent in 1910 to 48 per cent in 1940. Growth was due partly to expansion of existing metropolitan areas, but primarily to elevation of smaller urban places from city to metropolitan status. The *number* of metropolitan areas rose from 58 in 1910 to 140 in 1940.[7] Also very significant was the emergence of metropolitan development in the less urbanised regions: the South East (old South), the Plains, the Mountain region and the South West.[8] By 1940 metropolitan area formation and growth had become the primary type of development in all parts of the country.

The transformation of so many cities into metropolitan areas reflected the intense concentrating force of rural-to-urban migration. One possible course for urbanisation in this period was growth of villages and towns to city scale, producing a large increase in the number of foci of urban development. Instead, a radically different pattern evolved: the number of geographic centres of urbanisation remained fairly fixed as migration concentrated population in existing cities and metropolitan areas. Between 1920 and 1940 the fastest growing areas of the country were the geographic rings lying between one and ten miles from the centres of the metropolitan central cities of 1920. Cities between 25,000 and 50,000 population in 1920, just below metropolitan status, were second in rate of growth nationally. As these cities went above 50,000 they entered the Census Bureau's metropolitan classification and contributed to increasing the number of metropolitan areas.[9]

The appearance of metropolitan development in the predominantly rural and agricultural regions in this period was even more remarkable than the rapid progress of metropolitanisation in the industrial regions of New England, the Middle Atlantic states and the Great Lakes. Table I shows changes in the proportion of the

TABLE I   Proportion of regional population residing in
metropolitan areas, and number of metropolitan areas in each
region: 1910 and 1940

	1910		1940	
Region	Proportion of pop. residing in metro. areas %	Number of areas	Proportion of pop. residing in metro. areas %	Number of areas
New England	55	9	68	12
Middle Atlantic	60	13	77	23
Great Lakes	32	12	53	30
South-East	8	8	20	33
Plains	17	5	32	14
Mountain	17	2	22	3
South-West	7	4	26	14
Far West	41	5	63	11
US (all regions)[a]	31	58	48	140

[a] Continental US only, not including Alaska and Hawaii

Sources: Warren S. Thompson, *Population, The Growth of Metropolitan Districts in the U.S.: 1900–1940,* Washington, Bureau of the Census, 1947; US Census, *Historical Statistics, Colonial Times to 1970.*

States constituting each region: NEW ENGLAND: Maine, New Hampshire, Vermont, Massachusetts, Rhode Island, Connecticut; MIDDLE ATLANTIC: New York, New Jersey, Pennsylvania, Delaware, Maryland, District of Columbia; GREAT LAKES: Ohio, Indiana, Illinois, Michigan, Wisconsin; SOUTH-EAST: Virginia, West Virginia, North Carolina, South Carolina, Georgia, Florida, Kentucky, Tennessee, Alabama, Mississippi, Arkansas, Louisiana; PLAINS: Minnesota, Iowa, Kansas, Nebraska, Missouri, North Dakota, South Dakota; MOUNTAIN: Montana, Idaho, Wyoming, Utah, Colorado; SOUTH-WEST: Oklahoma, Texas, New Mexico, Arizona; FAR WEST: Washington, Oregon, Nevada, California.

population of each region living in metropolitan areas from 1910 to 1940, as well as the number of metropolitan areas in each region and the national proportions and totals.

The South-East, the states of the old South that formed the Confederacy and brought on the Civil War of 1861–65, had been settled for as long as the industrialised regions, but up to 1910 its pattern of settlement remained predominantly agricultural with few cities and little heavy industry. Only 8 per cent of the region's population lived in its 8 metropolitan areas. Between 1910 and 1940, a dramatic rejection of agricultural and rural life styles swept the region, facilitated by the rapid mechanisation of agricultural production as the available labour force declined. Rural birth rates remained high, but it was the cities that grew, swelled by rural-to-urban migration. By 1940 the South-East region had 33 metropolitan areas and the proportion of the region's population living in metropolitan areas had increased to 20 per cent. Most importantly, a pattern was established for young people born in rural areas to pursue their opportunities as adults in metropolitan areas either within the region or elsewhere in the country.

The South-West, with most of its population concentrated in the state of Texas, also experienced a dramatic shift toward a metropolitan settlement pattern. The number of metropolitan areas increased from 4 in 1910 to 14 in 1940, and the proportion of the population classified metropolitan from 7 to 26 per cent. Metropolitan settlement was not yet dominant by 1940, but the metropolitan population was growing rapidly while rural areas and small towns were stabilising or declining. These were the years of the great oil boom in Texas and Oklahoma. Growth associated with oil need not have been metropolitan, however. In part, corporations, large retailers and outside capital favoured metropolitan development, and in part, as in the South-East and other less urbanised regions, rural and small-town residents opted for life in the emerging metropolitan centres.

Metropolitan development established itself in the two other less urbanised regions, the Plains and the Mountain region, by 1940, but did not become dominant until the 1950s and 1960s. Agriculture and mining were the major industries here and both went into decline after the First World War. The Depression of the 1930s had its most severe impact on these regions. As population growth revived in the post-war years, it consisted almost entirely of metropolitan expansion.

By 1970, the Plains region had 20 metropolitan areas where 49 per cent of its population resided, and 59 per cent of the Mountain region's population was living in its 9 metropolitan areas. As in the South-East and South-West before 1940, metropolitan growth superimposed itself on an agricultural and resource-based settlement pattern that had stabilised. Post-war agriculture and mining adopted capital-intensive production methods that did not require increases in the labour force to raise productivity. Meanwhile metropolitan areas grew as a result of migration away from towns and rural areas within the two regions, and migration from other parts of the country. Colorado's population had become 72 per cent metropolitan by 1970 primarily because of the fantastic growth of the Denver metropolitan area. Denver's growth depended in part on the resources and agriculture of the regional economy, but more importantly on its connections to the national and international economies by way of the national system of metropolitan centres.[10]

The difficulty of accepting the metropolitan character of American settlement and American life styles since 1940 has been greatest in these four previously less urbanised regions. Many residents of suburban Phoenix or Dallas vehemently protest that metropolitan development in the South-West differs fundamentally from the suburbs of New York, Philadelphia or Chicago. While important differences exist, they have been much less a function of regional variation than of the timing of development. Metropolitan building of the 1920s tended to be similar in whatever region of the country it occurred. Residential suburbs developed before the First World War in widely distant metropolitan areas will tend to resemble each other more closely than they resemble suburbs in their own areas built in the 1920s or later.

Probably the most important reason metropolitan development did not encounter resistance as it spread to all regions of the country in the 1910–40 period was a desire not to be left out of the mainstream of national economic growth. By the 1920s ambitious interests among capital and labour had recognised the mutual advantages of the metropolitan settlement pattern. What regional resistance did occur was more the initiative of capital than of labour. For example, industrial and propertied white elites in the South-East were reluctant to draw large numbers of black migrants out of agricultural areas in their region into industry or into cities. As a result, most of the Great Migration of blacks in the 1910s and 1920s flowed out of the South-East region to cities in the North-East, Middle Atlantic and Great Lakes regions. South-East cities and industry did receive *white* out-migrants from agriculture and rural areas with enthusiasm, and metropolitan development became prominent in any case. The hundreds of thousands of blacks who left Alabama, Mississippi, Georgia and other South-East states for Pittsburgh or Cleveland were determined not to let their regional origins prevent them from missing the opportunities metropolitan development appeared to hold. Many rural whites from these states also followed the routes of the black migration to north-eastern and mid-western cities in this period, in pursuit of the same opportunities.[11]

METROPOLITAN AREAS ACQUIRE STRUCTURE: THE RISE OF THE SUBURBS AND THE CENTRAL BUSINESS DISTRICT, 1900–1930

The metropolitan area acquired its characteristic structure by a process of evolution from late nineteenth-century industrial city origins. The Census Bureau's metropolitan districts of 1910 were very large industrial cities that had expanded beyond their political boundaries. Their industrial growth was spreading around and beyond residential suburban towns established in the 1880s and 1890s. Electric streetcar lines were overwhelming villages in the nearby countryside with haphazard urban sprawl. Streetcars had turned the city centres into nightmares of wires and hopelessly snarled traffic. The need for a better arrangement was obvious, but new spatial patterns took time to emerge.

Late nineteenth-century industrial cities were extremely densely concentrated. Competition for central locations was intense. As industrial cities grew, their density increased. The number of residents per square mile living in central districts of American cities rose steadily from 1820 to peak levels in the 1890s. Population density in parts of New York City's Lower East Side in the 1890s approached 900 persons per acre, approximately 500,000 per square mile, probably the highest residential concentration ever achieved in modern history. Density declined toward the edges of the industrial city, but its boundary with the countryside was sharp. There were no zones of semi-urban transition separating country and city. In the 1880s a suburban style of house appeared and dominated new residential development at the expanding edges of large cities. But with the coming of the electric streetcar in the 1890s these districts lost their suburban qualities. Detached duplexes and triple-deckers, so fashionably different from the rows of centre city townhouses in the 1890s, were no longer considered suburban by 1920.[12]

A permanent differentiation between large cities and their suburban fringes did not begin to form until after 1900. Development patterns, land uses and building styles appeared that were very distinct from older, more central neighbourhoods. Later, in the 1920s and 1930s, when these areas experienced secondary development and steep increases in their density, they preserved their strong differentiation from central city patterns.

Formation of the metropolitan suburban fringe began with the appearance of three types of suburban development: manufacturing enclaves, working-class residential communities, and business-class residential communities. Manufacturers found the suburban fringe particularly attractive. Large industry had thrived in the centres of cities in the mid nineteenth century because wave upon wave of migrants provided cheap enthusiastic labour. Under the pressures of war, during the Civil War of 1861–5, the industrial working class became more organised and militant. Militance increased during the Depression of 1873–9, and national mass organisations formed in the 1880s. Then the Depression of 1893 set the scene for the Pullman Strike of 1894, a series of events approximating the proportions of a national general strike. The intensity of confrontation between capital and labour had become extreme. When prosperity returned in 1897, manufacturers building new plants looked to suburban locations as an escape from conflict and an opportunity to achieve a cooperative arrangement with their workers. Manufacturing enclaves, clusters of factories beyond the built-up area of the city, began to form.

Technology played an indispensable role in suburbanisation, but as means rather than cause. Up to 1890 coal was the prevailing source of power for industry. Urban factories had to locate close to railroad yards or docks where the coal could be delivered easily. The new suburban factories took advantage of the flexibility made possible by the introduction of high-voltage electrical systems in the late 1880s and the extremely rapid formation of large electric utility companies. Electricity was equally accessible and cheap anywhere within a utility company's network.

Electric streetcar systems facilitated the second type of suburban development: the working-class residential suburb. In 1888, Frank Sprague put into operation the first dependable city-wide electric streetcar network in Richmond, Virginia. By 1895, 850 cities and towns had built electric streetcar systems involving 10,000 total track miles. Streetcar companies extended their lines considerably beyond the built-up areas of the city. As they planned the lines, they bought up cheap land along the future streetcar routes. Once the systems were in operation, streetcar companies and their affiliated real estate enterprises reaped their biggest profits from resale of the land for home building and suburban community development.

Large-city electric streetcar companies built star-like systems reaching far out from the city centre, with cross-town connectors at medium distances. One fixed fare and free transfers was the typical rate structure, making the travel cost for a factory worker the same whether he rode in toward the centre on a single line, or transferred across and then out to a suburban factory. Additional small systems developed within the emerging suburban fringe as towns close to large cities built short streetcar lines in hopes of attracting manufacturers seeking suburban locations. Both kinds of streetcar networks stimulated the building of suburban working-class housing and the emergence of the working-class suburb as a fully formed community.

The third type of metropolitan suburban development, the business-class suburb, originated before the turn of the century. As the suburban fringe evolved, business-class suburbs proliferated rapidly. The wealthier reaches of the merchant, managerial and professional classes had established distant commuter towns as early as the 1850s, when steam railroads first became comfortable and convenient. Railroads commissioned prominent architects such as Henry Hobson Richardson to design commuter stations. The relation of land and house costs to commuting fares set parameters for business-class suburban growth. The very wealthy could afford both a town house and a country house. The next stratum sorted itself according to taste between those preferring moderately large town houses on very expensive city land and those choosing large suburban estates involving low land costs but sizeable annual railroad fare expense.

Around 1900 the railroads began installing electrified service twenty and sometimes thirty or more miles into the suburban fringe. High-speed 'inter-urban' electric trolley lines enriched the fringe network further. Fares were much lower than the old steam railroad service. Suburban residence at distances of fifteen miles, twenty or even farther became convenient and affordable for a broad business class.

While Ebenezer Howard and Patrick Geddes dreamed of deconcentration by means of garden cities entirely apart from England's industrial centres, American real estate developers were hurrying to make real the business-class vision of an urban village away from the city and yet completely tied to it for work, shopping and leisure. It was in one of these business-class villages, the Chicago suburb of Oak Park, that Frank Lloyd Wright began his career, building forerunners of his world famous 'Prairie' house for commuting business and professional men. Artistic genius aside, much of Wright's influence on American architecture must be credited to the fact that he was designing and building for the new suburban business class.

As the fringe proved favourable for industrial development and new working-class and business-class residential growth, enthusiasm grew for transforming the centre of the industrial city. The designers of the 1893 World's Columbian Exposition in Chicago, celebrating the four hundredth anniversary of Columbus' discovery of the New World, offered a prospect of what the new city centres might look like. Using plaster to imitate marble, they built a gleaming white city of administrative and retail palaces. The Exposition astounded 21 million visitors with the possibility that cities could be clean and open and beautiful. Daniel Burnham and his associates skilfully channelled the enthusiasm into a City Beautiful movement that contributed greatly to establishing professional city planning in the US. Burnham's plans for Washington, DC, San Francisco and Chicago, although never implemented with the scale or grandeur he specified, introduced a style of municipal rebuilding that dominated three decades of city development.[13]

Four groups of interests were particularly enthusiastic about a central district free of factories, railroad yards and shipping depots: banks, insurance companies, real estate owners and developers, and department stores and other retail merchants. Real estate developers built taller and taller speculative office buildings to house thousands of small ventures: sales offices, lawyers, accountants, wholesalers, printers, office supply outlets, shippers, secretarial services, messengers, bill collectors, stock brokers, advertising agents, manufacturers' representatives, employment agencies and even finders of lost persons. Land values rose, buildings went higher and higher, manufacturing departed, and central areas became central business districts.

Monopoly corporations played a specific role in the formation of the suburban fringe and the central business district. Monopolisation had been a reaction to excessive competition fuelled by excess manufacturing capacity. The new monopoly firms created in the turn

of the century merger movement were thus busier closing antiquated
factories than building new ones in their early years. Once they sorted
out their holdings and began to expand, monopoly corporations
contributed greatly to the suburbanising trend in manufacturing.
The plants monopoly corporations were closing tended to be at the
centres of the large cities. This helped prepare the ground for a new
pattern of central city uses and activities.

Monopoly corporations also played a leading role in establishing
the new pattern of uses, the central business district. Because they
had many plants and facilities to operate, monopoly corporations
separated managerial functions from operating activities and
concentrated them in one location, the corporate *central office*. The
central office might be attached to one of the firm's major factories, or
nearby in the city's office district. Between 1910 and 1930 practices
changed and large firms began seeking prestigious locations for their
central offices in the largest cities. Willard Thorp studied 1919
Census data on the central offices of 314 firms operating ten or more
separate manufacturing plants and found that more than half of them
were located in just six cities: New York, Chicago, Pittsburgh,
Boston, St. Louis and Cleveland. New York alone claimed 72 central
offices.[14]

Woolworth's, the monopoly 5 and 10 cent store chain, initiated the
fashion of prominently identifying a corporation's headquarters in
1913. They hired the renowned architect Cass Gilbert to design a
792-foot-high *Cathedral of Commerce* that held its title as the world's
tallest building for almost twenty years. In the 1920s Chrysler built a
magnificent headquarters tower in New York and soon after the
Rockefellers broke ground for Rockefeller Center, a whole complex of
office and retail buildings. Management of Standard Oil, the first
great monopoly and the origin of the Rockefellers' immense wealth,
had been handed over to professional managers by this time. The
family undertook Rockefeller Center as a speculative real estate
venture rather than as a corporate headquarters. The corporation
most prominently housed in the new centre was RCA, the Radio
Corporation of America.

Many monopoly firms preferred to be less flamboyant about their
central offices, but most favoured locating managerial activities in
central business districts. The fabulous William 'Billy' Durant,
founder of General Motors, loved to joke that he kept his office in his
hat; but Alfred Sloan, who steered GM past Henry Ford in the 1920s

and 1930s to make it the largest car producer in the world, understood the importance of making the corporation's offices in downtown Detroit secondary to a landmark headquarters building in New York City. Even firms with strong loyalties to smaller metropolitan centres adopted the new pattern and got involved with banks, real estate developers and retailers in developing a central business district for their home city.

THE METROPOLITAN AREA, c. 1929

By the end of the 1920s the physical structure of the American metropolitan area was established. The central district had been purged of industry and occupied by banks, insurance companies, commercial offices, real estate companies, brokers and corporate central offices. Accompanying these leading interests were thousands of small offices providing business services or conducting related functions. Department stores and retail shopping areas adjoined the business district in small and moderate sized metropolitan cities. In the large metropolitan cities department stores and retail shopping congregated in their own central district. Surrounding the central area, but within the city limits, one found rings and bisecting radial sectors comprised of rooming house districts, slums, ethnic enclaves, small shop and loft industrial areas, 'Negro' or 'coloured' black slums, fashionable apartment house neighbourhoods, and very exclusive clusters of business-class mansions and large houses.

The suburban fringe had assumed a distinctive form as well. In addition to the progress of the three major types of suburban settlement – manufacturing enclaves, working-class suburbs and business-class suburbs – the automobile had an increasingly powerful influence. Neither the automobile makers, nor the designers of the first parkways in the 1920s, nor the city planners anticipated the passionate love affair between metropolitan residents and the automobile. By the late 1920s, despite the lack of adequate highways, automobile commuting had become vital to suburban life. The foreign visitor standing on a streetcorner in early morning or late afternoon, 1929, would have had only one impression of metropolitan life: Americans were car crazy. Industrial areas, working-class residential areas and business-class suburban towns interspersed in mottled patterns throughout the fringe, with some tendency for new business-class development to locate at the far edges while new factories sprang up on undeveloped tracts within the built-up area. The motor truck became as crucial to suburban industry as the automobile was for suburban commuters and their families.

Turning to metropolitan social structure, *c.* 1929, one found two classes dominating the social topography, the business class and the working class. Industrial workers constituted a large part of the working class. To some extent employees of suburban factories earned higher wages than workers in older more central plants, but this was by no means a general rule. Working-class residential neighbourhoods and communities in the suburban fringe contained many more single family houses than central city neighbourhoods, but this resulted more from lower land and house costs in the fringe than from differences in average family income. Similarly for the business class, there were no overt social distinctions made between residents of older business-class neighbourhoods in the central city, and commuters living in the new business-class suburbs. The biggest differences were in house styles, neighbourhood appearance and commuting patterns. The fact that the central city business class rode in trollies and buses to work, while their suburban associates arrived in automobiles, was not grounds for suburban snobbery.

Intersecting the business-class/working-class division was a distinction between blue-collar workers, people who worked with tools and machines primarily in factories, and white-collar workers, people concerned with money, transactions and communications working primarily in offices and stores. The white-collar/blue-collar distinction signified the increasing importance of one's occupation as the basis for social standing, rather than the fate of being born into one class or the other. Membership in the business class had always been almost exclusively a matter of birth. Apart from a small proportion of self-made business men who had pressed upward from humble origins, the great majority of members of the business class had been born into business-class families. The working class consisted of everyone else, people dependent entirely on wages for their income.

Blue collar and *working class* were largely synonymous in the 1920s, the difference being that *blue collar* indicated one's occupation while *working class* referred to family origins and subjective class identification. It was the *white-collar* distinction that raised the difficult questions. *White collar* designated lower level occupations pursued in offices and stores: bookkeepers, secretaries, clerks, tellers. Up to the turn of the century these occupations were associated entirely with the business class, despite their low salaries and subservient status. They were filled almost invariably by people from business-class families; business-class mores, clothing fashions, speech and behaviour dictated their conduct and life style. Between the 1890s and the 1920s, the emergence of monopoly corporations and the related expansion of governmental bureaucracies and business services greatly swelled the need for this category of workers. Young people of working-class origins were drawn in. The term *white collar* came into use specifically to indicate that office and sales occupations were *no longer* synonymous with business-class origins. By the end of the 1920s, *white collar* implied that the person holding the position most probably grew up in a working-class family.

The emergence of a white-collar category of occupations and workers was inextricably linked with metropolitan development. Out of the tensions of the 1920s, between the business-class/working-class structuring of social classes and the white-collar/blue-collar structure of occupations, came the middle-class revolution of the late 1940s and 1950s that forms one of our two major themes. We will consider these white-collar beginnings of the middle class in greater detail in Chapter 2. Between the 1920s and the late 1940s, the Great Depression and the Second World War intervened. The pace of metropolitan development slowed and as the Depression continued a gloomy outlook on metropolitan living became prevalent.

DEPRESSION, WORLD WAR AND THE KEYNESIAN THEORY OF POST-WAR DEVELOPMENT

Americans date the Great Depression from the New York stock market crash of October 1929. Up to the crash, they believed the European economic crisis that began early in the 1920s was not going to affect them. The banking system spiralled downward for more than three years before collapsing totally in March 1933 in anticipation of federal intervention by the new Democratic President, Franklin D. Roosevelt. Federal measures succeeded in restoring stability to banking and finance, and New Deal programmes inspired a great deal of optimism about reducing unemployment and reviving industry. Yet in 1937 and 1938 employment and industrial production fell back to the depths they had plumbed in 1933.

As the economy continued to founder, expectations for long-term development lost their optimistic tone. Anticipation of 'recovery' and the return of 'prosperity' gave way to description of the continuing stagnation as the onset of the 'maturity' of the social system. Sociologist Roderick McKenzie, author of the major study of metropolitan communities commissioned by President Herbert Hoover's Research Committee on Social Trends, defended metropolitan development in 1933 against a vigorous *back-to-the-land* movement. 'Accommodation to present conditions of dislocation has largely taken the form of attempts to revert to a simpler social order', McKenzie wrote. While such impulses are understandable, he countered, 'our metropolitan society is too complex a mechanism to be adjusted by such expedients.' Instead, McKenzie enthusiastically advocated broad-ranging physical, economic and social planning.[15]

Later in the decade, however, after the National Industrial Recovery Act and other ambitious federal programmes had failed to spark an economic resurgence, analysts of metropolitan development turned to describing the national metropolitan settlement pattern as the structure of a maturing, stabilising social system. Slowly and steadily metropolitan areas would absorb the unemployed and adjust industrial production toward a moderated long-term equilibrium, free of the booms and crashes of pre-Depression capitalism. Rather than *recovering* from Depression, American society would adjust to a less dynamic, but also less disruptive, style of growth and social change than it had experienced over most of its history.

Talk of maturity and moderation proved premature. As Europe moved from aggression and appeasement to openly declared war, Roosevelt took the earliest opportunity to shift the US to a 'war basis' and negotiate 'Lend-Lease' agreements that translated into big orders for American heavy industry. The Second World War got the economy moving and revived optimism about long-term American development.

The Depression did not alter metropolitan settlement trends in any fundamental way. National population growth slowed, as did rural-to-urban migration, but the proportion of the population living in metropolitan areas continued to increase, reaching 47.8 per cent in 1940. The number of metropolitan areas increased from 97 to 140 between 1930 and 1940, due partly to the Census Bureau's revision of its definitions. The prominent demographer Warren Thompson prepared a major analysis of metropolitan growth from 1900 to 1940 for the Census Bureau that showed both the 140 metropolitan areas of 1940 and the 97 areas of 1930 growing faster than the non-metropolitan population during the 1930s. This meant that the *back-to-the-land* movement had not been very significant, despite the publicity it received in the depths of the Depression. As in the 1920s, the places experiencing the fastest growth continued to be the outer edges of the suburban fringes of metropolitan areas.[16]

Along with recovery from the Depression, and the revival of optimism about the nation's future, the war fostered an appreciation of the central role metropolitan areas would play in post-war economic and social development. The rejuvenating economic effects of government spending for the war effort helped convert liberal American economists to a radically new analysis of economic growth, the British economist John Maynard Keynes' *General Theory of Employment, Interest and Money*.

Keynes argued that investment oriented toward increasing the consumption of goods and services could be a means of preventing major depressions from occurring. The disasters of the 1920s and 1930s had demonstrated that capitalists' and bankers' natural inclinations did not tend in this direction, therefore government would have to assert a powerful influence. Keynes called for strong government oversight of money, banking and credit, and for the use of tax increases and public indebtedness (deficit spending) to finance direct government investment when private investment fell below the level necessary to sustain the growth of the economy. As Keynes' converts applied the theory to the US, metropolitan areas emerged as the physical and social context in which consumption-oriented investment should be planned. First and foremost, they advocated federal investment in redevelopment and housing construction in metropolitan central cities.[17]

Keynes did not argue that government investment must follow a metropolitan strategy. Keynes' influence in his native Britain helped to shape a post-war economic policy focused on coal, steel, railroads and other declining industries; its spatial perspective was regional rather than metropolitan. In the US, Keynesian economics and metropolitan development evolved a symbiotic relationship. Keynesian presidential and congressional advisers shaping national economy policy generally did not elaborate the metropolitan spatial context of their strategising. For a time, in the 1950s and 1960s, economic policy targeted lagging regions: Appalachia, the Ozarks (parts of Missouri, Arkansas and Oklahoma), the Four Corners in the South-West (where Utah, Colorado, Arizona and New Mexico meet), and others. Metropolitan development lay behind this effort however, for it was the lack of metropolitan urbanisation that caused these regions to trail behind the pace of national progress. The primary objective of post-war urban policy, 'saving the metropolitan central cities, was a function of *both* metropolitan development and the Keynesian approach to national economic policy. We will examine Keynesianism's role in urban policy in Chapter 3.

CONCLUSION

The scene is now set, as of 1940. Chapter 2 continues the settlement theme, describing the first of the two revolutions: the forging of a metropolitan middle class. Policy enters in Chapter 3. I have emphasised in this first chapter the most prominent factors and forces antecedent to settlement and policy in the metropolitan era, 1940–80: acceptance of the metropolitan area as a community; the joint enthusiasm of capital and labour for metropolitan development; the spread of metropolitan development to all major regions of the country; the formation of the suburban fringe and the central business district as the major features of metropolitan area structure; and the continuing strength of metropolitan trends through the Depression crisis.

Chapter 2 begins with the white-collar group and the sociologist who immortalised their contradictory role in the social structure of the 1940s, C. Wright Mills. Mills' expectations for white-collar people proved inaccurate, despite the acuteness of his analysis of their origins and circumstances. He could not imagine a social class made up of the likes of Kitty Foyle, salesgirl heroine of Christopher Morley's 1920s novel, or Willie Loman, fated hero of Arthur Miller's 1948 play, *Death of a Salesman*, rising to comfortable dominance over the American social system. 'The white-collar people slipped quietly into modern society', he wrote in 1951:

Whatever history they have had is a history without events;

whatever common interests they have had do not lead to unity: whatever future they have will not be of their own making. If they aspire at all it is to a middle course, at a time when no middle course is available, and hence to an illusory course in an imaginary society.[18]

I have disputed Mills' claims that white-collar aspirations were passive and that their perception of a middle course was illusory.

2. The First Metropolitan Revolution: Suburban Development and the Making of the Middle Class

Revolutionary social change is fundamental, and it is change animated by purpose and intention. The suburban development that began in the 1940s was revolutionary in two ways: it changed the type of community millions of Americans lived in, and it transformed the national social class structure. The change in community started as an escape from the big city and from city ways of living. The new suburbs acquired their distinctive character as they matured, in the 1950s and 1960s. The transformation of the class structure began in the realm of work and occupations, as white-collar workers sought a secure social position relative to the two established social classes, the business class and the working class. White-collar families made up much of the new suburban population, and the cultural patterns and social solidarity developing in suburban communities became increasingly associated with the white-collar occupational group. Eventually, suburban cultural changes and white-collar status aspirations fused and produced a shift in the basis of social class differentiation. Income and style of living supplanted occupation and economic status as the parameters defining the major social classes. A broad middle class emerged, encompassing considerably more than half the metropolitan population in the 1970s.

Suburban population growth since 1940 has been extraordinary. Some 20 million people lived in metropolitan suburban fringe areas in 1940, and 101 million in 1980 (see Table II). Metropolitan residents were not yet a majority of the nation's population in 1940: 33 per cent of the population lived in metropolitan central cities, and the suburban proportion was only 15 per cent; 52 per cent were non-metropolitan. By 1970 the suburban proportion had become the largest, 37 per cent. In 1980, 45 per cent of the nation's population was living in metropolitan suburban areas.

Table II   Metropolitan and non-metropolitan population:
1940–80

	1910	1940	1950	1960	1970	1980
Population (in millions)						
United States total		131.7	150.7	179.3	203.2	226.5
Metropolitan:		63.0	84.5	112.9	139.4	169.4
in central cities		42.8	49.4	58.0	63.8	67.9
in suburban fringes		20.2	35.1	54.9	75.6	101.5
Non-metropolitan		68.7	66.2	66.4	63.8	57.1
Per cent of total US						
Metropolitan:	31 %	47.8	56.1	62.9	68.6	74.8
in central cities		32.5	32.8	32.3	31.4	30.0
in suburban fringes		15.3	23.3	30.6	37.2	44.8
Non-metropolitan		52.2	43.9	37.1	31.4	25.2
United States total		100.0	100.0	100.0	100.0	100.0
Number of metropolitan areas	58	140	168	212	243	318

Sources: *U.S. Census of Population* for 1940 and 1950; for 1960, 1970 and 1980: *1980 Census of Population, Supplementary Reports*, 'Standard Metropolitan Statistical Areas and Standard Consolidated Statistical Areas: 1980', Table A.

The transformation of the class structure is more difficult to summarise. About one-third of the 59 million people at work in 1950 were white-collar: 5 million professional and technical workers, 7 million clerical workers, 4 million sales workers, and the lower 2–3 million of the 5 million managers, officials and proprietors. The upper echelons of the managers, officials and proprietors group still considered themselves the business class. The middle class that emerged during the 1950s and 1960s defined itself subjectively, rendering occupational categories an insufficient guide to class distinctions. When questioned by survey researchers, an increasing proportion of people with traditionally working-class occupations reported that they considered themselves middle class. Studies in 1952, 1956 and 1960 found that 35, 39 and 33 per cent of respondents considered themselves middle class. Comparable studies in 1964 and 1968 found 43 and 45 per cent characterising themselves as middle class, and a 1975 study reported 49 per cent. A 1963 study using somewhat less rigid questions found 66 per cent placing themselves in the middle class.

A fair summary of the survey research is that a middle class defined primarily in terms of white-collar occupations included about one-third of workers in the 1950s, while a middle class oriented toward income and life style, sometimes in contradiction with occupation, had come to include one-half of workers by the mid-1970s. The fact that the surveys covered only employed white males exaggerates the proportions somewhat. Unfortunately, surveys of all adults, white and minority, male and female, working and not working, introduce so many methodological and analytical difficulties that researchers have been reluctant to attempt them. Because the bulk of the middle class resides in metropolitan suburbs, the middle-class proportion of the metropolitan population is higher than the overall national percentages generated by these survey studies.[1]

The two kinds of revolutionary change originated as reactions to the social situation immediately following the Second World War. White-collar workers reacted to insecurity; their anomalous position between the business class and working class of the 1920s remained unresolved, despite fifteen years of depression and war. They sought a firm basis for defining their social status and pursuing upward advancement. The chapter begins by describing the circumstances and aspirations of white-collar workers in the early post-war period.

Capital's strategy for post-war economic expanion added tremendous momentum to white-collar forces, especially monopoly industrial capital. Between drawing in workers to produce machinery and consumer goods by labour-intensive methods, or automating physical production with capital-intensive technology and expanding the white-collar workforce involved in sales, promotion, advertising and management, capital took the white-collar path. Nation-wide coal and steel strikes in 1946, and the rise of national unions in more and more industries, encouraged this choice. The next section describes capital's options and their implications for industrial and white-collar workers.

The second reaction to post-war circumstances consisted of families deserting the city for homes in new suburban housing developments, aided and enticed by speculative builders of tract housing and shopping centres. The third section characterises the purposes of these families in terms of their desire to break the close connections of city neighbourhoods and establish an *isolated* structure of family life. Anonymity between neighbours, distance from relatives, the inward focus on children, leisure and home life, all enhanced the creation of new patterns of community culture in the metropolitan suburban fringe areas. For white-collar fathers, *isolated* family life served important functions relating to career aspirations. At first, in the late 1940s and early 1950s, white-collar forces and suburban community development remained distinct from each other, although many families were involved in both activities.

During the 1950s, white-collar and suburban development forces achieved some coordinated success. Post-war suburban developments began to receive recognition as a new community type, distinct from the business-class and working-class suburbs of the 1920s. And white-collar insecurity subsided as it became apparent that a new middle class was incorporating white-collar workers and the traditional business class into a single entity. The new middle class had its basis in cultural patterns and appearances, and the families of the new suburban communities were primarily responsible for creating the new culture. Monopoly industrial corporations and suburban builders and real estate speculators facilitated the establishment of middle-class culture by encouraging, and then rushing to satiate, emerging preferences in house design, shopping, automobiles, clothing, food, home appliances, leisure, entertainment, physical appearance. Sections four to eight of this chapter describe some prominent aspects of forging a middle class way of life in the suburbs of the 1950s: preferred styles of housing, the role of television, the ethic of *productivity* in home life, the central role of the public school in suburban communities, and the management of adolescent sexuality.

As the suburban middle-class revolution progressed, it shifted the basis upon which social class distinctions were made. Life style, and the income necessary to support it, displaced occupation as the principal determinant of social standing. First to go was the business class, originally grounded in family wealth, property or enterprises. Business owners and self-employed professionals began to be referred to as the *old* or traditional middle class in the 1950s, which preserved their separation from the white-collar workers with predominantly working-class origins forming the *new* middle class. In the 1960s, distinctions between *old* and *new* disappeared, replaced by income-based differentiations between *upper middle*, *middle middle* and *lower middle* classes. Then, in the late 1960s and 1970s, the occupational foundations of working-class identity crumbled, as policemen, fire fighters, skilled craftsmen and high-wage factory workers moved to middle-class suburban communities, wholeheartedly espoused middle-class culture, and subjectively identified themselves as middle class. The final section sketches the shift from occupational to income and life style distinctions.

Throughout I have emphasised that the forging of the middle class was a *metropolitan* revolution. Without the metropolitan context, especially the concentration of so much of the population in metropolitan areas at the time the Second World War ended, it is unlikely that such a large middle class could have emerged so rapidly. I have tried to show that the basis of the class system shifted, and a middle class became dominant, because people intentionally used the metropolitan context to raise their own social status and, if possible, to transform the national social system. It may seem incongruous to think of white-collar fathers of the 1950s pushing lawnmowers around their suburban backyards as the vanguard of a social revolution, but it should not be.

WHITE-COLLAR WORKERS AT THE END OF THE SECOND WORLD WAR

Let us pick up the white-collar workers where we left them at the end of Chapter 1, emerging from the Depression and the Second World War, and optimistic about their post-war future. Their social position, between the business class and the working class, remained insecure. Their numbers were growing, which militated toward adjustments in class definitions and boundaries.

C. Wright Mills, utilising the insights of Max Weber, was the first American sociologist to argue that the white-collar group would become a third social class as it grew. He confidently expected white-collar growth to continue, because he believed it was a function of a long-term economic trend. In his best-selling 1951 study *White Collar*, he wrote:

> The major shifts in occupations since the Civil War have assumed this industrial trend: as a proportion of the labor force, fewer individuals manipulate *things*, more handle *people* and *symbols*. This shift in needed skills is another way of describing the rise of the white-collar workers, for their characteristic skills involve the handling of paper and money and people. They are expert at dealing with people transiently and impersonally; they are masters of the commercial, professional, and technical relationship. The one thing they do not do is live by making things; rather, they live off the social machineries that organize and coordinate the people who do make things.[2]

Mills refers back to materialistic, *objective* definitions of social class in this passage. These older approaches differentiated the white-collar group from the traditional working class on the basis of their differing relationships to production, ownership and wealth. Mills also looks forward to his own interpretation, that the shift from an economy dominated by industry and the making of things, to one focused on money, symbols and the management of people, was transforming the entire basis of the social structure.

In *White Collar*, Mills argued that power, prestige, and individual goals such as 'success', had become a matter of symbols and appearances. Power, even in business, belonged to the man with the title on his office door; it had separated from ownership of the corporate assets or stock. Success had become an image, something for a man to assume, like a new suit of clothes. And because social prestige had also become a function of appearances, and their acknowledgement by others, social status had broken free of family origins and inherited class membership. Businessmen continued to constitute the business class, which Mills referred to as the entrepreneurial *old* middle class, but more by virtue of their occupations as business proprietors and managers than because of ownership or inheritance. Since prestige attached to occupations, rather than to family origins or wealth, it could no longer be 'absolutely set and unambivalent'. 'The enjoyment of prestige', Mills wrote, 'is often disturbed and uneasy, . . . the bases of prestige, the expressions of prestige claims, and the ways these claims are honored, are now subject to great strain, a strain which often puts men and women in a virtual status panic.'[3]

Mills anticipated that classes and class distinctions would solidify around fixed criteria for claiming and honouring prestige. He expected educational requirements for entry into occupations to become one important basis of the prestige system. 'Success' impressed him as the most desperately sought criterion, but he saw success as the ultimate in transitory appearances. In the bureaucratic world of white-collar occupations, success consisted of advancements created or erased by altering an organisation chart. Mills predicted that gradations between steps in bureaucratic hierarchies would become smaller and smaller. Salary differences would diminish as well. Career success might appear to be a firm foundation for social prestige and status mobility, but Mills warned that success would dissipate into a haze of superficial qualities and trivial distinctions.[4]

William H. Whyte, Jr gave Mills' conception of status grounded upon success a vivid illustration in his 1956 book *The Organization Man*. Whyte's new man represented not the typical American, but the American belief in mobility and success. The organisation man belonged neither to the traditional business class nor to the industrial working class. He worked for organisations, either monopoly corporations or governmental bureaucracies, and he lived in the suburbs. Whyte specified that he was describing the new ideology of American life, the 'social ethic' of a country dominated by corporations and bureaucracies.[5]

Whyte explored the psychological qualities prized by organisations and the use of psychological testing and evaluation to determine who should be promoted. Whyte's organisation man pursued success by shaping his personality to conform to the ideal psychological profile. He set out on his quest with one simple premise, 'that the goals of the individual [himself] and the goals of the organization will work out to be one and the same'. Whyte's analysis suggested that a status system based on occupational success was firmly entrenched by the mid 1950s.[6]

Mills and Whyte were describing the beginnings of the white-collar search for stable social position. Their belief that status was becoming increasingly subjective proved correct. In the late 1940s and early 1950s, white-collar efforts to gain control over the basis of social status were passive and somewhat self-destructive. Workers strove to *conform* to what success appeared to require. White-collar workers shied away from group organising or the formation of white-collar unions in order to avoid openly opposing corporate and bureaucratic values. Unions were for the factory workers they hoped to rise above in the prestige hierarchy. Only later, in the mid 1960s, did white-collar unions grow and become powerful among government and non-profit employees. White-collar unionism in private industry has yet to emerge.

The suburbs eventually proved more central to forging white-collar occupations and workers into a middle class than the ethic of success. Whyte recognised the crucial role suburban home life played for his organisation men and discussed it at length. Mills said nothing about suburbs in *White Collar*, despite his extensive critique of white-collar life styles. Just when white-collar workers began to move to the suburbs, corporate decisions about long-term economic strategy swelled their ranks tremendously. Success in the corporate hierarchy became far easier to obtain than Mills had expected because monopoly corporations acquired a voracious appetite for administrative and professional workers.

CAPITAL'S POST-WAR STRATEGY: THE OFFICE OR THE FACTORY?

When the Second World War ended in 1945, the American working class was hurtling along like a freight train going top speed. White male workers were fully employed or in the armed forces, war production had drawn in millions of women, and black workers had won entry to high-wage industrial jobs running machines and driving trucks. For most Americans the war had been an orgy of industrial expansion and prosperity. The clash of arms was remote and never seriously threatening. More people perished at home during the war years in automobile, industrial and household accidents than died in combat. The birth rate, which had been declining for 150 years, suddenly spurted upward in 1941. By 1946 the 'baby boom' was front page news: 2.5 million babies were born in 1939; 3.4 million were born in 1946 and 3.8 million in 1947. Capital's immediate post-war problem was not stimulating economic growth, but harnessing working-class dynamism in productive and profitable ways.

Channelling the dynamism into an expanded replica of the traditional industrial working class would have been very difficult. Industrial solidarity had reached dangerous levels during the war, as far as monopoly capital was concerned. Despite President Roosevelt's *no strike* doctrine, the United Auto Workers successfully organised Ford Motor Company in 1942 and the Congress of Industrial Organizations (CIO) made rapid progress.[7]

In 1946, with the war over, CIO unions tested their new power and President Truman chose to confront them. He intervened in a major steel strike and sent the army to break up an industry-wide coal strike of the United Mine Workers. Congress reacted as if the strikes threatened the heartbeat of the nation. They passed the Taft–Hartley Act in 1947, giving the President power to order striking unions back to work. The unions labelled it the 'slave labor' bill and persuaded Truman to veto it, but Congress quickly overrode the veto. John L. Lewis vowed that workers would never obey a presidential back-to-work injunction and Lewis' own United Mine Workers have maintained ever since that they have kept that promise.

Congress and the President handed capital a political victory over the unions, but the prospects for profit-making through traditional large-scale production were now inauspicious. Allowing working-class expansion to flow primarily into semi-skilled factory or mining occupations, now firmly controlled by unions, would directly increase union strength. If strikes and confrontations were to be avoided, union demands would have to be answered with wage increases and fringe benefits. Capital could bear the rising costs profitably only through exponential increases in production relative to the increasing size of the workforce, and that would require marketing and selling industrial products on a vastly greater scale. A profound long-run decision had to be made in 1947.

Capital avoided strengthening the working class and the unions by choosing a white-collar strategy, favouring the office over the factory. Rather than hiring more production workers and increasing physical output with their current machinery and technology, industrial corporations used engineers, technicians and managers to revamp production so that fewer factory workers were needed, even as output expanded. *Automation* became the popular term for this trend in factory modernisation.

Increased output had to be sold at prices that generated profits. Lowering prices might have undermined oligopolistic market relationships and triggered destructive competition wars. Instead, monopoly manufacturers expanded their advertising, marketing and product development staffs and attempted to sell more products at existing or possibly higher prices. This effort generated even greater demand for white-collar workers than the reorganisation of production. Corporations learned to market Rice Krispies and Chevrolets to the public *before* hiring additional assembly-line workers to produce them. The costs for development, advertising and marketing embodied in each unit of product often exceeded the unit cost of raw materials and labour. Effective white-collar expansion on the selling end of manufacturing enterprise proved the key to realising profits in post-war industry.

For reasons of production, and of pricing and sales, industrial capital preferred to absorb post-war working-class energies in white-collar office jobs. In addition, emphasising the office over the factory made it possible to increase wages and benefits for factory workers and stabilise relations with the unions. Monopoly corporations and industrial unions evolved a system of *productivity bargaining* in which workers' wage and benefit demands were financed by increased physical productivity per worker. Contract terms won at the bargaining table constantly improved, and workers endured the wear and tear of faster assembly lines and more stressful work individually and silently, at least in the 1950s.

Unions paid little attention to the stabilisation of factory employment that accompanied corporate emphasis on white-collar expansion. Unions concerned themselves only with employed workers, even workers laid off temporarily lost their union membership unless they chose to pay the dues out of their own pockets. Nor did industrial unions attempt to organise white-collar workers. Only considerably later, in the 1970s, did unions begin to recognise that the narrow focus on job security and economic needs of production workers had weakened the working class and undermined the unions' own political power.

Returning veterans and young people of the late 1940s appeared to prefer white-collar opportunities to factory employment. Veterans' enthusiasm for the education programme of the *G.I. Bill of Rights*, through which they could obtain financing for tuition and family living expenses while earning a college degree, was one indication of a strong desire to escape a life of factory labour. Given the unhappy experiences of college graduates in the depression years, there was

little assurance that the investment in higher education would lead to
higher income or greater economic security than industrial work. Yet
tens of thousands of veterans swarmed onto college and university
campuses, despite the risk that white-collar success might elude
them. The proportion of young people completing high school, which
first became significant in relation to the white-collar expansion of the
1920s, continued to increase steadily in the late 1940s and 1950s.
Most high school graduates entered sales or clerical occupations. A
growing minority went on to college or advanced technical training.
The factory acquired a negative aura; increasingly the young people
entering factory work in the post-war period were high school
'drop-outs'. Most were regretful about missed opportunities.

THE SUBURBAN EXODUS AND THE ISOLATED FAMILY

GI benefits also included a mortgage subsidy programme that
allowed returning veterans to purchase homes on extremely liberal
terms. The Federal Housing Administration, created during the New
Deal, provided mortgage insurance that greatly reduced risks for
home builders and mortgage lenders: banks, savings and loan
associations and insurance companies. Enticed by these two federal
programmes, builders began constructing single family homes in the
fringes of metropolitan areas and young city couples and families
appeared to buy them. By 1949, the construction rate was 1.25 million
houses per year and a suburban housing boom was in full swing.[8]

'Levittown' emerged as the popular image of the new suburban
development. William Levitt pioneered the technique of building
several thousand houses on town-sized tracts of very cheap land.
Vanity inspired him to name these instant communities after himself.
Levitt undertook his first project in the Long Island suburbs of New
York City in the late 1940s. He started the second soon after in the
Pennsylvania suburbs of Philadelphia. In the mid 1950s he built
another well-known Levittown in Philadelphia's New Jersey
suburban area. Small companies building fewer than 100 homes a
year constructed the vast majority of new post-war suburban homes,
but it was Levitt and the few other very large builders who captured
the popular imagination. A family could reserve a lot and have a
house built in Levittown, New Jersey in 1955 with no more than a

$100 downpayment and assurance that their annual income exceeded $5,500. The national median family income at that time was about $5,000, putting Levitt's terms within reach of several million young city families.[9]

Levittowns and smaller suburban developments capitalised on the desire of young couples to escape the tight relationships among relatives, friends and neighbours characteristic of city neighbourhoods. New suburbanites emphasised the opportunity to 'own your own home' as their primary motivation, but the opportunity for privacy among anonymous neighbours was clearly what made owning a single family suburban house on its own piece of land attractive. The structure of post-war suburban families can best be described as 'isolated', an arrangement that facilitated attainment of long-run family objectives.[10]

The most important of these objectives was social and economic advancement. Isolated structure, including only a husband and wife and their children, streamlined the family and focused their energies on career success for the husband and father. Moving to the suburbs distanced young couples from their parents, the most threatening potential drain on economic and psychological resources. Parents bore the scars of the Depression and tended to fear the risks involved in mortgage borrowing and home ownership. Immigrant and working-class parents were accustomed to depending on relatives and city neighbourhood cultural mores for social and economic security. Grounding a young family's long-term wellbeing entirely on the husband's career at work was alien to these traditions, making parents sceptical of suburban life.

Isolated structure concentrated the wife and mother's day-to-day activities and thoughts on her husband and children. Wives did not work, especially while any of the children were small. This compensated for some advantages the suburban family sacrificed when it abandoned the close family and neighbourhood life of the city. Suburban wives could not depend on their mothers, relatives and childhood friends for psychological support or child-care assistance. Not working provided them with the time to handle these burdens alone. Mustering the necessary emotional strength was a problem they struggled with as best they could.

Norms concerning isolation from parents, and wives' not working, gained strength from the rapid evolution of new child-rearing principles. Guiding parents in caring for their children may have been less important than the role the new principles played in mandating parental behaviour appropriate to isolated family structure. Benjamin Spock's *Baby and Child Care*, the bible of suburban child-rearing in the 1950s and 1960s, served indirectly as a guide to organising day-to-day life in an isolated family and functioning within it as husband and wife, father and mother.[11]

Introduction of Freudian principles as child-rearing standards lent Spock and other experts much of their legitimacy. Psychologist Erik Erikson translated Freudian theory directly into popular prescriptions for child-rearing. Working to avoid the sexual repression Freud had identified as the great evil of family life for children, Erikson, Spock and their allies became famous for encouraging flexibility, permissiveness and toleration of sexual acting out. At the same time, however, their books made it clear that the presence of adults other than the father and mother in the home, including grandparents, would interfere with efforts to create the non-repressive environment required for the children's proper psychological development. Freudian theory of child development turned upon formation and subsequent severing of intense sexually-grounded attachments to mother and father. The everyday presence of grandparents or other adults would intrude upon these processes and inevitably distort them, with damaging consequences for the child's developing personality. The message to mothers in particular was to exclude parents from living in the home and even to minimise the wife's mother's (the children's grandmother) involvement as a frequent baby sitter. Approaches based on Freudian theory suggested that anonymous adults were preferable to grandmothers or other relatives for child-care assistance.[12]

The new principles of child-rearing helped the suburban wife adapt to an isolated family structure. The principles provided an explanation as to why grandparents should be excluded from the home, why wives should not work during child-rearing years, and why isolated family life among anonymous neighbours was beneficial for one's children. Spock later endured severe criticism for having prescribed that mothers should not work in order to be at home with their children. For example, concerning Freudian sexual acting out toward mother and father between the ages of three and six, Spock counselled the young mother: 'These strong romantic attachments help children to grow spiritually and to acquire wholesome feelings toward the opposite sex that will later guide them into good marriages.' In short, Heaven help her if she failed over a *three-year period*, for the consequence might be permanent destruction of the child's capacity for happiness.[13]

Census data from prototypical suburban communities of the 1950s reveal the prevalence of isolated family structure. Nearly the entire population of Levittown, New Jersey, almost 12,000 people, consisted of husband and wife families with an average of two children under eighteen years of age. No more than one family in six had one of the couple's parents or other relatives living with them. Almost every family owned its own home, and 65 per cent of males pursued white-collar occupations. Of married women living with their husbands only 16 per cent worked, and of those with children under six years of age only 4 per cent worked. The picture was similar in Park Forest, Illinois, the Chicago suburb studied by William H. Whyte for *The Organization Man*. Virtually everyone lived in families of isolated structure with approximately two children under eighteen. No more than one family in nine had a parent or other relative living with them; 83 per cent of males had white-collar occupations; married women's labour force participation was 20 per cent, and for women with children under six it was 6 per cent. In contrast, in the turn of the century business-class Chicago suburb of Oak Park, more than sixty years old by the 1950s, husbands, wives and children under eighteen living together in families constituted only 75 per cent of a population of more than 60,000. Husband and wife families averaged only one child under eighteen, while more than half of husband-wife families may have had a parent or other relative living with them. The proportion of married women with children under six who worked was 10 per cent, similar to that in Levittown or Park Forest, while 31 per cent of all married women worked, considerably more than in Levittown or Park Forest. Except for families with young children, Oak Park presented far greater diversity in family structure than the new post-war suburbs.[14]

Many husbands and fathers of new suburban families were white-collar workers, but in its initial stages suburban development was not considered a white-collar phenomenon. William Whyte's *Organization Man* was the first prominent analysis to connect the white-collar quest for occupational advancement with the aspirations of new suburbanites. Whyte conceded that most residents of the new suburbs were working class, but he insisted that 'organization men' and their families were determining the course of new trends. He supported his claims with a detailed description of Park Forest, Illinois, prefacing them with the assertion that 'the values of Park Forest . . . are harbingers of the way it's going to be'.[15]

Park Forest consisted initially of two-bedroom garden apartment complexes and a shopping centre on 2,400 acres of former cornfields thirty miles from downtown Chicago. Later single family homes were added. The first residents arrived in 1948 and by 1956 the population was 25,000. The average adult, considering both men and women, had more than two years of education beyond high school. Whyte's representative sampling of new families in 1955 included:

research chemist, Sinclair Oil Company
salesman, Swift and Co. (monopoly meat packers)
major, Fifth Army
investigator, Federal Bureau of Investigation
purchasing agent, Ford Motor Company
industrial psychologist, Swift and Co.
space salesman (advertising), *Business Week* magazine
underwriter, Prudential Life Insurance Company
salesman, Dupont Company (monopoly chemicals and paint)
buyer, Carson, Pirie, Scott store (downtown Chicago department store)
trainee, Burroughs Adding Machine Company
lieutenant colonel, Fifth Army
research engineer, Continental Can Co. (monopoly can manufacturer)
engineer, Western Electric (manufacturing branch, AT&T)
sales trainee, Atlas Box Company
engineer, General Electric
pilot, American Airlines
public relations assistant, Acme Steel Company
teacher, Rich High School
labor-relations assistant, Ford Motor Company
writer, Time, Inc. (*Time* magazine)
accountant, Gulf Oil Company
copywriter, Chicago advertising agency

All of these are distinctly white-collar occupations. However, Whyte had not studied Park Forest because it was typical of the new suburban population. It interested him because he believed it represented the vanguard of emerging suburban culture.[16]

Whyte argued that his organisation men were shaping the isolated structure family and its suburban life style into mechanisms for supporting their own white-collar career advancement. Such a claim was premature in 1956; the evolution of the isolated structure family, and of life styles in the new suburbs, was extremely open-ended in the early post-war period. But from the mid 1950s onward, evolving suburban culture and white-collar status aspirations did become coordinated. By the 1960s suburban culture and white-collar occupational trends were perceived as aspects of a single social development: the forging of a new middle class. The next several sections describe elements of emerging suburban culture and their role in the emergence of the middle class.

THE NEW CULTURE: MIDDLE CLASS HOUSES

Most prominent as instrument, symbol and artifact of the new suburban culture was the detached single family suburban house on its grassy plot. The house styles favoured by post-war suburbanites evolved in conjunction with the day-to-day activities of the isolated structure family. The differences from the typical business-class suburban house of the 1920s were considerable, and very revealing of the cultural changes under way.

Distinct bedrooms for a husband's or wife's parents, or for live-in servants, common features of business-class suburban houses, completely disappeared. Bedroom types shrank to a bare minimum: 'master' bedroom, almost invariably for double bed; child's bedroom; and 'guest room', sometimes promoted as a dual-purpose bedroom and 'study' to be furnished with a 'sleeper couch' rather than a bed. All traces of the nineteenth century 'parlor' for formal entertaining disappeared. Varying combinations of living room, dining room, kitchen and 'family' room emerged, including the living room–dining room, the 'eat-in' kitchen, and the living room–family room with space for both adult and child activities. Numbers of bathrooms increased, with toilet, sink and tub-with-shower compressed into a single room. Closets abounded.

The relative distribution of construction expenditure reflected various priorities of post-war suburban families. Multiple bathrooms were very expensive, yet much desired. Closets, although not expensive in and of themselves, required that the overall size of the house be larger in order to keep the closets from eating up space within rooms. Another priority was eliminating stairs, either through the single-level 'ranch' style, or the one-and-a-half story 'split level' and 'raised ranch' designs. These covered more ground area, and therefore necessitated larger lots, than the popular two-story 'colonial' or neo-Elizabethan houses of the 1920s. For buyers with more money to spend, priority went to the large 'eat-in' kitchen, and to separate bedrooms for each child. Separation of living room from dining room was less important. A style of living evolved in which meals became less and less distinct as culturally significant activities. A defined room for dining thus declined in usefulness.

The new suburban house styles emphasised both family unity and individuality. By the onset of adolescence at the latest, all children required a room of their own. Sharing of bedrooms by boys and girls was frowned upon even for infants. Child-rearing norms encouraged developing the child's sense of responsibility for tasks and property. Having one's own room provided setting and rationale for this process. 'Cleaning up your room' became a central children's activity, especially from a parental perspective. The eat-in kitchen and the family room served the need for familial 'togetherness', one of many new concepts of the 1950s. Given the isolation of the suburban family both socially and physically, joint family activities had to expand in significance as the justification for enduring isolation's hardships. Rooms for interacting with visitors and non-resident relations, such as living rooms and dining rooms, could therefore disappear as the locus of activity shifted to eating and recreational rooms suitable *only* for family members. Television, already prevalent by 1950, concentrated activity even more intensely in the 'family' room where the set resided.

THE NEW CULTURE: TELEVISION AND FAMILY LIFE

Looking back from a hundred years in the future, the 1950s will stand out as the Age of Television. Initially, mistaken beliefs that TV programmes and advertising exerted powerful psychological influence over the viewers distorted understanding of the role of television in family life and cultural development. The advertising industry was obsessed with 'hidden' persuasion in the early years, believing that television could sell styles of living through the long-term influence of linking a company's products to a popular weekly programme. The assumption that TV was selling products *to* its bemused, passive viewers hindered the development of a more accurate understanding of television's role. In the mid 1960s, Marshall McLuhan achieved renown for pointing out what should have been obvious from the beginning: television is a psychologically 'cool' medium with little power to alter behaviour directly.[17]

Television alleviated some drawbacks of isolated family life in suburbs. It was a minimally adequate substitute for activities that were convenient and inexpensive in a dense city community, but became time-consuming and costly in the suburbs. Film-going, for example, declined catastrophically in the 1950s and television was supposedly the reason. But cinemas would undoubtedly have suffered severely even without television as the dispersion of their potential audience into a suburban settlement pattern increased the expense and effort of attending film shows. Theatres, amusement parks and other forms of 'live' entertainment suffered as well. Bars and taverns experienced declining patronage, and for the patrons who remained an important attraction was being able to watch TV away from home and family. Whether substituting TV for live entertainment and community events degraded the quality of cultural life was a question debated at great length. The viewers seemed satisfied, judging by the number of hours spent in front of the set. Studies showed that adult viewing averaged 2½ hours a day.[18]

Television provided families with a sense of participation in a common national culture. Television narrowed and homogenised cultural experiences in order to appeal to the largest possible audience. The television and advertising industries learned how to create programmes and commercial practices that reflected widely held social aspirations. For white-collar and suburban families, television both proposed and confirmed the emergence of the new middle class. For the advertising industry, and for manufacturers of consumer products, television functioned as a mode of obtaining information from viewers about how family life was changing and what products the changes might favour. Television allowed advertisers and manufacturers to interact with viewers at home in front of their sets in the mutual creation of a middle-class culture and its essential consumer products.

The most revealing of these mutually developed products was the TV dinner: a compartmentalised aluminium tray containing entrée, vegetable and potatoes or other starch, sealed and sold frozen in a cardboard package. Preparation consisted merely of heating in an oven and serving, no intermediate defrosting was necessary. When used with paper napkins, plastic cups and plastic utensils, as was customary, no washing or clean-up was required. The function of going to such lengths in order to provide the ultimate in simplicity was to offer a meal that could be prepared, eaten and disposed of entirely in the midst of watching television. The point was not so much to reduce the bother of meals as to conveniently combine eating and television watching. The TV dinner was a response to desires to integrate the ordinary activities of day-to-day family life with the emerging cultural patterns being disseminated by means of television.

Television helped isolated structure families to build a way of life for themselves that would satisfy their needs and also clearly signify their position in the social structure. Out of the mutual experimentation of viewers and advertisers came a reconstitution of everyday habits to emphasise the primacy of home life as the basis for social status. Cleanliness became an obsession, especially the glossiness of kitchen floors and enamel-coated appliances, the 'whiter than white' of laundered linens, the 'closeness' of the husband's shave, the gleam of teeth brushed religiously morning and night, and the suppression of bodily odours with special soaps, underarm deodorants and 'feminine' menstrual napkins. Television encouraged competitiveness about personal and home cleanliness that provided the aspiring family with a basis for confirming their ascension on the prestige hierarchy. They could verify their social standing to themselves through the appearance, and smell, of their home, their clothing, and their bodies. Almost any product facilitating neatness, cleanliness and order was a likely possibility for Madison Avenue promotion and viewer acceptance: greaseless cosmetics, do-it-yourself house paint, no-effort automobile waxes, spray can dusting compounds, spray air fresheners, and also powered implements such as clothes dryers, dishwashers, lawnmowers and snow-blowing machines.

Characters and family life portrayed on television aided the development of a culture suited to isolated families by presenting timeless models of day-to-day and year-by-year existence. The absence of change differed radically from nineteenth-century bourgeois family life, or business-class family life in the 1920s, where everything turned upon the progress of the family business, on very wide networks of relations, and upon the milestones of life and their rites of passage: birth, baptism, marriage, illness and death. Producers of situation comedies and adventure melodramas carefully purged their starring family's lives of such drastic changes: Ozzie and Harriet's boys, Ricky and David, remained perpetual teenagers; Beaver was always about ten-and-a-half; and when Lucy and Desi put the real-life birth of their son into an episode of their programme, it became a profound event in the history of television.

Gunsmoke, one of the longest running and most popular shows in TV history, employed a formula that completely reversed the customary relationship between the family and the milestones of life. Matt Dillon, Kitty and Chester played roles resembling father, loyal wife and obedient son, but without the ties of marriage, sex or even overt affection. Weekly episodes filled with the despair, joy, greed, transformation, or sudden death of transient characters surged and ebbed around their rocklike triangle, causing not a ripple of change for the three permanent figures. As in all the many serial programmes portraying unchanging family life, the objective was to assure the viewers that their own isolated family life style was not abnormal or psychologically incomplete.

THE NEW CULTURE: THE PRODUCTIVE HOME

As the new culture took shape, aspiring families used it to signify their social standing and to unite with others in solidifying their new status. A middle class based on symbols and subjective appearances, of the sort anticipated by C. Wright Mills, incorporated the traditional business class, the white-collar group, and aspiring working-class families into a single entity. Unlike the three older occupational and ownership-based groups, whose foundations were in the world of work, the new middle class was primarily cultural and had its foundations in the home and the residential community, especially the new suburban communities. The new culture associated with isolated structure families, suburbs and television became the cultural basis of the new middle class.

Aspiring families used the new culture to assert middle-class status and to forge middle-class unity. This assertiveness took the form of an ethic of productive home life; acquiring and maintaining symbols and implements of the new culture became the means of joining and building the new middle class. Families espousing the productive ethic in day-to-day home activity believed they were achieving, and then defending, a foothold in the new middle class.

New suburban communities provided the best setting for productive home life. Suburbs in which the majority of families adopted the new culture acquired reputations as middle-class communities. In return for their efforts, families gained secure middle-class status by virtue of residence in a middle-class town. It was on this basis that suburbanites threw themselves into cultivating the appearance of their homes, mowing the lawn, rooting out crabgrass, pruning the trees, repainting trim and shutters, repaving the driveway. Indoors, equal diligence went into vacuuming, floor polishing, enamel scrubbing, laundering and dusting. Powered appliances eased the physical effort of these tasks, but tended to increase the total energy and time devoted to productive home activities. Despite the fact that much of it was accomplished during 'leisure' hours, home productivity was hard work.

Building middle-class communities was the most important means of forging the new middle class. Metropolitan development had spread to all regions of the country by the 1950s, providing accessible suburban settings for the middle-class aspirations of most of the population. The social highway to middle-class status in Tennessee, or Kansas, ran through construction and growth of suburban communities in the existing metropolitan centres, and promotion of growth of smaller cities to metropolitan size. The new culture and its ethic of productive home life were available to aspiring families as tools for creating middle-class communities and joining the emerging national middle class. High standards of house and lot maintenance in a suburban town could attract new residents with strong aspirations and improve the community's social reputation. The ultimate objective of endless hours mowing the lawn and fertilising the trees was to entice a family of higher income and status than one's own to buy the house next door and improve the standing of the community, however infinitesimally.[19]

THE NEW CULTURE: SCHOOLS AND CHILDREN'S ACHIEVEMENT

Schools were central to community improvement efforts in the new suburbs. Parents regarded education as the essential mechanism for assuring their children middle-class status as adults. Parents looked to the schools to socialise children to middle-class culture so that they became enthusiastic, hard-working and ambitious. Parents demanded that the schools promote individual achievement in their children. The key to better achievement appeared to be more sophisticated, more expensive schools, and parents therefore mobilised community concern to improve them. They voted to raise property taxes in order to increase school expenditures, they approved bond issues to finance extravagant buildings, and they organised volunteer activities to support educational efforts, usually through Parent Teacher Associations (PTAs).

National norms of achievement, based on standardised testing, measured the success of the educational process. Parents expected schools to generate above-average test scores by their children, both individually and in community-wide averages. Middle-class communities sought highly trained teachers skilled in promoting student achievement on tests and inspiring children with the values of the new culture. Parents invested time and concern at home pressuring children to achieve in school. They expected to see the combination of their own efforts, town expenditures on school costs, and teachers' application of pedagogical methods in class reappear as appropriately high scores on the national tests. Whether or not these mechanistic expectations represented 'quality' in education, they were the kind of effectiveness ambitious parents demanded from their community schools.

By the 1960s middle-class parents became obsessed with anxiety that future admission to middle-class status would be limited to holders of college and university degrees. College entrance examinations, 'College Boards', became the new measure of school quality and status-conscious parents demanded that high schools prepare their children to excel in the competition for college admission. Middle-class parents equated the grades their children achieved in school with their prospects for success in college, and beyond college in future careers. Failure in school prefigured failure in adult life.

THE NEW CULTURE: TEENAGERS AND GOING STEADY

The new culture also evolved patterns of adolescent maturing and sexuality appropriate to a middle class founded on life style and appearances. Romantic attachment, pregnancy, childbirth, or marriage with an inappropriate partner endangered a young adult's chances of finishing college, beginning a successful career, and buying a home and establishing a family in a middle-class community. The new culture minimised these dangers by setting apart the 'teen' years between twelve and twenty as a period for experimentation. Teenage sexuality, infatuation, love, clothing, food, music, were tolerated and even indulged. Later, middle-class children would put aside such behaviour and become 'adults', especially in selecting marriage partners. Teenage 'going steady', boys and girls forming extremely intense monogamous love attachments carrying no implied promise that marriage would follow, gained acceptance with parents. Going steady found favour with middle-class parents exactly because of the cultural understanding that it was not a pre-marital attachment.

With the development of the teenage years as an experimental stage of life, middle-class parents did not need to dominate the social structure of early adult life in the way that business-class parents ruled high schools and leisure activities in the 1920s. The pre-Depression high school was a social labyrinth of dress codes, cliques, fraternities and sororities, exclusive dances and parties, all closely supervised by business-class parents. Working-class students could aspire to enter these preliminary institutions of business-class life, but almost invariably acceptance was denied them. Rejection initiated them in the bitter realities of class differences. In their study of culture and social class in the 1920s, using Muncie, Indiana, as a representative community, sociologists Robert and Helen Lynd described the great significance attaching to clothes among high school students. Lack of appropriately expensive and fashionable clothing exposed working-class children to embarrassment and rejection, frequently leading to their abandoning high school entirely. Numerous working-class mothers told the Lynds' interviewers that their daughters refused to go to high school because they could not afford the silk stockings mandated by the business-class cliques, or because they had only home-sewn dresses to wear.[20]

In contrast, the suburban high school of the 1950s could be an almost classless social democracy. Cultural change now authorised parents to break attachments formed by 'going steady' in the teen years, providing a guarantee that inter-class mingling would not permanently compromise the child's social progress as an adult. Children going on to college understood the importance of treating it as entry into a wholly different world from high school, severing teenage affections in order to be free for new sexual matches and social opportunities. The middle-class children who revolted against parental authority and married their teenage loves were led to believe that the consquence would be almost certain inability to succeed in a middle-class career. Typically parents who had saved to finance their children's college education would refuse to support them if they married, making college, career and middle-class success into a symbolic lifetime thrown away on romantic infatuation. Teenage marriage became identified more and more exclusively with the working class. This further eased the apprehension of middle-class parents about their children's intimacy with working-class children in teenage high school society. Differing class practices helped ensure that a middle-class child paired with a working-class partner in high school would not end up trapped in a debilitating cross-class marriage.

James Dean's popular film *Rebel Without A Cause* (1955), based on a sophisticated novel of the same title, used the transition from the pre-Depression business-class domination of high school life to the classless teenage democracy of the 1950s as its underlying theme. Dean played the child of a business-class family recently moved to modern California from an unidentified town still languishing in the old culture. He appears for the first day at his new high school in jacket and tie, standard pre-Depression dress code attire, and is as out of place as if he were wearing doublet, hose and Elizabethan ruffles. The students dictate what is to be worn here and their preferred uniform consists of black slacks, open collars and rolled-up sleeves.

Beneath a story line involving the need for Dean to prove his manliness, in competition with the working-class 'hoods' who dominate the teenage social structure, ran a theme of parental failure to perceive the demise of the older business-class mores and replace them with role models appropriate for children of the new middle class. A secondary plot, involving pop-singing star Sal Mineo, crudely underscored this theme. Mineo's character lives with a housekeeper in a mansion while his wealthy, irresponsible parents are abroad leading a hedonistic existence. Mineo attaches himself to Dean in the guise of orphan child desperately searching for a father who, culturally, has yet to evolve. Dean's character, who also needs such a new-style father, eventually transforms himself into the new middle-class prototype in the course of the story. Natalie Wood played the female character Dean wins away from her working-class clique, and the film closes with intimations that they will go on to become the new kind of parents the teenagers of the 1950s require.

American Graffiti, produced in the 1973, provides a nostalgic retrospective portrait of early teenage culture. The plot follows the summer antics of the 1962 graduating class of a California high school, and again the underlying theme is the separateness and classless democracy of the teenage world. Middle-class and working-class children mix together socially and sexually, all in a spirit of irresponsible fun. The two-class reality of the adult world reasserts itself at the end as the lead character, played by Richard Dreyfuss, departs by air for an unspecified eastern college while the closing credits spell out the distinctly working-class futures awaiting his companions.

FROM OCCUPATION TO INCOME: MIDDLE-CLASS STATUS AS A STYLE OF LIVING

As the new culture became pervasive, and the suburban, middle-class revolution progressed, they did more than establish a new occupational or economic category between the traditional business class above and the industrial working class below. Economically-grounded classes had dominated the pre-Depression social structure in large part because the culture of that era was industrial and extremely production-oriented. Factory production and machine-synchronised labour exerted powerful influences on cultural imagination, encouraging identification with one's economic class as the basis upon which individuals, families and cultural groups integrated themselves with the social system as a whole. In the post-war period, as a culturally-grounded middle class grew larger than either of the traditional economic classes, it contributed to dissolving the industrial focus of economic and social life. By the late 1960s it was apparent that the Industrial Age had come to an end and some as yet untitled 'post-industrial' society had begun to take shape.

The displacement of industrial culture weakened the economic and occupational foundations upon which status distinctions and community social structures had been based before the Depression and the Second World War. At first, in the 1940s and 1950s, middle-class status rested upon professional and white-collar occupations staffing the increasingly complex corporations and bureaucracies of the advanced industrial economy. Aspiring families used the new post-war suburbs to support and protect their collective efforts at forging the white-collar occupational group into a permanent middle class.

During the 1950s the new culture associated with suburban communities, isolated family structure, and productive home life worked a complementary transformation in the realm of business, work and occupations. Rather than struggling to preserve the traditional industrial distinctions between the blue-collared machine worker in the factory, the pink-bloused file clerk in the office and the white-coated engineer in the research lab, the business world turned to encouraging change in the social structure and anticipating the desires of the new middle class for new products and services. Television was essential to this shift in strategy because it allowed business to perceive cultural changes more accurately, and react to them more quickly, than had been possible with previous communications media.

Occupational and production-oriented distinctions declined in importance as life style and appearances became sufficient to signify membership in the new middle class. Increasingly, any family that chose to buy a home in a reputedly middle-class community, behave in a middle-class manner, and maintain all appearances of being middle class, could gain acceptance in the new middle class, regardless of the parents' occupations. An electrician married to a secretary could live next door to an accountant, dentist or advertising copywriter on fairly equal terms, providing their income was sufficient to afford a similar life style.

As more and more higher wage blue-collar people chose to take advantage of opportunities to live a middle-class way of life, income supplanted occupation as the means of achieving middle-class standing. Families whose income placed them in the middle ranks tended to adopt a middle-class life style and identify themselves as middle class. The new importance of income and life style induced movements within numerous occupations to raise salary levels so that the income the occupation provided correlated better with its purported social status. White-collar public employees, especially schoolteachers, took up unionism with a vengeance in the mid 1960s as a means of boosting their income to the level of business-sector occupations requiring similar education, experience and responsibility. Much of the impetus sending wives into the labour force in the 1960s and 1970s came from desires to strengthen the family's hold on middle-class status. Needs for additional income to 'make ends meet' frequently included paying the mortgage and taxes on a larger house in a more definitively middle-class suburb.

People with traditionally working-class occupations who wanted to preserve the solidarity of the working class found themselves in contradictory circumstances. The incentives to work hard at transforming suburban communities to middle-class standards and appearances were strong. 'Working-class' suburbs became increasingly anomalous because no prototype of a self-confident, improving working-class community gained widespread cultural recognition. Neither manufacturers nor the advertising industry showed much interest in developing products for a distinctive middle-income life style that was recognisably working-class.

Some culturally experimental products did appear, and were aggressively taken up by higher wage working-class families: the so-called leisure suit, recreational vans and 'campers', four-wheel-drive vehicles evolved from the military jeep, snowmobiles, outboard engines for small boats, peaked caps emblazoned with the corporate symbols of truck and heavy equipment manufacturers, electric organs for home music-making. However, working-class aspirations and manufacturer's product initiatives failed to coalesce around a *complete* working-class life style, leaving ambitious working-class families no medium for expressing their status aspirations except middle-class culture, products, houses and communities. Another complication was that most higher wage factory workers longed to see their children go to college and escape the blue-collar work world entirely. In so far as mixing culturally with white-collar and professional families improved their children's educational chances, working-class parents were willing to forgo efforts to create a distinctive working-class alternative to the new suburban, middle-class culture.[21]

CLASS AND COMMUNITY UNITED: THE MIDDLE-CLASS SUBURBS

The success of the suburban, middle-class revolution became complete during the 1960s, when the social status of suburban communities, and by extension the status of their residents, began to be calculated by their distance from the central city. Income was the means of supporting a middle-class way of life, but overt signs of one's income, such as expensive automobiles or extravagant clothing, acquired only a marginal role in rituals of claiming, and receiving recognition of, social standing. Instead, middle-class standing became associated with suburban communities, and communities farther out in the suburban fringe successfully asserted a higher status than those closer to the city.

As the distance-status correlation became established, it functioned prescriptively. Ambitious families with rising incomes sought homes in communities farther out in the fringe, and developers interested in building for the higher income buyer located their tracts of larger, more expensive homes as far out as their courage allowed. The quest for distance burdened husbands and fathers with longer and longer commuting to and from their central city offices, but the hardship quickly became a badge of pride and another sign of rising status. Social critic A. C. Spectorsky revealingly observed that it was men in the advertising industry who were most obsessed with the distance-status symbolism. Spectorsky immortalised the association of advertising and media with Madison Avenue and made Westport, Connecticut, an hour and a quarter from Manhattan by commuter train, infamous as their preferred home community. He called his new breed 'exurbanites', and their residential zone 'exurbia', to indicate that their status ambitions had carried them beyond all conventional notions of the metropolitan fringe.[22]

As the relationship between social status and residential location within the metropolitan community strengthened, it reflected the extent to which social class determination had become detached from the world of production and occupations, and reconstituted on the basis of culture, life style, income and subjective aspiration. A new middle class had used the community structure of the metropolitan area to establish itself as the dominant entity in the national social system. While occupational status was not entirely displaced, class became primarily a function of community of residence and of life style, and the community structure of metropolitan areas became the organising mechanism for the national social structure.

'Suburban' and 'middle class' became synonymous, despite the fact that more than one-third of the suburban population continued to be working class by occupation and by self-identification. Such is the power of a successful social revolution, that it can obscure the persisting elements of the previous social structure. The rise of a suburban middle class to dominance over all other classes and groupings in American society was a revolution made possible by the emergence of a metropolitan settlement pattern in the decades up to the 1940s. Suburban transformation, in turn, set the stage for a second metropolitan revolution, the rebellion of the central city black communities in the mid 1960s. We will consider the central city rebellion in Chapter 5.

Chapter 3 begins the policy theme, carrying the policy story from its origins in Roosevelt's New Deal to the height of central city renewal in the 1960s. Chapter 4 describes city life in the 1950s, emphasising three factors that later became prominent in the urban crisis of the early 1970s: race, ethnicity and poverty. Chapter 4's assessment of conditions before the turbulence of the 1960s will aid the evaluation of the urban crisis in Chapter 6. Our tracing of the suburban, middle-class revolution has carried us chronologically past these other developments in settlement and policy. As we go back to the late 1930s and move forward again to the 1970s, we will be observing the impact of the suburbs and the new middle class on the city, on urban policy, and on national life.

3. Saving the Central City

The objective of the first national urban policy was metropolitan central city revitalisation. This chapter describes the origins of national urban policy, the emergence of the 'saving the central cities' objective, and the establishment and operation of revitalisation programmes. Chronologically, it returns to the 1930s and President Roosevelt's New Deal and moves forward through the years of post-war suburban development discussed in Chapter 2, concluding in the mid 1960s when central city renewal was at its height.

This is the first of three chapters emphasising our policy theme and it begins with a brief discussion of settlement policy in general. *Urban* policy is only one of numerous approaches a nation can take regarding the forces of settlement: family change, work and lifestyle change, migration and community formation.

A specifically *urban* settlement policy originated in concern about distress in the cities at the depths of the Depression. Initially, the Roosevelt administration focused on banking, agriculture and manufacturing in its efforts to confront the Depression crisis. Urban policy began with an admission that cities had been neglected and a commitment to attend to the needs of the urban population.

Once settlement policy had been cast in urban terms, three factors dominated the formulation of urban policy: housing, city real estate and its owners and investors, and the impact of federal taxes on urban development. The construction industry was greatly interested in the housing question; the banking and insurances industries influenced much of what was done about urban real estate; and income tax subsidies gave middle- and upper-income home owners an increasing stake in federal decisions affecting urban areas.

Urban policy took shape as part of the Keynesian revolution in policy-making. Enthusiasm for British economist John Maynard Keynes' theory of national economic development and planning inspired Congress to adopt a general economic development policy in

1946 and to consider approaches to other policy areas designed to promote capital investment and economic growth. By the mid 1940s Congress was discussing urban policy in development terms. It was in this context that they selected metropolitan central city revitalisation as the objective of national urban policy.

The next four sections of the chapter describe the progress of central city redevelopment efforts. The initial federal programme, presented as Title I of the Housing Act of 1949, failed to elicit sufficient participation by the cities. By its fifth and final year, only $100 million was committed to projects, one-fifth of the $500 million authorised to be spent. Revisions incorporated in the Housing Act of 1954 introduced *urban renewal* and subordinated housing construction goals to more comprehensive central city development objectives. Innovative mayors were able to use urban renewal to better advantage; later their successes brought them national prominence as the 'renewal mayors'. The city-planning profession evolved a theory of *comprehensive planning* suitable for coordinating numerous urban renewal projects in different areas of a central city. Comprehensive planning theory also provided much needed coordination between urban renewal programmes and the federal inter-state highway programme introduced in 1956.

The chapter concludes with a brief evaluation of the independence of federal urban policy-making from powerful economic and political interests. Was central city revitalisation 'capitalist planning'; did it directly serve the needs of capital? Alternatively, was the objective of 'saving the central cities' arrived at by predominantly democratic and rational processes? Can the national urban policy of the 1940s and 1950s be described as an effort to plan logically and responsibly for the public interest? I have argued that it can. Later, in Chapters 6 and 7, we will evaluate the logical and rational character of urban policy a second time, as urban renewal concluded and the 'saving the central cities' objective was abandoned.

SETTLEMENT POLICY BEFORE THE URBAN ERA

National urban policy for the United States dates from 1937, when the Urbanism Committee of President Franklin Roosevelt's National Resources Committee presented its report, *Our Cities, Their Role in the National Economy*. Roosevelt almost certainly never read the report and

Congress never debated its recommendations. Yet *Our Cities* became a landmark because the President had allowed an official statement to appear arguing that the federal government should concern itself with urban policy issues. The reference to the economy in the report's title is indicative of how cautiously this first step toward a national urban policy was taken. The National Resources Committee would not authorise its Urbanism Committee to claim that cities deserved federal attention on their own merits. Economic distress caused by the Depression was the report's principal concern. Cities were important secondarily, as places where the majority of the population lived, and therefore where much distress was concentrated and compounded.

Urban policy is only one of the various forms that national settlement policy can assume. The social importance of cities, or even a preponderance of urban dwellers in the national population, does not necessarily compel the federal government to cast its settlement policy in urban terms. Nineteenth-century settlement policy followed the lead of population movement. The Northwest Ordinance, which guided settlement and eventual statehood in the territory that became the states of Ohio, Indiana, Illinois and Michigan, preceded the writing of the federal Constitution in 1787. The Ordinance's principles were adopted as the basis for all subsequent territorial organisation and statehood.

Westward expansion was the theme of Secretary of the Treasury Albert Gallatin's 1810 report on canals, roads and national development. Independent settlement of Texas while it was officially part of Mexico led, in conjunction with other factors, to the Mexican War of 1846 and seizure of the south-western area later formed into the states of Utah, Nevada, Arizona, New Mexico and California. Western settlement policy dispute brought on the Civil War. The Republican Party organised itself and gained control of the federal government in the 1860 elections not to destroy slavery and southern slave-based society for abstract reasons, but because slave society threatened to continue expanding into the western territories. The fact that slaves in the West would become a free and nominally equal black population when slavery was abolished, as even Southerners believed it eventually would be, spurred the Union armies as much as their hatred for slavery as an institution in their merciless devastation of the Confederacy. The Republican slogan for the western territories: 'Free Soil, Free Labor, Free Men', had an implied meaning of: 'White

Soil, White Labor, White Men' that everyone understood, North and South, white and black, free and slave.[2]

An important exception to following the lead of population movement arose in the case of urbanisation. The federal structure of national government in the US demands that policies relate not only to large or majority segments of the population, but also to a majority of states. It was not until 1920 that the urban population surpassed the rural in size, and even then the majority of states remained predominantly rural. Urbanisation was highly concentrated in the north-eastern, middle Atlantic, and Great Lakes regions.

Many historians and commentators have argued that a strong anti-urban cultural tradition spawned a powerful resistance to conceding that America had become an urban society. Jefferson took the lead here as an intellectual influence, followed by a parade of figures including Emerson, Thoreau, Abraham Lincoln and Mark Twain. William Jennings Bryan boasted that the cities would spring up again after being destroyed, if farms and rural society remained sound. Franklin Roosevelt owed his electoral success partly to his image as a gentleman farmer.

Others, notably the urban historian Charles Glaab, have cast doubt on the strength of anti-urbanism, pointing out that much of the enthusiasm for western settlement consisted of expectations about founding great cities. Speculators rushed to acquire title to the land at the juncture of the Ohio and Mississippi rivers, where the city of Cairo, Illinois, now stands, convinced that the nation's greatest metropolis would soon arise on their site. St. Louis, at the confluence of the Mississippi and Missouri rivers, grew to enjoy a future foreseen for a hundred similarly desirable locations. Charles Dickens' most prominent portrayal of the United States is the western town speculation swindle in *Martin Chuzzlewit*. Dickens modelled the incident after schemes involving Cairo, which he had visited. He was rumoured to have invested and lost a considerable sum on an early Cairo venture that went bankrupt.[3]

The dominant factor in national settlement policy in the late nineteenth century was open encouragement of European immigration, almost all of which flowed to cities. More than one-third of all large city residents in 1910 were foreign born. Part of the anti-urban tradition was a belief that cities would breed the decadent and anti-democratic influences characteristic of Europe. Yet such beliefs did not generate significant opposition to immigration.

Anti-foreign rhetoric in the Populist movement of the 1890s did more to alienate urban voters from the Populist cause than to build support for restricting immigration. When strict limits *were* placed on immigration immediately following the First World War, concern about the undesirable influence of immigrant-populated cities was not an important factor.

James Bryce, the British political commentator whose *American Commonwealth*, originally published in 1887, became the bible of academic political science, warned that city politics inevitably became corrupt whenever the population included a significant proportion of immigrants. But Bryce's remedy for the immigration problem was aggressive leadership by the city's natural political and social elite, combined with political education and rapid assimilation of immigrants as fully equal citizens. Bryce considered immigrants a problem because of the ways existing corrupt elements in urban politics could manipulate them, not because they brought with them European pathologies dangerous to republican government. Nor did Bryce advocate limiting immigration. Even Woodrow Wilson, whose contributions to founding American political science included a racist belief in the political superiority of the Anglo-Saxon, Germanic and Swiss peoples, did not cultivate an anti-urban bias or recommend restricting immigration.[4]

Allowing the free flow of millions of immigrants to the cities between the 1870s and the 1920s functioned in national policy terms as a *quid pro quo* with industrial and urban interests. Immigration provided them with a labour force they much desired. In return, they did not demand federal government concern for city problems.

When urban concerns did become the focus of national politics, in the Progressive era, the federal role consisted of reforms that rationalised economic and political institutions and relationships: direct election of Senators, federal income taxes, regularisation of competition and monopoly, pure food and drug legislation, abolition of child labour, voting rights for women, and so on. Progressive philosophy assigned specifically urban reforms to city government. Strong city self-government, municipal home rule, was the cornerstone of urban Progressivism. Progressive political theorists argued vigorously that what the Founding Fathers meant by the 'separation of powers' they considered so crucial to the success of the federal Constitution included not just the traditional separation between executive, legislative and judicial powers, but also the separation of powers among federal, state and municipal governments. The Progressives' strongest indictment of the political failings inherited from the late nineteenth century focused on failure to provide large cities with sufficient powers of self-government to accommodate the needs of the urban population.[5]

THE BEGINNINGS OF AN URBAN POLICY

The federal government finally initiated a specifically urban policy in the context of the Depression crisis and the politics of the New Deal. From one perspective, it would seem obvious that settlement policy and policy for future national development should take an urban form at that juncture in American history. The urban population had recently become the majority, and the distress and suffering caused by the Depression appeared most severe in cities. The central strength in Roosevelt's electoral coalition consisted of big city Democratic political machines and masses of urban working-class voters. The historical tradition that portrays Franklin Roosevelt as the ultimate political pragmatist concludes from these circumstances that the social and political strength of urban forces made an urban settlement policy Roosevelt's only feasible choice.[6]

Political advantage was only one factor encouraging formulation of an urban policy, however. Similar political circumstances prevailed during the Depression of 1893–7, including strong Democratic machines in the cities. Yet for the 1896 election the Democrats rejected Grover Cleveland, an incumbent President with a strong urban following, in favour of William Jennings Bryan, merger with the Populist movement, and a stridently anti-urban campaign.

Roosevelt's personal inclinations about confronting the Depression ran toward rural resettlement to reverse what he considered an imbalance between urban and industrial, and rural and agricultural, aspects of national society. Mark Gelfand has pointed out that Roosevelt targeted his programmes on urban residents and interests, rather than on cities and their systemic problems. No structural programmes were proposed for cities comparable to such rural and regional development projects as the Rural Electrification Administration or the Tennessee Valley Authority. The New Deal was capable of encouraging, and responding to, urban electoral support without becoming predominantly urban in focus.[7]

The most powerful force pressuring the federal government to design an urban policy was a belief that the industrial and urban form of settlement represented the final stage of US development, at least for the foreseeable future. It is only in retrospect, from beyond the 1950s and 1960s, that the Great Depression appears as a prolonged hesitation in long-term development. Policy planners and analysts working during the course of the Depression tended to project characteristics of the current situation as permanent features of future decades. When the crisis failed to respond to Roosevelt's initial programmes, and especially when unemployment spiked back up to 25 per cent in 1937, discussions of the future began to include less and less talk of recovery and more and more consideration that development had achieved its mature form. Many believed that development had run its course and that the 1940s, 1950s and beyond would see only gradual adjustment and accommodation to the established urban industrial social and economic structure. Birth rates during the Depression fell to very low levels and demographers encouraged the idea that development had entered its final stage by estimating low birth rates for as far into the future as they could forecast. As slow adjustment proceeded, unemployment would moderate and labour, industry and agriculture would move toward a stable equilibrium. Federal urban policy under these circumstances would resemble federal agricultural or natural resource policy; it would be a policy of management and conservation for a prominent and largely unchanging sector of national life.

The group responsible for proposing and defining New Deal settlement policy, the National Resources Committee, began its work under a weak mandate. The Committee descended from efforts by professional social scientists in the 1920s to establish a working relationship with the federal government. President Hoover had authorised formation of a voluntary President's Research Committee on Social Trends, to prepare reports that would 'supply a basis for the formulation of large national policies looking to the next phase in the nation's development'. The Committee was not expecting the stock market crash that occurred soon after its' work began, or the Depression that followed. By the time Hoover received the Committee's final report, in the autumn of 1932, prospects for the next phase of national development had changed drastically.[8]

Yet the Depression convinced Committee members that a clearly articulated development policy was more necessary than ever. They persuaded Roosevelt to continue the work of the Social Trends group by appointing a permanent committee reporting to the President. Roosevelt had the greatest difficulty with proposals to use the word 'planning' in the Committee's name. 'National Resources Committee' represented a concession to his fears that any hint of planning would set off howls of protest about preparations for a Roosevelt dictatorship.

The National Resources Committee dedicated itself to moving the President and the federal government toward formally adopting a national development policy. The members were not committed to any specific policy, only to policy as a process. To them, the most important aspect of their first report, *Regional Factors in National Planning and Development*, presented in 1935, was its broaching of the possibility of national development planning. When their proposal of a regional framework for planning met with mixed responses, they made little effort to promote regionalism further. Consideration of an urban policy was placed in the hands of a subcommittee on urbanism, presumably to avoid suggesting that the main Committee had any special preference for an urban focus in national development planning. When the Urbanism Committee drafted a recommendation for a permanent federal bureau of urban affairs, the National Resources Committee vetoed it and directed that no reference be made in the final report even to the possibility of an urban bureau. The Committee members believed, quite correctly, that if and when the federal government adopted an explicit development policy, the focus would not be selected because of pressure from a powerful interest, whether urban, regional, agricultural, environmental or industrial.[9]

OUR CITIES: THE URBANISM COMMITTEE'S REPORT

The Urbanism Committee's public report adhered to the neutral strategy ordained by the National Resources Committee for all its publications. If the federal government were to establish a development policy, the *Our Cities* report argued, our social scientific research suggests that policy about structures and types of settlement, present and future, should be urban in orientation.

Following a strong statement that urbanisation was the form

assumed by national settlement in the nation's 'maturity', the
Committee wrote, under the heading 'Cities and Public Policy':

> Compared to the attention that has been devoted to agriculture and
> the rural phase of American life, that part of America which is
> symbolized by the city has been almost completely neglected and
> has never fully emerged into our national consciousness. . . . As
> long as the United States was principally a rural and agricultural
> country, as long as our economy was relatively primitive, local and
> self-sufficient, as long as our rich natural resources were scarcely
> known or exploited, and as long as a relatively secure and
> expanding life was within the reach of even a rapidly increasing
> population, it was to be expected that our outlook and policies
> should have been largely rural. But since the city has come to play
> such a preponderant role in our national existence, it becomes
> imperative that it acquire a central position in the formulation of
> national policy.[10]

As policy, the report was primarily descriptive. It delineated past
development and the situation as of 1937 from an urban perspective.
Like all national policies, its major function was to define an outlook,
a framework for discussion and decision-making. The *Our Cities*
report signalled that the federal government was now prepared to
hear social and economic issues presented as urban problems.
Beyond this, the report's content and logic are interesting but only
marginally important. Louis Wirth supervised much of the research
and his sociological theory of urbanism pervades the text. Wirth used
the fact that the majority of the nation's population was now urban to
argue that cities and urban issues should receive primary attention
because the majority of Americans were now 'city' men with
personalities and social relations 'distinctive from those of the country
man'. If rural or small-town life were for some reason more desirable,
national policy should be formulated with that principle in mind.
However, the report argued, urban life had clearly become dominant:

> It may well be that the future of our civilization will in large
> measure depend not upon man's ability to escape from the city but
> upon his ability to master and use the forces that move and control
> it. It is doubtful whether without the city we can hope to enjoy the

plane of living that contemporary civilization makes possible. The central problem of national life in regard to cities is a problem of creating those conditions that are required to make cities livable for human beings in a machine age.[11]

The pessimism about urban life inherent in this statement was typical of Wirth's approach. Scepticism toward city life persisted throughout the course of post-war urban policy. Regardless of successes in each major federal programme, subsequent programmes would be prefaced by new forebodings of social distress and deterioration. Continuing pessimism was not inherited from Wirth or the *Our Cities* report, but it may have played an important role in justifying federal urban policy.

OTHER ORIGINS OF URBAN POLICY

In addition to the question of national settlement policy and the appropriate federal role in development, three other pressing national concerns contributed to the emergence of an urban policy: housing; the relative profitability of real estate compared with industrial capital and other forms of investment; and taxation and its effects on urban development. Each factor became prominent in national urban policy for reasons specific to its own history. In the case of tax policy, the interrelation with urban questions was excluded from urban policy controversy for more than twenty years, despite the powerful indirect influence of tax policy on the effectiveness of federal urban programmes. Housing policy probably became more urban in focus than it should have, given the tremendous need for better rural housing. Urban development became so prominent in the post-war period in part because it aided major interests in these independent spheres in furthering their purposes.

To many, housing was a more pressing issue than all other aspects of urban policy put together. Housing construction stagnated in the 1920s and the supply of adequate working-class housing shrank to dangerously low levels during the Depression. A distinct housing interest coalesced around Senator Robert Wagner of New York, who became its champion. The group included progressive social reformers, urban labour unions, social service professionals and agencies, and a great mass of working-class people. Their objective was federally-financed public housing. After considerable hesitancy on the part of Roosevelt and many Democrats in Congress, they were rewarded with passage of the Housing Act of 1937, popularly known as the Wagner–Steagall Act. The Act created the United States Housing Authority, designed to loan federal money to local housing agencies to assist them in the assembling, development and administration of slum clearance and low-rent housing construction projects. Between then and 1972, when the Nixon administration introduced a new approach to housing subsidies, Congress appropriated almost $4 billion for the programme and slightly less than 1 million units of housing were constructed. The wording of the Act did not favour cities over towns or rural areas, but about two-thirds of the units were eventually built in cities of over 50,000 and less than one-fifth in towns under 10,000. This was approximately what Wagner and his associates had hoped would occur. Up to 1970, 12 per cent of all units constructred were in either New York City or Chicago.[12]

Public housing had powerful opponents and some of the central aspects of urban policy resulted from their efforts to stifle the low-rent housing programme. The National Association of Real Estate Boards led the opposition, representing owners of city land and buildings, especially apartment buildings. Part of their campaign involved attacking public housing as a threat to private provision and ownership of housing. Part was tied in with long-standing conflict between the real estate interests and the progressive housing interests, including confrontation over zoning regulation, rent control, building codes, health regulation, building inspection, and landlord–tenant legal relations.

Most dangerous of all, for the real estate interests, was the threat posed by the 1937 Housing Act programmes to the long-term profitability of investment in city land and residential housing. The progressive housing groups supporting subsidised public housing looked at city slums and blighted areas as a problem of inadequate and dangerous housing for working-class people. The real estate interests also recognised slums, and blighting of sound residential neighbourhoods, as serious housing problems. However, as deterioration worsened slums had to be cleared, preparing the way for new development. In the long run, in other words, slums and blight represented new opportunities to real estate interests. By associating slum clearance exclusively with federally subsidised construction of low-rent public housing, the Housing Act not only threatened to drive private owners out of the working-class housing business, but hampered real estate interests in obtaining federal slum clearance programmes for private redevelopment, whether housing, commercial, or other uses.

The public housing programme strongly implied that low-income people should continue to live in the central areas of cities where slums tended to form. While real estate interests were not necessarily opposed to this for the time being, giving low-income people an exclusive claim on central areas of the city would severely limit long-term development options. Above all, the profitability of city real estate depended upon flexibility of uses. Real estate interests needed as much freedom as possible to convert properties and neighbourhoods from housing to office use to commercial use and back again as prospects changed over several decades.

The real estate interests moved to counter the threat from public housing programmes by subsuming them within more comprehensive proposals for slum clearance and urban development. While they joined in the larger defence of capitalism and private ownership against the socialistic tendencies of the New Deal, real estate investors were eager to obtain federal programmes subsidising and facilitating private urban investment and development. Their opposition to public housing programmes was actually secondary to their concern for the profitability of capital invested in urban real estate. They wanted federal policies and programmes similar to those benefiting other forms of capital: minerals and natural resources, agriculture, heavy industry and transportation. The Depression had a disastrous impact on urban property values. The more serious long-term danger for urban real estate interests, however, was that federal efforts to lift the country out of the Depression would ignore the problems of cities. New Deal programmes concentrated on reviving agriculture and manufacturing. When the Second World War began, industry and agriculture were favoured again. If the war ended with the economy booming but with large city downtown areas still mired in Depression, what hope would there be of restoring urban real estate investment to a profitable basis? The urban policy focus that eventually emerged in the late 1940s, an 'urban renewal' campaign to save the metropolitan central cities, was even more desperately important to real estate owners than it was to the working-class city dwellers usually thought of as the principal intended beneficiaries.

The third factor, federal taxation and subsidies in relation to individuals and families, contributed to the emergence of an urban policy in a complicated manner. Above all, the Depression was a financial crisis, and reviving the banking system after its collapse in early 1933 was a central New Deal objective. Congress established the Federal Home Loan Bank Board (FHLBB) in 1932 to provide supervision and emergency assistance for savings and loan associations and other institutions with major investments in home mortgages. Roosevelt publicised the funding given to this agency as 'emergency relief' for homeowners with mortgages, but in fact the primary purpose was to help the lending institutions. As more and more federal support flowed to the mortgage-granting institutions, homeowners benefited as well because more funds became available to borrow for purchasing or refinancing houses.[13]

The Federal Housing Administration (FHA) was established in 1934 to directly insure loans on housing by banks, insurance companies and secondary mortgage market lenders. Here too, helping and protecting the lending institutions was the immediate objective. The popularity of the Bank Board and FHA programmes as solutions to finance and banking problems resulted in abundant federal subsidisation of the kinds of families owning mortgaged homes: white-collar and high-wage, working-class people. The FHA and FHLBB quickly gained independent control of their activities. The narrow self-interest of the lending institutions dominated internal agency decision-making. The agencies assisted lending institutions in restricting insured mortgages to the safest borrowers: primarily white single family home buyers with secure employment in stable neighbourhoods or, once building resumed after the war, new suburban developments.

In short, because of the vast amounts of money involved, a federal programme subsidising home mortgage borrowers as a means of aiding banking and insurance capital came to play a more influential role in federal housing and development policy than either the public housing programme or the direct efforts to initiate urban development programmes. A revealing indicator of the primacy of banking interests in urban policy is the fact that throughout the course of federal involvement the House of Representatives has assigned control of urban affairs to its Committee on Banking and Currency.[14]

Another tremendously important federal tax and subsidy policy affecting urban development has been the exemption of mortgage loan interest and local property tax expenses from federal income taxation. Established for reasons having little to do with homeownership and nothing at all with urban policy, the mortgage and property tax exemptions enjoyed by home owners were quite small in the 1930s when federal income tax rates were very low. With the war, taxes rose and in the 1950s they rose further. Each increase in tax rates converted every mortgage interest or property tax dollar a homeowner could exempt from federal income tax into a larger and larger subsidy to homeownership: 10 cents per dollar when federal tax rates were 10 per cent, 25 cents per dollar of mortgage interest or taxes at 25 per cent tax rate, and so on.

These federal subsidies, known today as 'tax expenditures', began to amount to several billions of dollars a year in the 1950s. This was more money by far than the federal government was paying out in direct expenditures under urban renewal or other programmes. Economist Henry Aaron estimated the amount of subsidy for the year 1966 at approximately $7 billion in increased federal income tax that homeowners would have had to pay if their investments and loans for their homes had been taxed in the same manner as other kinds of assets. Aaron estimated for a hypothetical 1972 comparison between a homeowner and a home renter, each with a gross income of $15,000 and a family of four, that the tax rules were providing the homeowner with a subsidy of $594.[15]

While everyone was aware of the size and significance of the federal income tax subsidy to homeowners, urban policy debate did not expand to include discussion of its effects, relative to other programmes and federal expenditures, until the 1970s. One reason the effects were not discussed sooner was because the tax subsidy increased in proportion to a homeowner's income due to the progressive rate structure of the federal income tax. The bulk of the benefits was flowing to the rich and the upper middle class, and neither Congress nor most other interests involved in urban policy controversy was inclined to meddle with that state of affairs. Needless to say, several billions of dollars a year in subsidy for owning homes rather than renting housing had considerable impact on settlement patterns and private housing construction within urban areas.

THE KEYNESIAN REVOLUTION AND POLICY FOR DEVELOPMENT

Roosevelt's New Deal committed the federal government to organising national revival from the Depression. What post-Depression society would be like was considered beyond the control of any single force or group, whether government, banking and finance, industry, or even business and government in partnership. Projecting a Depression-like urban industrial equilibrium as the mature stage of development, as the National Resources Committee did in *Our Cities* and other reports, was a way of officially ending the economic crisis with an absolute minimum of federal expenditure, action, or institutional reconstruction. Regardless of how constrained the federal government's role might be, however, it was committed to *development*. Once the freedom of preparing for war allowed policy controversies to flower and expand, development became the objective of policy. It was in this political and intellectual climate that John Maynard Keynes' theory of a politically managed economy revolutionised policy discussion in the US. The effect on urban policy was to combine diverse controversies into one broad debate about urban development, which in turn formed a major subheading of general national development policy.

Keynes' *General Theory of Employment, Interest and Money* excited Americans because he argued that prosperous capitalist expansion could be initiated and sustained by managing investment and consumption. US economists had demoralised themselves miserably struggling to combat the Depression by tinkering with production and wholesale prices of producers' durable goods. Keynes encouraged them to stand at a new vantage point and attack problems in new ways. Converts to Keynesianism immediately recognised that urban areas were excellent targets for a policy intent upon spending federal money to stimulate and structure consumption. Perhaps the very first American policy statement grounded in Keynesian theory was Guy Greer and Alvin Hansen's *Urban Redevelopment and Housing – A Plan for Post-War*, published in 1941. Where experts on cities had been cautious about broadening urban questions into issues of general national concern, Greer and Hansen examined urban areas as targets for national policies about investment, consumption and economic growth and concluded that a comprehensive national urban development policy was needed.

While it is appropriate to single out their pamphlet as the beginning of the evolution of urban development policy, it is also important to remember that the development focus came to dominate urban policy because of the Keynesian revolution in policy discussion, not because urban development proved superior on its own merits to other approaches to urban questions.[16]

Hansen and Greer assigned the National Resources Planning Board (successor to the National Resources Committee) the role of supervising urban development policy in their proposed scheme. Keynesianism also captured the imagination of many Board members, and by 1945 they had become the leading advocates of Keynesian policy-making in the federal government. Congress staged a major debate on the Keynesian orientation to policy-making in its 1945 session, but failed to pass the proposed law mandating *full employment* as the goal of federal economic policy. Keynesians achieved a more limited success the following year. The word 'full' had to be deleted from the law's title; instead the 1946 Act established a Council of Economic Advisors to design policy for the President that would achieve 'maximum employment, production and purchasing power'. Congress backed away from a strong commitment to a policy goal, but they could not reverse the revolution that had occurred in the terms of policy controversy.[17]

SAVING THE CENTRAL CITY, AN URBAN DEVELOPMENT POLICY

The Keynesian revolution established economic development as the federal government's chief policy concern. Settlement policy now became a question of improving the spatial organisation of economic activity. The metropolitan area gained acceptance as the appropriate settlement pattern for large urban centres virtually by default. Whether smaller centres could also be classified as metropolitan in structure was decided in the 1950s. President Eisenhower's Bureau of the Budget seized official responsibility for defining metropolitan areas from the Census Bureau in hopes of coordinating the policy implications of settlement statistics with their general political strategy. The Budget Bureau favoured a monolithic metropolitan area definition, one that treated both the New York metropolis of more than 10 million and central cities of 50,000 with modest suburban populations as the same kind of economic and social community. Placing the Budget Bureau in charge of determining the desired national settlement pattern terminated meaningful controversy. For policy purposes, the country now consisted of two kinds of settlements: metropolitan and non-metropolitan. Spatial development policy could relate to one or the other, or both.

With issues of national spatial structure excluded from debate, urban policy discussion centred upon the metropolitan area. Settlement and development policy for non-metropolitan parts of the country were treated separately from urban questions. National economic development policy assumed that economic development would manifest itself spatially as metropolitan growth. Urban policy therefore became a question of what constituted an appropriate metropolitan policy. Saving the central cities of metropolitan areas emerged as the major objective of urban policy as the response to this question. Left to its own economic incentives, new residential, commercial, or industrial development seemed to seek out sparsely settled land toward the edges of metropolitan areas, or central locations in small metropolitan areas. Post-war development might bypass larger and older central cities, leading to decay at the core of metropolitan areas that could eventually hamper national economic growth.

The major interests anxious to influence urban policy reorchestrated their programmes on the theme of saving the central city. The National Association of Real Estate Boards (NAREB) was already concentrating its efforts on deteriorated areas of large cities. Even before Greer and Hansen's Keynesian pamphlet appeared, NAREB put forward a document on housing and blighted areas calling for as much as $40 billion in federal assistance to private urban reconstruction. NAREB incorporated its opposition to public housing in the scheme by lobbying to constrain the activities of federal and local public housing agencies as much as possible, excluding them entirely from programmes involving land acquisition, slum clearance and redevelopment. In 1943 NAREB's research branch, the Urban Land Institute, got Senator Wagner to sponsor a Neighborhood Development Act. Greer, Hansen and others prevailed upon Senator Elbert Thomas of Utah to present their proposal: a Federal Urban Redevelopment Act. The housing interests mobilised to ensure that low-rent public housing remained the dominant element in federal urban programmes.[18]

Congress finally authorised central city redevelopment programmes in the Housing Act of 1949. Title I: 'Slum Clearance and Community Development and Redevelopment' provided $1 billion in loans and $500 million in direct grants for planning, acquiring and clearing land, and preparing sites for new uses. Programmes would be administered by independent 'local public agencies', LPAs as they were later known, in each city. In response to the real estate interests, local public housing agencies were excluded from acting as redevelopment agencies. Congress declined to conclude the struggle between the real estate and the housing interests, however. Title I projects had to be 'predominantly residential'. The Act included a 'National Housing Policy and Goal' statement: 'a decent home' and a 'suitable living environment' for every American family. This goal was to be attained primarily by encouraging private enterprise to meet the need for housing, governmental assistance being confined to slum clearance, alleviation of 'blight' and provision of public housing for families too poor to afford private market rents. In retrospect, it is remarkable that confrontation between real estate and housing interests at the city level did not completely stalemate the Title I programme.[19]

URBAN REDEVELOPMENT: THE FIRST FIVE YEARS

The Title I redevelopment programme was not a federal handout and cities did not rush to participate. The programme's terms presented as many drawbacks as advantages. Title I offered cities funds to purchase slum property at its market value, clear it of structures, prepare it for new uses, and 'write down' the resale price to a level comparable with the cost of empty suburban land. In practice, the market price of land in slums was a fiction, for most slum property was not in demand. The money for buying slum property would be going partly to owner occupants of multi-family dwellings, but also to absentee landlords, 'slumlords', especially in the largest cities. The money for clearance and preparation would go to construction companies. And the benefits from artificially lowered resale prices would accrue to the new developer: a large real estate investor, commercial management company or department store for example. If upper- or upper-middle income apartments were planned, resale write downs would ultimately benefit the city's wealthier tenants by lowering their rents. Meanwhile, unless appropriate numbers of new public housing units were included in the project plan, the slum clearance would be reducing the amount of housing available to low-income people, thereby either driving them out of the city entirely or forcing up their rents in other neighbourhoods. Title I guarantees that families driven out by slum clearance would obtain relocation assistance proved largely ineffective.

Mayors had to calculate very carefully to determine whether urban renewal would benefit them politically. An aging, declining city could only be 'saved' under Title I if someone at the city level organised the redevelopment scheme, most of which necessarily had to consist of convincing large real estate and development interests to invest in major projects at locations currently plagued by slums and blight. Unless everything came together exactly, a mayor could labour for years and end up having the inadvertent failure of redevelopment ruin his political career. On the other hand, there was no practical way a city's real estate and commercial interests could initiate and oversee Title I redevelopment without the enthusiastic cooperation of the city's political leaders.

In the first four years only $105 million of the $500 million in Title I grant money was even tentatively allocated to projects. The real estate interests recognised that nothing of significance would be accomplished until the law was rewritten. The election of Dwight Eisenhower in November 1952 represented a severe setback for the public housing interests. Eisenhower was philosophically opposed to 'socialistic' programmes such as low-rent public housing. He was, however, sympathetic to revising the redevelopment programme. Early in 1953 he appointed a President's Advisory Committee on Government Housing Policies and Programs out of which came proposed changes eventually written into the 1954 reauthorisation of redevelopment.[20]

URBAN RENEWAL: THE 1954 REVISIONS

What is familiarly referred to as urban renewal consisted of programmes designed under the revised provisions in the Housing Act of 1954. Public housing sustained the expected setback. The number of units authorised for construction was reduced to 10,000 per year, compared with 800,000 over six years in the 1949 legislation.

Redevelopment capital grant authorisations increased to $400 million over two years, compared with $500 million for the five years 1950–4 (of which about $400 million had not been spent). By 1968 Congress had authorised $10 billion for redevelopment under the 1954 revised provisions.[21]

The new provisions encouraged city political leaders to use the redevelopment programme as the basis for planning city-wide economic and social renewal. A considerable proportion of each project grant could be expended on planning and administration. A proposal was most likely to be funded if the applying city could show that the project was coordinated with a comprehensive plan for the whole city. The 1954 provisions required that a 'workable program' for combatting slums and blight be prepared, although cities were not held to carrying out the programme they submitted. Most importantly for the real estate interests, the federal Urban Renewal Administration was authorised to expend up to 10 per cent of programme funds on non-residential projects. By 1965 Congress had raised the non-residential proportion to 35 per cent. And Congress revised and expanded FHA programmes to cover rehabilitation of existing housing, including rental housing, in hopes of encouraging FHA activity in conjunction with urban renewal projects.[22]

1954 Housing Act urban renewal looked much more inviting to mayors. The new guidelines and opportunities made it worth the effort to attempt what renewing an aging central city necessitated. On the political side, mayors had to mobilise a broad alliance of real estate owners, developers, commercial and office business interests, banks, construction industry companies and unions, and electoral factions. On the administrative side, they had to develop the capability to plan and carry out projects involving coordinated efforts by virtually all operating departments, plus contract work by numerous private firms. Administrative control from Washington was remarkably liberal where the larger purposes of renewal projects were concerned; regulation was strict primarily about determining the market value of properties to be purchased, and avoiding corruption in the selection of contractors. It was up to the cities and the private developers to use the programme for worthwhile ends.

Central business district revitalisation aroused the greatest enthusiasm as a comprehensive urban renewal scheme. Current owners and investors in centrally located properties naturally had intense personal interests in concentrating metropolitan area offices, department stores, and other high-rent uses in a central business district. Penn Center, the Pennsylvania Railroad Company's privately financed renewal project adjacent to its main station in the centre of Philadelphia, undertaken in the late 1940s, provided a prototype for multi-block, high-rise office and commercial renewal. Planners studied Penn Center for land use design ideas and as a case-study in investment profitability. Another new development of the late 1940s, the suburban shopping centre, presented competition for downtown commercial ventures. Department store chains planning expansion tended to assume that their total sales potential throughout a metropolitan area had a fixed limit. What they had to determine was whether that potential would be more effectively exploited with a large central business district store, with several suburban stores, or with a combination of locations. During the late 1950s and early 1960s many cities used urban renewal to turn their central downtown areas into central business district complexes, including office buildings, banks, department stores and speciality retail shops, hotels, convention centres, theatres and even sports stadiums. Without urban renewal, some of this development might have located in the suburban fringe. Many mayors and central business district real estate owners believed they were fostering development that would not have occurred at all in the absence of urban renewal.

Mayors who were able to organise strong coalitions of political factions and development interests scored the most impressive successes with the urban renewal programme. David Lawrence, elected mayor of Pittsburgh for the first time in 1945, forged and led a downtown revitalisation coalition even before urban renewal was available. Lawrence was a Democrat struggling to retain political control that had been wrested from the Republicans, led by the powerful Mellon family, during the Depression. When the Mellons proposed to clear the 'Point' area at the centre of Pittsburgh, where Fort Duquesne once stood, of aging industrial uses and revive the downtown, Lawrence supported their plan and then negotiated an alliance between their business and development forces and his working-class political machine. The allied interests proposed a grandiose 'Pittsburgh Renaissance' and expanded the Mellon plan into 'Gateway Center', a $50 million office building complex. Clearance and construction proceeded rapidly and the completed project proved quite profitable commercially. The political benefits

Lawrence accrued from the Center's success encouraged other mayors to form similar alliances with commercial and real estate interests as their strategy for urban renewal.

Using the coalition strategy pioneered by Lawrence, a considerable list of mayors became famous as masters of downtown renaissance: Arthur Naftalin in Minneapolis, Ivan Allen in Atlanta, Richard Lee in New Haven, John Collins and Kevin White in Boston, and Joseph Clark and Richardson Dilworth in Philadelphia. Much of Richard Daley's success as mayor of Chicago derived not from his power as the last great 'machine' boss, but from his leadership of a central business district renewal coalition including real estate owners, banks, department stores, and some monopoly corporations with headquarters in Chicago.[23]

New Haven, Connecticut, was one of the first cities to complete renewal projects covering a major proportion of its' downtown area. Critics proclaimed it a success, by and large, and generalised from New Haven's experience that central business district renewal was worthwhile. Like Lawrence, New Haven's Dick Lee was a Democratic mayor who orchestrated renewal by drawing real estate, banking, commercial and business leaders, many of whom were major supporters of the Republican party, into the initial publicising of the renewal effort. Later, as projects for each section of the downtown area were prepared and submitted to Washington for approval, Lee coaxed and pleaded with whoever was interested in developing something to become involved. Yale University and the regional Bell Telephone subsidiary, the two largest employers in the city, saved several projects at crucial moments. The Telephone company purchased a considerable proportion of the renewed parcels and relocated regional office and equipment facilities to New Haven in order to make use of them. At one point, when no developer could be found for an important parcel, Lee organised an independent public authority to build a 'coliseum' on the site. Yale University carried the mortgages for a commercial mall, hotel, office tower and department store project when the original developer went bankrupt. On another occasion the university helped out by buying two aging public high schools and using the land for new dormitories. All the renewal mayors prided themselves on this kind of resourcefulness.

COMPREHENSIVE PLANNING FOR METROPOLITAN CENTRAL CITIES

Urban renewal provided city planners with the opportunity to promote complete models of good city design for the central city of a metropolitan area. The federal policy commitment to saving the central cities and the multi-billion dollar Congressional authorisation of renewal funds elevated city planners to positions of substantial political influence over a nation-wide urban development process. Planned urban development was to be concentrated in the metropolitan central cities and plans were needed. Planners responded by rapidly elaborating the theory and method of 'comprehensive' planning.

Comprehensive planning provided a framework for coordinating urban renewal projects with the economic and social functions of the central city. Inherent in comprehensive planning theory were assumptions about the spatial distribution of activities throughout the metropolitan area, with emphasis on activities that ought to be concentrated in the central city. Locational tendencies became unwritten norms, which comprehensive planning methods systematically elicited through analytic determination of a city's 'goals'. Because comprehensive planning specified that goal determination was above all a process, goals came to be set in practice in accord with the enthusiasm of the potential users of the city: industrial, residential, commercial, institutional and so on.[24]

In cities where an aggressive mayor was working to forge a renewal coalition with real estate, banking, and development interests, comprehensive planning process generated city-wide goals and plans that varied little from city to city. A central business district (CBD) dominated virtually all plans prepared by comprehensive methods. The city centre should be cleared of industrial and residential land uses in favour of high-rise office buildings housing banks, corporate headquarters, financial and business service companies, wholesale trade offices, transportation and communication company offices, insurance companies, advertising and media. Department stores and speciality retail shops should also concentrate in the CBD. According to one widely approved comprehensive planning theory, all economic activities requiring face-to-face interaction should locate in a central district where meetings were easiest and cheapest to facilitate. Other economic functions could be spread more broadly over the city and metropolitan area, especially very general activities such as food shopping or residences. Industry also, according to this theory, need not concentrate in the city, especially if the output of a plant was destined primarily for national or world-wide markets. Once the central business district plan was generally accepted, other claimants on the city could be located in relation to the CBD and to each other.[25]

Comprehensive planning severely constrained the uses urban renewal projects might practically propose for any given city area or neighbourhood. Central business district development usually called for conversion of declining residential and industrial areas. Typically CBD urban renewal projects would call for complete elimination of residential and industrial uses. Residential uses would be identified with specifically residential neighbourhoods, which would then form a second class of projects separate from the central business district projects. Comprehensive planning advocated 'separation of uses', arguing that blight occurred when 'incompatible' uses or activities interfered with each other at the same location. For example, commercial activity, especially involving truck deliveries, was believed to 'blight' residential areas. Residential neighbourhood projects strove to maximise the residential character of a city area by rerouting commercial and through commuter traffic, relocating stores to the edges or entirely outside the area, and excluding industrial and office uses. Parks, schools, libraries and neighbourhood centres would be added or improved to enhance the quality of residential life.

A third sort of area, often designated an 'inner ring' surrounding the central business district, might be targeted for mixed residential and commercial uses: apartment houses intermixed with shops, professional offices, restaurants and bars. Two other common project types were institutional complexes for universities or medical centres, and specialised industrial areas for firms anxious to remain in the central city. The Urban Renewal Administration preferred that each project set one major objective for a carefully delineated area of the city. The best justification for specialisation in one area was interdependence with other specialised uses in other areas within the context of a comprehensive plan for the whole city. Cities with a well-defined comprehensive plan would apply to fund five, ten or even more separate urban renewal projects for as many separate areas of the city. Economist William Stull's 1978 analysis of projects in nine selected cities found an average of twelve projects in each city. About one-quarter were downtown projects, slightly more than half were residential neighbourhood projects, and the rest were a mixture of residential-commercial, institutional and industrial projects. In dollar terms, Stull found that one-third of all funds went to the downtown projects, one-third to neighbourhood residential, and one-third to the other three types. The total for all grants to the nine cities, as of 1977, was $1,729 million.[26]

COMPREHENSIVE CITY PLANNING AND THE INTERSTATE HIGHWAY PROGRAMME

Comprehensive planning was particularly important in coordinating urban development with national transportation planning. Strange as it may sound for a nation obsessed with the automobile, Congress authorised a 41,000-mile interstate highway system in 1956 without any mention of its effect on urban areas. Cities used comprehensive planning methods to connect highway construction funded as part of the interstate system with renewal projects funded by urban redevelopment programmes. Of $27 billion spent on highway construction from 1956 to 1966, $15 billion went to roadways in urban areas. This was a much larger proportion than many Congressional proponents of the interstate system had intended. City planners evolved a beltway and spoke design for the interstates within a metropolitan area: one north-south and one east-west highway connecting the area with the national interstate system, and a ring highway around the central city at a distance of five to ten miles out into the suburban fringe. The portions of the direct highways across the diameters of the ring, or beltway, provided main commuting arteries into central business district boulevards, streets and parking facilities.[27]

Upon completion of the renewal projects and the interstates, an illusion appeared that wise planners at the federal level had devised and implemented a combined transportation and central city revitalisation programme to promote metropolitan development. In fact, the purposive content and coordination of the two programmes arose almost entirely from city plans and efforts. Far from being a grand national enterprise, or a fantastic conspiracy by special interests, as some critics charged, the form taken by metropolitan development, and the specific concentration of federal subsidies on saving the central city, were consequences for the most part of efforts by large-city political and economic interests.

Comprehensive planning was not fundamentally enamoured of the automobile. It ended up encouraging great use of automobiles for commuting for pragmatic reasons: the highway programme was available and could be effectively coordinated with central business district development. Sometimes, in their haste to seize federal monies, planners lost sight of central city revitalisation's grand objectives and levelled a beautiful neighbourhood to build a commuter highway into the CBD. Boston's curious geography resulted in several disastrous clearance projects and a maze of elevated roadways and bridges. San Francisco came close to suffering the same fate, but was saved to some extent by a protest movement that forced a partially completed expressway to be dismantled. Critics of commuter expressways never appropriately conceded the advantages of automobile commuting for the suburban family in terms of time, flexibility when changing jobs, and expense. After an initial acceleration up to the mid 1960s, auto commuting to central city downtowns moderated as the beltways encouraged suburban relocation of workplaces and jobs. Eventually, critics may conclude that the interstate highway programme built just enough roadways for good metropolitan traffic circulation. The images of monstrous steel and concrete ribbons strangling the life out of the cities may age and fade.[28]

CENTRAL CITY REVITALISATION AS CAPITALIST PLANNING

We will consider the success of urban redevelopment at appropriate places in the next several chapters. Whether the cities were 'saved' depends upon one's expectations. Policy is not authoritarian planning, it is only a political orientation for a complex social and economic system. Ten years after urban renewal began in earnest, President Lyndon Johnson proclaimed that poverty was the nation's most compelling dilemma, especially poverty in large cities. Some interpreted central city poverty as a direct failing of urban renewal, charging that the 'save the central cities' policy had been an exercise in deception. Experts on migration and family restructuring sensed that central city poverty was not so much a result of policies and programmes as an issue rising to prominence because urban renewal had made the large city a focus of national attention. Hitherto invisible poor people were now in the political spotlight motioning to be seen and heard.

Beyond programmatic successes or failures, we want to know whether policies and plans accomplished anything by democratic criteria. One influential critique of capitalist society asserts that capital controls development to an extent that supresses popular aspirations, distorting the course of social change away from fulfilment of human needs. Apart from the influence specific capitalist interests exerted on urban policy, can we perceive the controlling hand of capital in the broad course urban policy has followed since 1937? If the commitment to metropolitan central city renewal is the evidence on which an answer can be based, then that answer is clearly 'No'. The two largest concentrations of capitalist power, large financial institutions and monopoly manufacturing corporations, watched the emergence and determination of national urban policy with indifference. While numerous examples of powerful families attempting to influence renewal in a city can be found, such as the Mellons with their banking and oil interests (Gulf Oil) in Pittsburgh or the Rockefellers in New York City, the prevailing concern of manufacturing and finance capital has been national economic growth and metropolitan development. What happened to central cities mattered only to the extent that city deterioration might hinder metropolitan and national growth.

In class terms as well, saving the large cities ran counter to the existing distribution of wealth and power. Urban renewal benefited some of the most conservative classes imaginable: owners of slum real estate, banks with investments in declining city real estate, secondary mortgage lenders. In so far as federal funds flowed to these people, it was being diverted from investment in basic research, manufacturing innovation, production expansion or job creation. The classes benefited most by urban renewal identify politically with the Republican Party. Yet the Democrats did not criticise the emerging urban policy because it was benefiting primarily Republican interests. No historians have concluded that Eisenhower reformed and expanded the redevelopment programme in order to make it more attractive to interests within his own Republican party.

The relation of central city revitalisation to the larger purposes of capital becomes apparent from the structure of the urban renewal programme. Capital's interests in policy were served by broad

Keynesian economic and social management. Capital's concern about settlement patterns focused on metropolitan areas. Central city revitalisation mattered to the extent that national economic and social development was faltering, or because central city renewal seemed important to metropolitan development. Urban renewal provided a programme that made federal funds available for central cities to draw assistance as they found it beneficial. In practice, even once the programme was in operation, political and economic interests in each city had to provide detailed justification for every renewal dollar requested. Once the highway programme was also available, and comprehensive planning had evolved into a sophisticated process for preparing and evaluating renewal proposals, urban renewal became a large bureaucratic system in which the federal Urban Renewal Administration and the President's Bureau of the Budget accepted, delayed or rejected projects largely in terms of their contribution to improving the flow of economic activity in metropolitan areas. Where a willing, skilled and educated labour force was available in the suburban fringe, where highways were planned or in place for easy commuting to the central business district, and where the mayor and the city's development interests were enthusiastic about a major project, the federal URA, with Budget Bureau approval, had the power to finance removal of two kinds of obstacles: the expense of buying out existing property owners on a project site, and the inability of banks and other investors to free their capital from existing uses and make it available for the new projects. These were the very specific ways that urban renewal impacted cities and metropolitan areas, and the details are important to understanding its usefulness to capital.[29]

In the larger scheme of post-war capitalist development, urban renewal was a facilitating programme, and not a particularly expensive one. Saving the central cities was conditional; it depended upon the extent to which metropolitan development required central city renewal. Within these parameters, the renewal mayors demonstrated some imaginative schemes cities could try. Later, after migration and metropolitan social change had time to react to federal urban policy and programmes, the terms of confrontation between policy and settlement that are our general theme became better defined. Having examined urban policy as it initially evolved from the mid 1930s to the mid 1950s, let us go back to migration and metropolitan structure as they progressed into the turbulent 1960s.

4. City Life in Metropolitan Areas

In 1950, sociologist David Riesman provided a compelling metaphor for city life in post-war metropolitan areas: the 'lonely crowd'. The book carrying the ironic phrase as its title became a best seller. Riesman meant to suggest that when people perceive their society as an anonymous mass, the image of the individual reflected back to them will necessarily be cold, colourless and impersonal. Industrial urban society, Riesman explained, separated the individual from traditional culture transmitted down generations through families and communities. In place of tradition and culture, the modern social system emphasised education and occupation as the basis for the individual's connection to society. Riesman labelled such a character type: 'other directed', meaning an individual functioning by responding to important *others*: supervisors, colleagues, institutions, information in the media, political leaders. Other-directed individuals had to respond appropriately to complex, dynamic situations; they could not rely on inherited cultural mores or even on techniques of self-reliance. Riesman called self-reliance 'inner direction' and associated it with the ambitious, pious bourgeoisie of early nineteenth-century Europe and America. In contrast, other-directed behaviour was highly functional for modern white-collar workers in large bureaucracies.[1]

Although Riesman did not intend it, readers interpreted his argument to mean that *home life* in the suburbs provided the only effective counterforce to the alienating power of industrial urban society. Humanity would be preserved in post-war America only through leisure, play and sexuality away from the city. A second common conclusion, also contrary to Riesman's intentions, was that individuals compelled to live in the city as well as work there, who never enjoyed respite from the urban industrial system, would become entirely 'other-directed', losing all capability for emotion, spontaneity or creativity. Other-directed city dwellers would become systemic beings indistinguishable from each other in appearance or behaviour. Very like ants, they would be motivated by stimuli communicating the needs of the mass and highly adaptable to whatever behaviour might be necessary. Many imagined Riesman was arguing that the transformation was far advanced and that the lonely crowd of city people was already beyond hope.

Riesman's book marked a milestone of cultural change, for its popularity indicated that informed social opinion had assumed a detached perspective on the city. City life would henceforth be observed from a higher or outer vantage, not from personal experience. The city dweller was undergoing a transition from subject to object of cultural reflection, moving out of the centre of social concern to become an 'other'. The faces in the lonely crowd, apartment dwellers, people who rode on subways to work, children playing on asphalt with no trees to climb, were no longer typical Americans.

How accurate were perceptions of the city by these detached observers? In the early 1970s, worsening conditions in most large, older cities were interpreted as a generalised urban 'crisis'. The search for causes of the crisis led back to the cities of the 1950s, but objective analysis was impossible. Between the 1950s and the 1970s, the riots of the 1960s intervened, shocking and sensitising observers of city life. After the riots, it did not matter whether life in big city neighbourhoods in the 1950s had been stable and tolerable, or possibly even enjoyable. Every pre-riot *fact* now carried a politically-charged implication. The mis-interpreters of Riesman's *Lonely Crowd* already felt detached and indifferent about city life. The riots rendered city conditions and city people of the 1950s even more 'other' and alien.

This chapter's account of the city in the 1950s and early 1960s attempts to contend with these difficulties. We will examine life in metropolitan central cities on its own terms, and also in terms of the major factors that became prominent in the search for causes of the urban crisis of the early 1970s: race, ethnicity and poverty. This second aspect of the discussion will be valuable later, when we consider the policy controversy over the urban crisis (Chapter 6).

The chapter begins with a consideration of the city-planning profession's vision of American city life in the 1950s. American city planning had constructed its ideals under the influence of the English 'garden city' movement. Most prominent in the American movement was the group of planners led by Clarence Stein, beginning in the 1920s. Planners provided authoritative standards of city design that were widely accepted. Their ideals and principles defined what was *good*, and what was undesirable, for the informed public and also for planing urban renewal.

In the early 1960s, the planners' vision of what constituted *good* city life came under attack for ignoring desirable features of working-class and poor neighbourhoods in large cities. Two important critics, Jane Jacobs and Herbert Gans, called upon the city-planning profession to reconsider its principles. Their charges were sympathetically received by some planners and grudgingly acknowledged by others. Somewhat revised principles of good city design emerged from the confrontation.

Jacobs and Gans raised questions about social and political bias in planning. What planners saw when they looked at city neighbourhoods depended to a considerable extent on *who they were*, socially and politically. Observation carried with it implications that could lead to dramatic consequences when decisions were made about clearing 'slums' or locating new expressways into downtown areas.

The critique of planning ideals eventually centred on three aspects of big-city life: race, ethnicity, and poverty. Later, during the controversy over the urban crisis, the status of these three factors in the 1950s took on added significance as the preconditions of central city deterioration in the 1970s. What had conditions in the 1950s actually been like? The next sections of this chapter evaluate race, ethnicity and poverty in light of later assertions concerning the causes of the urban crisis. Each section also emphasises settlement forces: black migration out of the rural South and community formation in northern and western cities, immigration to cities and the relation of immigration to ethnic groupings and neighbourhoods in the 1950s, poverty as a 'culture' of city living similar to ethnic culture.

Finally, I have assembled a positive description of city life in the 1950s. Before the riots of the 1960s, and the urban crisis of the 1970s, city dwellers simply lived their lives. As Chapter 5 will explain, the rioting was not anticipated or foreshadowed. Nor is it clear that the deterioration of the early 1970s had its origins in the conditions of the 1950s. In 1978 President Carter advocated that policy stop trying to reverse the urban crisis and restore the stability of city life before the riots. This section tries to capture the best of what that stability was like. Whether policy has the option of restoring it, as Carter rhetorically suggested, is a moot question; the 1950s cannot be revived.

THE CITY PLANNERS' VISION OF THE CITY: THE AMERICAN GARDEN CITY MOVEMENT

Post-war suburban development, and the creation of a suburban, middle-class culture, described in Chapter 2, differentiated metropolitan life into city and suburban variants. The city remained the dominant place of work, but suburban living became increasingly preferable, in large part because it offered distance and respite from work. In so far as separation from the world of work and commerce made suburban living desirable, city living acquired a negative character. The pejorative interpretation readers gave to Riesman's lonely crowd of other-directed individuals was one indication of emerging attitudes toward the city.

City planners stood against this darkening mood as the leading proponents of city living. However, planners were not fully prepared for confrontation with suburban ideals. The prevailing ideals and principles of good city design in the 1950s derived most directly from the 'Garden City' movement in English planning. Ebenezer Howard had first advocated building 'garden cities' at the turn of the century as a solution to the excessive congestion of industrial London, Manchester and Liverpool. Howard proposed combining industry, commerce, residence, and also agriculture, in free-standing small cities beyond commuting distance from the existing metropolitan centres. In the 1920s, the first 'New Towns' were built, incorporating many of Howard's principles for good city location and design.

Clarence Stein, Lewis Mumford, Henry Wright and their associates, a group of forward-looking planners, initiated an American Garden City movement in the 1920s. Their objectives involved more than promoting English-style New Towns in the US, however. Their primary concern was to revolutionise the individual city resident's experience of the urban environment. They made no plans to shield their projects from oncoming urban development, and as a result, practical considerations seemed always to require that their neighbourhood and community experiments be located within, or on the fringes of, existing metropolitan areas.

Looking back twenty years from 1950, Stein commented on Radburn, New Jersey, his group's first attempt to build a complete town:

> In our minds' eye we still had the theme that Ebenezer Howard had created so vividly in his book *Garden Cities of Tomorrow*. We believed thoroughly in green belts [broad forested areas separating new urban development from existing large cities], and towns of a limited size planned for work as well as living. We did not fully recognize that our main interest after our Sunnyside experience had been transferred to a more pressing need, that of a town in which people could live peacefully with the automobile – or rather in spite of it.

The chosen site was only sixteen miles from Manhattan and even in 1929, when the surrounding area was largely agricultural, 70 per cent of the original residents commuted to work in New York City. By 1960, post-war suburban development completely engulfed Radburn.[2]

The effort to transplant Garden City ideals to the US spawned two quite separate innovations. The Stein group's original project, Sunnyside Gardens, Queens, a row and apartment house complex in a residential section of New York City, introduced multi-block developments for dense areas of large cities. Sunnyside Gardens retained the existing grid of streets and avenues, but Radburn and later projects replaced the grid with the 'superblock': streets bounding areas as large as five or ten conventional city blocks, allowing residential structures to be situated in a park-like setting of grass, trees and walkways. Hillside Homes, a 1932 New York City apartment house complex billed as 'a complete, integrated neighborhood within the larger framework' of a densely settled city, reveals how much the mammoth public housing projects of the 1940s and 1950s owe to the US Garden City movement. Hillside featured 'safe green courts', community rooms, nursery school rooms, playgrounds and club rooms, plus a large 'Assembly Room', all designed by the Stein group to sustain a community life they considered absent from traditional grid-street, tenement house neighbourhoods.

The second tradition initiated by the Stein group was a sporadic enthusiasm for suburban new towns. The Stein group's new towns appeared closer to the English Garden City tradition in community design than their city projects, but ultimately they did little to bring the Garden City influence to bear on US suburban development. Because none of them were built at a distance from existing metropolitan areas, the Stein group's new towns failed to carry on the Garden City effort to counter excessive metropolitan concentration. Instead, American developers perceived them as model planned suburbs intended to encourage suburban development on a community rather than a subdivision scale.

The Stein group's influence peaked in 1935 when Roosevelt authorised federal construction of 'Greenbelt Towns', three of which were eventually completed. While Stein and others believed that Radburn and the Greenbelt towns contributed positively to the tradition of suburban development evolving after the war, their impact was in fact probably nil. Neither developers nor local or state governments adopted the practice of constructing whole suburban communities. There is little evidence that the few developers who did build entire communities, such as Levitt, gave much thought to the Stein group's examples.

Attempts to revive the New Towns tradition in the 1960s only re-emphasised how completely US suburban building had evolved its own notions of the value of space, trees and grass, while ignoring metropolitan deconcentration. The two most publicised *new* new towns, Reston, Virginia, and Columbia, Maryland, were both within the suburban fringes of major metropolitan areas (Washington and Baltimore). And while both towns emphasised industry and offices to facilitate living and working in a unified community, this meant something very different in the 1960s, when factories and office complexes were springing up everywhere in metropolitan suburban fringes. Finally, and ironically, the new new towns of the 1960s had even less impact on development patterns than the Stein projects of the 1920s and 1930s. The replicas and successors of Reston and Columbia failed to appear.

THE CRITIQUE OF 'GARDEN CITY' PLANNING: JANE JACOBS AND HERBERT GANS

Public housing design and early urban renewal planning employed the principles and design techniques of the American Garden City movement. During the 1950s, as the earliest public housing projects aged, it became painfully apparent that grass, trees, careful planning, sound construction and ample provision for community activities did not automatically transform slum residents into denizens of Utopia. Many planners defended the approaches based on Garden City principles, but doubts were increasing. Too often life in public projects seemed more bleak and oppressive than the slums urban renewal had cleared away.

In 1961, Jane Jacobs, an amateur urbanist in the eyes of professional planners, aroused a great stir by accusing Stein, Wright, Mumford and their followers of destroying the mechanisms that made cities work. Jacobs lumped the Stein group and Ebenezer Howard together with the French architect and planner Le Courbusier and the American City Beautiful planning tradition into a caricature of American planning in the 1950s: 'a sort of Radiant Garden City Beautiful'. Planning was supposedly improving city life by separating different uses from each other, entombing each use in superblocks of concrete, steel and glass, and expecting people to order their lives according to places, using each planned space exclusively for its intended activity. Jacobs argued that day-to-day life in these rigid environments was sterile, uninteresting and even dangerous. Superblocks minimised the use of streets and sidewalks, she explained, and thus invited criminal elements to attack the few remaining pedestrians.

Jacobs wrote her book, *The Death and Life of Great American Cities*, partly out of anger at the professional planners who had proposed to redesign and redevelop her own Greenwich village neighbourhood in New York City. The planners had found the White Horse Tavern, frequented by poet Dylan Thomas, incompatible with the predominantly residential character of its block. Even more objectionable was the nearby Women's House of Detention, which the planners condemned as ugly, dangerous and totally at odds with the neighbourhood's residential and retail activities.

Jacobs attacked this kind of planning for losing touch with what made city living desirable. Under the principle of separation of 'incompatible' uses, planners had identified exactly the features that made her neighbourhood unique and interesting, and proposed to remove them. She filled her book with examples of similar destructiveness by planners all over New York City and in other cities. By building ever more sophisticated principles upon the separation of uses axiom, planners had committed themselves to eliminating *diversity*. They had forgotten that diversity was what made city neighbourhoods lively, safe, and attractive to work in, live in or visit.[3]

Jacobs' book threw the planning profession into confusion. Devastatingly accurate criticism from an uncredentialed outsider was embarrassing and dangerous. Many planners tried to minimise the damage by pretending that Jacobs' principles were already commonplace. Readers were hearing about them first from her because professional planners lacked the time to explain new trends to the general public. In fact, the planning profession never accepted Jacobs' critique in the spirit she intended. First they praised her for proclaiming that separation of uses was destroying what was most valuable in dense city environments. Then they reformulated her principles of diverse uses into neighbourhood planning rules every bit as rigid and lifeless as the separation of use rules she had condemned.

Sociologist Herbert Gans' *The Urban Villagers*, a study of Boston's West End neighbourhood, presented another influential defence of city life. Gans' project began as a sociological analysis of ethnic neighbourhood dynamics, but he also knew that Boston's urban renewal plans called for complete destruction of the West End. After the clearance was carried out, Gans' positive portrayal of neighbourhood life became an epitaph, and a denunciation of the total clearance renewal strategy.[4]

THE IMPLICATIONS OF OBSERVATION

As with Jacobs' critique, the response to *The Urban Villagers* was very emotional. Gans and Jacobs had exposed a bias in the Garden City planning tradition against the spontaneity and diversity of working-class and poor neighbourhoods. In the name of eliminating slums and blight, planners were making war on city life styles that centred in the streets and on sidewalks, mixing work, business, eating, play and family life all together. Yet ultimately Gans and Jacobs reinforced the planning profession's inherent bias, by arguing that the errors they had condemned could be avoided through *better* planning principles. In the end, Jane Jacobs put her faith in well-planned physical environments to create desirable city life, just as the Garden city tradition had. 'The task is to promote the city life of city people, housed, let us hope, in concentrations both dense enough *and* diverse enough to offer them a decent chance at developing city life.'[5]

Gans and Jacobs continued to assert the validity of objective, professional observation by planners and social scientists. Although they sparked controversy over differing urban values and ideals, neither was willing to abandon the search for one common set of values that planning could use to serve all classes, races and groups of city residents. Both Gans and Jacobs dealt extensively with what later came to be called 'ethnic' neighbourhoods, yet neither would concede the possibility that the desirable features they praised were generated by cultural networks and traditions rather than by the physical arrangement of streets, buildings and activities.

Gans openly admitted that West End life resembled life in the Italian villages from which much of its population had emigrated. As a planning manifesto, however, *The Urban Villagers* downplayed the possibility that cultural factors made the West End example unsuitable for generalisation as a neighbourhood planning model. Jacobs perceived the danger for the planning enterprise more clearly and attempted to counter it with explicit denials. 'Some observers of city life,' she wrote in her central chapter on neighbourhoods,

> noting that strong city neighborhoods are so frequently ethnic communities – especially communities of Italians, Poles, Jews or Irish – have speculated that a cohesive ethnic base is required for a city neighbourhood that works as a social unit. In effect, this is to say that only hyphenated-Americans are capable of local self-government in big cities. I think this is absurd.[6]

Planning's bias had more serious implications than Jacobs' rebuttal suggests, however. When Martin Luther King mobilised more than 200,000 people for the March on Washington in August 1963, many of the marchers came from Birmingham and Montgomery, Alabama, Atlanta, Georgia, and other centres of civil rights activism in the South. But equally large numbers came from metropolitan central cities in the North and mid-West. The March dramatised what the

Census of 1960 had shown: 40 per cent of the nation's black population were living outside the South, and nine-tenths of the non-Southern group were living in cities. Black migration out of the rural South to large cities during the Second World War and immediately following had been charted and recognised, but the continuation of migration throughout the 1950s was ignored by planners, developers and sociologists arguing the future of central cities. The Census revealed that Washington, DC, had a majority black population and that Cleveland and Detroit, both 29 per cent black, would have black majorities by 1970 if the trends of the 1950s continued. Planners, and others, who believed consensus about values could be achieved and then used to guide urban renewal and long-range city planning, had yet to confront the implications of race and ethnicity.

Looking back from the 1970s, it was difficult to understand how informed observers and concerned professional planners of the 1950s could have suppressed racial and ethnic differences so forcefully. Poverty also underwent re-examination. Urban renewal had treated poverty as if it were entirely a physical problem of neighbourhoods and substandard housing. Many planners who had done early renewal work later felt remorse over their failure to consider the social and personal problems of the people displaced by slum clearance.

When the biases of observation were exposed, ten years after, it was difficult to reinterpret the status of racial, ethnic and poverty factors in city life. And conditions in the 1950s were not merely of historical interest. 'Facts' about race, ethnicity and poverty before the riots of the 1960s, and the urban crisis of the early 1970s, carried powerful implications for the policy controversy about *causes* of the urban crisis. Let us consider the three factors in detail and then attempt a comprehensive description of city life in the 1950s and early 1960s.

RACE

Race became a major factor in metropolitan central city development for the same reason that status aspirations were crucial in shaping the suburban fringe. Black Americans chose central cities as the terrain on which to reconstitute their standing in national society. To understand their struggle, we must remember that in racist societies race is problematic only to the white, dominant race. For black people, their race is the basis of their solidarity and strength. The objectives of struggle in the post-war era were the same as during slavery and since Emancipation: freedom and equality. These goals were not synonymous with the disappearance of black people as a social group, however, as much liberal ideology of the 1940s and 1950s assumed. Part of the race problem, especially in social science, was the inability of whites to conceive of black Americans as something other than 'white people with black skins', as if differences in physical appearance were the source of the race problem.

At first, during the Second World War and in the civil rights struggles of the 1950s, blacks experienced their advances as movement away from the preceding caste-like system of legal segregation, 'Jim Crow', the colour line, separate facilities, dual justice and wanton racist violence and murder. The thousands of black soldiers who fought with furious bravery in the war were totally segregated in Negro units; it was not until 1948 that President Truman integrated the military by executive order. The Supreme Court did not outlaw legally segregated school systems until 1954. The first effective federal civil rights law passed Congress in 1964.

Then, during the 1960s, black struggle changed character suddenly and profoundly. The term 'Negro' went out of use, replaced by a far more positive self-conception as 'black people'. Less apparent to whites, but tremendously important to racial solidarity, was the attack upon status distinctions among blacks based on skin tone. 'Black is beautiful' resembled an advertising slogan to most whites, but to black people it meant the end of a pernicious snobbery in which Negro high society prided itself on lightness of skin colour. As far as race was concerned, whether socially, economically or politically, all black people became equal in a way that they had never been before. The urban riots or 'rebellions' of the mid 1960s had a great deal to do with this transformation. We will consider them separately in Chapter 5. Here we must elaborate the contradictions that a socially and politically united black community posed to Riesman's 'lonely crowd' and to planners' belief in consensus about city life.[7]

As with aspiring working-class families of the 1940s seeking a new class standing in the suburbs, the significance of race begins with migration. Blacks launched their first assault on the national social system with the Great Migration, beginning around 1910 and continuing through the 1920s. In 1910, the black population outside the South was very small, only 1.6 per cent of the total non-Southern population, but highly urbanised. Of black people outside the South, 79 per cent lived in cities. The vast majority of blacks, 90 per cent, still lived in the South and were predominantly rural; only 22 per cent of Southern blacks lived in cities. The Great Migration consisted of rural Southern blacks moving primarily to very large cities in the North and West. Net migration out of the South between 1910 and 1940 was 1,750,000, meaning emigration to the North and West was equal in size to one-fifth of the South's black population in 1910. This ranks the Great Migration as one of the most dramatic mass migrations in modern history. The proportion of the nation's black population living in the South declined to 76 per cent by 1940, while the proportion living in the North and West increased from 10 per cent in 1910 to 24 per cent in 1940. Since most of the migrants went to cities, the proportion of blacks in the North and West living in cities increased to almost 90 per cent by 1940, with the bulk of the urban group living in the very largest cities. There was also migration from the rural South to Southern cities. The proportion of Southern blacks living in cities increased from 22 per cent in 1910 to 37 per cent in 1940.[8]

The Great Migration established major black communities in the largest Northern cities. New York City's 1940 black population of 458,000 constituted 17 per cent of all black people living outside the South. Another 30 per cent of blacks in the North and West lived in just five other cities: Chicago, Philadelphia, Detroit, Cleveland and Pittsburgh. Chicago's black community had a population of 278,000, Philadelphia: 251,000, Detroit: 149,000, Cleveland: 84,500, and Pittsburgh: 62,000. Extreme concentration in one or two neighbourhoods appeared as discrimination and segregation from one perspective, but as essential strategy from another. Concentration gave black communities the strength of numbers to expand by tipping the racial balance in blocks at their edges, driving whites out and freeing housing for black occupancy. Less concentrated settlement patterns would have exposed isolated families or blocks of people to pressure, violence and arson from their white neighbours.

The First World War provided black workers with their first opportunities to obtain high-wage jobs in heavy industry. With the supply of European immigrants cut off, certain industries began to draw in black workers, most notably steel and meat-packing. Often black workers entered an industry initially as strikebreakers. Unions frequently attacked them for playing into bosses' hands and dividing the union movement when it most needed to be united. Blacks responded that their interest was in jobs; if the unions were truly interested in labour solidarity they should bring black workers into new industries by way of union membership. Then black strikebreaking would cease.

Following the war, Congress established severe limits on immigration for the first time. This made the wartime situation permanent; black workers became industry's principal source of new labour for the indefinite future. More industries, including the prestigious auto industry, drew in black workers during the 1920s. Henry Ford enthusiastically hired blacks at his new River Rouge complex in Dearborn, using the Sociological Department to handle whatever problems might arise. The Sociological Department encouraged them to live in the nearby black community of Inkster, where it could conveniently monitor and discipline their behaviour off the job. Drinking or marital conflict at home were grounds for dismissal from one's job.

The Second World War sparked a second Great Migration, but it lacked the fanfare of a mass movement. Industry expanded very rapidly beginning in 1940 and black workers had opportunities to entrench themselves permanently, especially where seniority determined the order of promotion and layoff. Industry resisted massive influxes of blacks, despite the desperate need for workers. Companies tried to maintain a caste system in which blacks were excluded from high-wage production line jobs. The nominal excuse was that white workers would not tolerate competition from blacks that might undermine wage rates gained through long and arduous struggle. A. Phillip Randolph, head of the Brotherhood of Sleeping Car Porters and the most prominent black labour leader, embarrassed the federal government into forcing admission of blacks to production jobs by threatening to lead a massive 'March on Washington' in 1942.[9]

Again, migration targeted very large industrial centres, which now included Los Angeles, San Diego and other Pacific coast cities. Los Angeles' black population expanded more than two and a half times, from 64,000 to 171,000, between 1940 and 1950. The bulk of new migration out of the South went to the cities where significant black communities had been established, and they registered striking increases: the black population of Detroit more than doubled to

301,000; Chicago's black community grew 77 per cent to 492,000, Cleveland: 75 per cent growth to 148,000, New York: 62 per cent to 742,000, Philadelphia: 50 per cent to 376,000, and Pittsburgh: 32 per cent to 82,000.

The war ended, and the 1940s came to a close, but migration persisted. Black communities in the metropolitan central cities expanded into new neighbourhoods. Jackie Robinson made his appearance as the first black player in major league baseball in 1948. At approximately the same time, ordinary black people in the cities began to shed their invisibility. The migration of the 1940s and 1950s ultimately proved far larger in absolute numbers than the Great Migration. The added effects of natural population increase within established black communities made the situation revealed by the 1960 Census profoundly striking. In Chicago, Detroit, New York, Philadelphia, Washington, Cleveland, blacks were becoming not just the largest 'minority' group, but the largest socially conscious group of any kind. The total white population might still constitute a majority, but whites attached little positive significance to their racial commonality. Only ethnicity among whites was comparable to the racial solidarity of central city black communities, and now, suddenly, whites realised that blacks were overshadowing all the traditional big city rivals: Irish, Italians, Jews, Poles. The more than 1 million blacks constituted 14 per cent of New York City's 1960 population, while first and second generation Irish numbered only 312,000, Italians 859,000, and Puerto Ricans 613,000. Jews maintained an advantage, at approximately 1.5 million, but their lead was rapidly shrinking. Chicago's 23 per cent black population of 813,000 far exceeded its 259,000 first and second generation Poles, the largest white ethnic group. And blacks in Washington, DC, were an absolute majority.

Reaction to the new status of blacks in the central cities took two forms. Planners, social scientists, and concerned whites struggled to reconcile black cultural mores, behaviour and attitudes with the belief in consensus about urban values, as Gans and Jacobs had done with ethnicity. Only partial accommodation was achieved, however, and the incongruencies emerged in the guise of a sudden new concern about urban 'poverty'. While 'black' never became completely synonymous with 'poor', 'poverty' functioned as a code word for any and all social problems attributed to the black community. Blacks were encouraged to define and explain whatever discontents they felt for the social system in terms of poverty. This definition had the effect of distancing blacks with steady employment, especially those of middle-class means, from blacks with 'problems' such as single parent families, unemployment, low wages, bad housing, lack of education, or physical disabilities. Those with aspirations to advance were encouraged to realise their talents and abilities, to take maximum advantage of educational and occupational opportunities. The underlying message was to shape oneself and one's children in a white middle-class mould. Those who could not find opportunities, or could not turn them to personal advantage, were branded with 'poverty' as if it were the mark of Cain.

The second form of reaction was the rise of the 'new ethnicity'. Suddenly the distribution of urban services and benefits became a competition between blacks and whatever religious, cultural or national groups could mobilise internal solidarity and strength. Poles, Italians and Jews asserted early claims. The Irish, having just achieved the sublime satisfaction of seeing one of their own elected President, tended to bow out of the new ethnic struggle and blend into the new middle class as much as possible. Where they appeared in sufficient numbers, non-Caucasian peoples other than blacks also came to be defined in ethnic terms; Puerto Ricans, Mexicans, Japanese, and Chinese all suddenly became equivalent to the European groups distinguished on grounds of language, nationality, culture and religion. In ethnic terms, blacks became the latest in the succession of groups thrown into the 'melting pot' of American society.

Since to a considerable extent social science had announced the successful conclusion of the assimilation process during the 1950s, the new ethnicity involved some vigorous ideological back-pedalling. Riesman's whole notion of an other-directed individual depended fundamentally on the disappearance of ethnic claims and inheritances. Historian Oscar Handlin, Riesman's colleague at Harvard, had managed almost singlehandedly to convince professional American historians that assimilation had triumphed and that ethnicity had breathed its last as a significant political, social or cultural force. By the mid 1960s historians were puzzling over how they could ever have countenanced the extreme generalisations that social history asserted in the 1950s.

Let us consider ethnicity and poverty on their own terms, in addition to their importance as reactions to the emergence of race. For apart from their significance in ideological and analytical controversy in the 1950s and 1960s, lack of economic means, and group solidarity based on common nationality, language, culture and religion, exerted powerful influences on city life.

ETHNICITY

America's ethnic groups originated in emigration, frequently with expectations of returning to beloved homelands. Of roughly 20 million arrivals in the 'new' immigration of 1880–1917, approximately one-third eventually emigrated again. Those who remained found themselves conglomerated into groups considerably larger and more heterogenous than their personal allegiances to language and nationality. 'Italians' became a label for people whose foreignness to each other within Italy was more pronounced than that of English and Irish. Jews from Poland, Lithuania, Czechoslovakia, Russia, Romania, and Hungary, Yiddish-speaking or not, differing in religious practices as broadly as Protestants from Catholics, all became one and the same in contradistinction to Poles, Hungarians, Slavs, Czechs, and Russians of Roman Catholic, Eastern Orthodox or national Catholic religion. No straightforward principles of language, nationality, religion or culture applied to all cases, nor did groups generally evolve from alliances among sets of smaller collectivities, such as natives of the same region or province. Alienation from common enemies drove people together as often as they chose to seek affinity with each other.

After the severe legal restriction of immigration in 1921, ethnicity assumed a stable pattern along generational lines. Those who were already adults by the 1920s adopted rigid personal and family identifications. Their allegiances constituted the major ethnicities recognised in the 1950s. Children of these adults, born approximately between 1905 and 1940, formed a distinct 'second generation'. Persistence of ethnicity through the 1950s and beyond depended upon their aspirations and choices, and upon pressures within the social system as a whole relating to groups, races and classes.

Sociologist Will Herberg perceptively observed as early as 1955 that post-war suburbanites had a passion for church, temple, meeting house and synagogue building, but not for ethnic purposes. Herberg went so far as to argue that even the great separtions between catholicism, protestantism and judaism no longer had any important significance, that they had evolved toward each other and become, for practical purposes, 'branches' of a single 'American' religion. While this broad charge was provocative, Herberg was entirely correct about the convergence in the beliefs, practices and customs of all denominations and 'religions', especially in the suburbs. Catholics and Jews increasingly followed Protestant practice, as husbands, wives and children attended a 'service' conducted by a functionary on a weekly 'sabbath'. Protestants minimised the importance of individual struggle to avoid eternal damnation and increasingly emphasised collecting funds to build churches rivalling Catholic structures in size and expense. Herberg argued that the new emphasis on religion represented an effort to support culturally neutral institutions for socialising children that would minimise ethnic identification among the 'third' generation, children born after 1939.[10]

Second- and third-generation immigrants in cities manipulated their ethnicity to personal and group advantage. The dual character of ethnic identification pervades *Beyond the Melting Pot*, Nathan Glazer and Daniel Moynihan's 1963 study of groups in New York City. 'Ethnic groups . . .' they wrote, 'even after distinctive language, customs, and culture are lost, as they largely were in the second generation, and even more fully in the third generation, are continually recreated by new experiences in America. . . . A man is connected to his group by ties of family and friendship. But he is also connected by ties of *interest*. The ethnic groups in New York are also *interest groups*.' Ethnic groups functioned as networks of businesses and political factions. Ethnic 'neighborhoods' consisted of landlords, small businessmen, political leaders and resident families asserting their common interests in ethnic terms. The combination of territorial and social unity could be powerful.[11]

Ethnicity in the 1950s had little connection with any country of origin. Ethnic identification played an important socialisation role for many third-generation children, especially in large city 'ethnic' neighbourhoods, but not for the purpose of preserving ties to the cultural homeland. The Second World War had so changed the political constellations of Europe and Asia that the only real concerns were for relatives still living there, often in hopes of rescuing them from 'behind the Iron Curtain' in Poland or Hungary, or from poverty and turmoil in post-war Italy or Greece. Ethnicity's principal function was as an alternative to education and the white-collar occupational structure. In conjunction with property holding and small business, ethnic networks provided employment opportunities, business possibilities, political connections and social ties. Families solidly entrenched in an ethnically organised neighbourhood could raise their children to enter a comfortable, boisterous, emotional society that had severely constrained opportunities in comparison with the corporate, white-collar world, but that did not demand ambition for one's individual success and career advancement. For those without property or business ties, life in the ethnic neighbourhood could be an alternative to factory work and other anonymous unpleasant working-class jobs. The 'high school dropout' with little ambition to work or marry, could depend on his parents for economic support and still preserve a modicum of self-respect within neighbourhood society.

Ethnicity lent structure to politics in large cities by providing a basis for party loyalty and activism. Once attached to a particular party or political leader, an ethnic group's social solidarity could operate as political unity as well. Ethnic antagonisms strengthened group political identification by forcing the opposing groups into opposite parties. Italians in large cities tended to be Republicans in the 1920s, and still in the 1950s, largely because the Irish were such aggressive Democrats. Jews might be either Democrats or Republicans, depending upon the state of affairs among other ethnic factions; often both parties would have a sizeable Jewish group. At the neighbourhood or 'precinct' level, structures were microscopically intricate and political ethnicity became an arcane science.

The rewards of political activism came primarily through city employment. Groups struggled to establish claims on particular departments. The 'Irish' cop or fireman was much more than a myth. Even after the introduction of civil service merit examinations for entry, groups successfully monopolised employment, especially where members of the group occupied managerial positions. Jews dominated public school teaching and administration in New York City, for example, to the extent that approximately 90 per cent of all teachers in the early 1960s were Jewish. Italians concentrated in the sanitation department, somewhat by default, due to lack of success in police and fire. And from a negative perspective, people who identified themselves in ethnic terms usually attributed unsatisfactory service from the municipal bureaucracy to discrimination. Political scientist Ira Katznelson found in a political survey of northern Manhattan residents in the early 1970s that a large majority believed the city government administered services in an ethnically discriminatory manner. Needless to say, almost everyone holding such beliefs reported that their own ethnic group was the most frequent victim of the bureaucracy's malign intentionality.[12]

As for culture and tradition, ethnicity's significance became increasingly controversial. Ethnic neighbourhoods in large cities certainly had distinctive cultural and traditional features: restaurants, types of stores, religious institutions, festivals, clubs and societies, sports, children's games, styles of dress. But investigation of such cultural behaviours by sociologists showed that the 'cultural' aspect tended to be a function of the existence of an ethnic group, rather than the group surviving in order to preserve a culture and its tradition. Gerald Suttles' study of 'Taylor Street' neighbourhood in Chicago in the early 1960s revealed distinct ethnic groups: Italians, 'Negroes', Puerto Ricans and Mexicans primarily. There was no question that the groups differed in religion, language, gestures, clothing, types of businesses, patterns of 'street life', approaches to education, sexual behaviour, food and recreation. But more importantly Suttles determined that practices regularly changed for all groups over the several years of his study.

Overt behaviour in public varied most frequently, especially among teenagers and young adults. Clothing, gestures, language and recreational activities altered even to the point that distinctive styles migrated from group to group. As the basis of behaviour at a particular historical moment, Suttles argued, the specifics of ethnicity were largely a function of the neighbourhood and city-wide social environment within which each ethnic group situated itself. Prominent in each group's social environment were other ethnic groups competing to adapt and prosper. The crucial function of ethnicity, Suttles generalised, was to stabilise social relations in an uncertain, dangerous world, to provide a 'moral order' where social values lacked the strength to maintain community peace and harmony.[13]

Described in Suttles' terms, ethnicity constituted an alternative social system to the world of white-collar occupations, socialisation through education, and status based on career success, salary income and suburban residence. Suttles was particular in limiting his claims to 'slum' neighbourhoods, however. He believed that an ethnically grounded social order prevailed only among people excluded, or overlooked, for some reason by the educational, occupational, status-conscious metropolitan social system. As concern for urban 'poverty', the third of our factors, grew in the early 1960s, analysis of ethnicity and culture became intertwined with attempts to explain the origins and persistence of poverty. Suttles had not set out to study ethnicity in order to use his findings to explain urban poverty, but inevitably his cultural analysis was dragged into the poverty debate. Short of indicting the entire economic system, poverty was difficult to explain without resort to 'cultural' mechanisms.

POVERTY

Poverty as a factor in post-war city life bore little resemblance to any conventional understanding of economic deprivation in other countries or historical periods. By nineteenth-century standards, post-war American cities had no class of poor people. The federal government's 'poverty line', the income level below which a family of husband, wife and two children were officially classified as 'poor', corresponded to a standard of material wellbeing achieved only by high-wage industrial workers in the 1910s and 1920s. Poverty was a policy term intended to describe people whose income lagged behind the minimum they could be expected to earn if appropriately employed. Poverty encompassed the residue left over after employment, unemployment insurance, relief, social security, workmen's compensation and other public and charitable programmes had provided people with income, resources and services.

The chief principle underlying the policy conception of poverty was that the combination of economic activities and social programmes available by the 1960s had become capable of lifting and sustaining everyone in the society above a calculable minimum level. As it designed economic policies and social programmes, according to this principle, the federal government was inherently setting this minimum level. 'Poverty' consisted of falling below the calculated minimum income. People found to be in poverty, according to this definition, were then studied to determine whether their poverty resulted from failings of the economic system, from oversights or maladministration of social programmes, or from some other source.

Once poverty was understood in this policy-oriented fashion, it could be efficiently and fairly speedily eradicated.

Concern about poverty in the 1960s derived directly from confidence in the power and capability of an expanding economy harnessed to an enlightened federal policy machine. President John Kennedy came into office in 1961 determined to make significant social advances. Kennedy 'discovered' poverty, by his own report, from reading social democrat Michael Harrington's *The Other America*. President Lyndon Johnson took up the concern with poverty as an issue on which to quickly build his record for the November 1964 election. While the flamboyant rhetoric of the 'Great Society' was cranked up on one side, advisers furiously threw together and pushed through Congress the Economic Opportunity Act of 1964. Johnson conducted his 'War on Poverty' very much like a war in the sense that he began mobilising forces to attack the purported enemy before determining the nature of the threat or the best strategies to combat it.

Careful analysis of poverty began in the latter part of 1964. Policy experts categorised the people living below the poverty level in relation to major programmes the Johnson administration hoped to initiate. For example, much of the 'income gap' found among the elderly could be attributed to costs arising from health problems. Solution: add a federally subsidised medical insurance system, Medicare, to Social Security, and add federal medical relief, Medicaid, to the welfare system. Federal medical subsidy programmes were far from a new idea in 1964, but proposing them as strategies for the War on Poverty led to their adoption where previous proposals had died in Congressional committees.

There was a similar response to the discovery of income shortfalls due to insufficient support provisions in the main Social Security programme: old age, survivors and disability insurance (OASDI). Analysis revealed that one-third of all poor families in 1962 were headed by a person 65 or older, and that an additional 2.7 million elderly living apart from relatives had incomes of less than $1,500 a year. In other words, a federal programme, OASDI, was itself the *cause* of poverty for millions of people because the support levels it provided were too low. Solution: increase OASDI benefits, which was done five different times between 1964 and 1974.[14]

The major thrust of the War on Poverty was not bolstering existing programmes, however, but identifying and confronting causes of poverty that continued to elude both an expanding economy and a concerned federal policy apparatus. Poverty came to be conceptualised as a consequence of barriers walling off certain kinds and classes of people from jobs, social services and income transfer or 'maintenance' programmes. The most obvious barrier was racial discrimination against blacks and minorities. This the Johnson administration confronted with the Civil Rights Act of 1964, which introduced 'affirmative action' in hiring and established the Equal Employment Opportunity Commission to adjudicate and remedy discrimination at work.

Having provided legal guarantees that everyone able and willing to work would have an equal opportunity to obtain a job and advance in it, the poverty programme's designers moved on to two potentially fundamental barriers confining people in poverty: lack of appropriate acculturation to the world of work, and lack of skills corresponding to the available jobs. The War on Poverty attacked the first with Project Headstart and the second with the Job Corps and other job training programmes. Finally, the Johnson administration postulated that poverty could persist within entire neighbourhoods of cities, because the residents had traditionally been excluded from the political system and had lost the will and the means to demand equal participation in political and social programmes. Demoralisation on a neighbourhood or 'community' level, according to this analysis, contributed to individual loss of self-respect, weakening people's determination to obtain employment and persevere in a rigorously competitive economy. Reversing this neighbourhood dilemma took the form of the most controversial aspects of the War on Poverty: 'community action', and the overarching mandate in all the poverty programmes for 'maximum feasible participation' by poor people in planning and administering programmes and organisations.

Inherent in the analysis and the programmes lay two kinds of assumptions about poverty. One was the 'culture of poverty' theory associated with the anthropologist Oscar Lewis. Lewis first developed his theory while studying poor families in Mexico City in the 1950s. Lewis had little interest in federal policy debate, but he did not dissuade others from elaborating his argument into a set of policy assumptions. Poverty conceptualised as a 'culture' resembled ethnicity in many ways; the 'culture of poverty' rhetoric postulated that in certain situations poor people living together in city neighbourhoods constructed a curious form of solidarity and common behaviours as a means of protecting themselves in a hostile environment. Poverty, according to this argument, was the ethnicity of the poor. Thus the culture of poverty argument implied that poor people socialised their children into poverty as a way of life, not out of perversity but as their only hope for survival. Specialists wrote of generation after generation in families and neighbourhoods caught in the 'downward spiral' or 'unbreakable cycle' of poverty. Some argued that federal social security and welfare intensified the problem. Because welfare and social security provided a spare but adequate minimum, children growing up in welfare families too easily fell into welfare as a permanent way of life, especially if their poverty was so all pervasive as to appear to them in the manner that other children experienced culture, either ethnic or mainstream American.

The second set of assumptions asserted that weakness in *family structure* lay at the heart of the poverty problem. In part, the family structure arguments tried to explain how a 'culture' of poverty could emerge. These arguments suggested that where adversity in a neighbourhood led to collapse of many families, leaving a large proportion of children growing up without a stable two-parent home environment, the effects could become cumulative. An entire generation of a neighbourhood's children could become socialised to patterns of family life and social adaptation uniquely specialised for coping with poverty. Then if the next generation of children also encountered no forceful intervention from political change, economic development, or governmental programmes, the isolation of the neighbourhood would intensify and patterns of coping would become psychologically ingrained in families and culturally entrenched in neighbourhood life.

Another type of family structure argument proposed that family structure could become the source of poverty in circumstances where forces of other kinds, other than poverty, had initially weakened the family. Prominent among these arguments was Daniel Moynihan's *The Negro Family, The Case for National Action*, a report he prepared in his role as Assistant Secretary of Labor for Policy Planning and Research in the Johnson administration in March, 1965.[15] Moynihan considered black people in his report as if they were the latest in a succession of ethnic groups entering American urban society at the bottom and struggling to rise and prosper. He presented evidence to show that they were not rising as other groups had done. Rather, he argued, 'the fabric of Negro society' was deteriorating, and the reason was 'the deterioration of the Negro family', which Moynihan called 'the fundamental source of weakness of the Negro community at the present time'. Culturally, Moynihan suggested, the United States was assimilating varying immigrant family structures and producing a single American 'family system'. Yet 'one truly great discontinuity in family structure' remained:

> that between the white world in general and that of the Negro American. The white family has achieved a high degree of stability and is maintaining that stability. By contrast, the family structure of lower class Negroes is highly unstable, and in many urban centers is approaching a complete breakdown.[16]

Moynihan explained the deterioration of the Negro family in terms of the history of oppression, during slavery and since, endured by black Americans. Family structure weakened by centuries of oppression was susceptible to complete disintegration under the hardships of poverty, exposing black communities in large cities to unique dangers of falling into the 'cycle of poverty'. In regard to the various theories of poverty, such logic made it difficult to determine whether Moynihan believed that there were two kinds of families, white and 'Negro', and thus two kinds of poverty, or whether he was merely underwriting the family theory of the cycle of poverty and adding to it the proposition that differing past experiences of ethnic and racial groups could affect their ability to cope with poverty in post-war metropolitan areas. In all likelihood Moynihan made his explanatory logic ambiguous with the exact intention of stirring up controversy about racism and family structure.

The various assumptions about sources of poverty identified two more types of people who diverged from the prototypical city dweller for whom planners had hoped to construct a consensus about urban values and good urban design. In addition to blacks and ethnics, poverty theory postulated 'poor people', who were trapped in poverty in cultural terms, and 'the Negro poor', whom Moynihan suggested should be classified separately from either the white and ethnic poor on the one hand or non-poor blacks on the other. Much of the controversy among poverty theorists stemmed not from analytical disagreements but from differing preferences about whom federal War on Poverty programmes should benefit. Black commentators found Moynihan's argument especially frustrating. They recognised

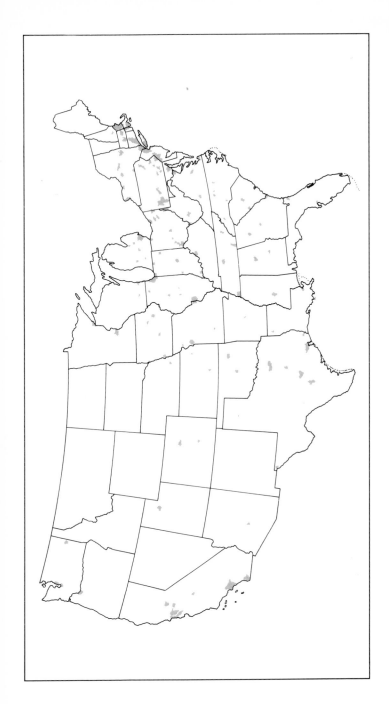

1. Metropolitan districts: 1940. The Census Bureau delineated 140 districts, an increase of almost 50% over the 96 districts identified in the 1930 Census. The fact that the Depression dominated the 1930–1940 decade made the increase particularly remarkable.

2. Jacob Lawrence, *The Migration of the Negro, No. 58* (1940–41), 'In the North, the Negro had better educational facilities.' Tempera on gesso on composition board, 12″ × 18″. As World War II and the Second Great Migration were beginning, Jacob Lawrence looked back to the experience of the Great Migration of the World War I period in a series of 60 paintings. Collection, The Museum of Modern Art, New York.

3. Jacob Lawrence, *The Ironers* (1943). Laundering and ironing, in commercial launderies and at home, were important sources of income for black women newly arrived in northern and western cities from the rural South during the Second Great Migration.

4. Edward Hopper, *Sunlight in a Cafeteria* (1958). It is presumed that the cafeteria is in New York City. Yale University Art Gallery, Bequest of Stephen Carlton Clark, B.A. 1903.

5. Edward Hopper, *First Row Orchestra* (1951). The absence of an orchestra pit suggests that this is a dramatic play, not a musical comedy. It is presumed that the theater is in New York City. Hirshhorn Museum and Sculpture Garden, Smithsonian Institution.

6. Aerial view of Levittown, Long Island, New York; 14 December 1949. The site is approximately 25 miles from Manhattan, far beyond the farthest suburbs of the 1920s. UPI/Bettman Archive.

7. Village Creek, Norwalk, Connecticut. The cooperatively owned, racially integrated community of Village Creek began development in the 1950s. Fifty miles from Manhattan, but close to an excellent commuter railroad service, the community functioned as a suburb of New York City for many of its residents.

8. New Haven, Connecticut. Aerial view of Oak Street area showing buildings later demolished for the Oak Street Connector. 1958. The New Haven Colony Historical Society.

9. Oak Street Connector and portions of four Urban Renewal projects, New Haven. The photograph was taken from approximately the same position as the aerial photograph above. Of the buildings in the centre of the aerial photo, only the United Illuminating Company building (the white cupola to the left and slightly above the center) remains standing and visible.

10. New Haven, Connecticut. Oak Street Project — Before, 1956. Oak Street was New Haven's first urban renewal project and among the earliest nationwide. The photograph is a distinctive illustration of 'slums and blight.' The New Haven Colony Historical Society.

11. Levittown, Pennsylvania, 23 June 1952. 'The Joe Shugarts, first family to move into the sprawling 16,000-family housing project built to serve employees of the new U.S. Steel plant near Trenton, N.J.' UPI/Bettman Archive.

12. Police Ineffective Here; Cleveland, 19 July 1966. 'Store owners gave up trying to protect their goods here July 19th. A Negro (left), boldly carries off a fan as others (right) walk off with clothing. One woman was killed and 15 persons were injured during rioting on Cleveland's east side.' UPI/Bettman Archive.

13. Scene of Violence; Detroit, 25 July 1967. 'The gutted remains of buildings (left) attest to the destruction caused by two days of rioting in Detroit's west side. At least 23 persons killed and more than a thousand injured.' UPI/Bettman Archive.

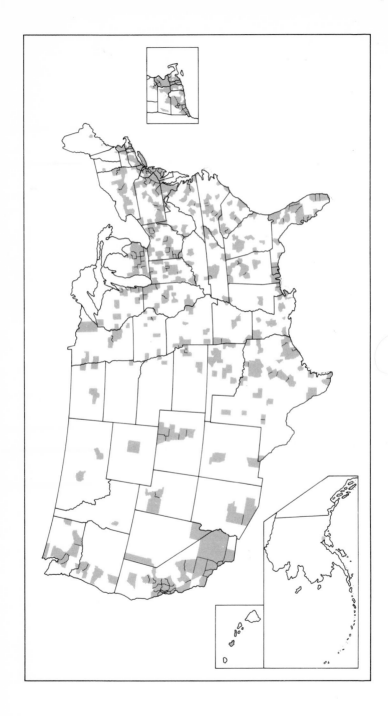

14. Standard Consolidated Statistical Areas and Standard Metropolitan Statistical Areas of the United States: 1980. The Census Bureau delineated 318 metropolitan areas, 316 in the 'continental' states and one each in Alaska and Hawaii. Consolidated areas consist of two or more adjacent metropolitan areas.

that his objective was to convince Johnson to target the War on Poverty primarily on the black poor in big cities. Yet the implications of his arguments disturbed them. For example, prominent civil rights leader James Farmer wrote in New York City's major black newspaper, the *Amsterdam News*:

> [Moynihan's] well-enough intentioned analysis provides the fuel for a new racism . . . it succeeds in taking the real tragedy of black poverty and serving it up as an essentially salacious 'discovery' suggesting that Negro mental health should be the first order of business in a civil rights revolution. Nowhere does Moynihan suggest that there may be something wrong in an 'orderly and normal' white family structure that is weaned on race hatred and passes the word 'nigger' from generation to generation.

Farmer went on to point out that by attributing black poverty to weakness in family structure, Moynihan was blaming blacks for their own poverty. Many commentators made similar criticisms of the culture of poverty arguments. For the moment, however, the War on Poverty was advancing; controversy about definitions and causes could await evidence from successes and failures of poverty programmes.[17]

CITY LIFE DESCRIBED

Following the pattern of our discussion of aspiring families in the suburbs, depiction of city life in the 1950s and early 1960s must specify whether the collection of types identified by political concern with race, ethnicity and poverty represents assorted victims of social processes, or whether we can treat urban blacks, ethnics and poor people as groups engaged in struggle for their own advancement. While neither aspect of the question can be dismissed, it seems appropriate to set aside policy's interest in social process when attempting to describe the social state of affairs. Although ethnicity involved cultural elements brought in from other countries, Glazer and Moynihan were correct to point out that ethnic groups in the 1950s were 'not a survival from the age of mass immigration'; they were 'a new social form'. Similarly for blacks and poor people, their lives in post-war cities included a strong sense of group solidarity and common interest. Suburbs served the new middle class as communities. City slums were communities as well, places where people lived out their ambitions, cherished their hopes and made the most of their opportunities.[18]

City life in the 1950s had a serene stability that the New York City artist Edward Hopper captured in his paintings. Institutional complexity provided workers, shoppers and residents with distinct roles to play, allowing them anonymity and privacy within the protective clothing, gestures and conversation of outward social appearance. *Sunlight in a Cafeteria*, painted in 1958, shows a man and a woman seated at separate tables. The woman sits in thought, having a cup of coffee or tea. The man smokes a cigarette and gazes in her direction, without staring directly. Sunlight fills the cafeteria through the large front window, but the view from inside is entirely dominated by a nondescript grey building across the street. The city's massive weight presses down, yet within the patch of sunlight quiet contemplation and human drama transpire. The woman is dressed for shopping, the man wears a suit for the office. They do not speak to each other, nor is it likely they would in life. But the tension of sexuality is present and a sense of shared emotion. It is an experience only life in a large city can provide.[19]

Hopper's *First Row Orchestra*, painted in 1951, presents well-to-do couples in formal dress settling in their seats before a play. The curtain and stage fill two-thirds of the painting, heightening anticipation of the drama they are about to see. They do not speak or look at each other. An intense cultural experience is about to begin, but for the moment expectant calm prevails. The ritual aspect of theatre performance is apparent, and the excitement of creativity as well. The scene's appearance is as simple as its meaning is worldly and sophisticated.[20]

Viewers and critics have identified a profound 'loneliness' in Hopper's paintings that would make them ideal illustrations for Riesman's *Lonely Crowd*. Hopper disputed this assessment of his emotional portrayal of city life, although he did not reject loneliness as a factor. 'The loneliness thing is overdone', he commented.[21]

Similar controversy surrounded the stereotypes in C. Wright Mills' *White Collar* (1951). Mills gave his descriptions an ironic, negative tone; the salesgirl in the department store was 'self-alienated' because psychological selling technique demanded she use her personality as a tool. Mills quotes an observer's description:

She wears a fixed smile on her made-up face, and it never varies, no matter to whom she speaks. I never heard her laugh spontaneously or naturally. Either she is frowning or her face is devoid of any expression. When a customer approaches, she immediately assumes her hard, forced smile. It amazes me because, although I know that the smiles of most salesgirls are unreal, I've never seen such calculation given to the timing of a smile. I myself tried to copy such an expression, but I am unable to keep such a smile on my face if it is not sincerely and genuinely motivated.[22]

Mills' negative evaluation is open to question, however. His notions of 'spontaneity', 'nature', 'sincerity' and 'genuine motivation' are highly pejorative. 'Self-alienation' is also immersion in the flows of money and commodities, an experience in contact with the artificial embodiment of human needs and desire, with its packaging and transfer in exchange for wages earned under compulsion of exploitation. To condemn urban commodity capitalism for its money values and its artifice, as Mills unrelentingly does, should not mean that working and living in the city is therefore 'unnatural' or 'insincere'. If anything, the pretence of 'nature' underlying life in the 1950s suburb was more deserving of contempt. At least the artificiality of the department store did not disguise itself as something other than what it was.

City life flourished in restaurants, fashionable clothing stores, art museums, zoos, libraries, and especially bars, cafes and nightclubs. Atop Rockefeller Center, headquarters of NBC television network and other control centres of industry, commerce and media, Count Basie and his black band played jazz in the Rainbow Room, an elegant 'supper club'. Apartment dwellers at 860 Lake Shore Drive, Chicago, Ludwig Mies Van de Rohe's introduction of International style architecture to America, looked out over Lake Michigan at the sunrise, and took their children down the Museum of Science and Industry's replica of a coal mine on Sunday afternoon. Abercrombie and Fitch sold hunting and fishing equipment to wealthy sportsmen; business executives practised golf strokes on their office rugs between appointments; boys of all ages took afternoons off to go to the ball park. Baseball teams personified the life of their cities: 'Dem Bums' the Brooklyn Dodgers, the BoSox (Boston), Cards (St. Louis), Reds (Cincinnati), Tigers (Detroit), Cubs (Chicago) and Senators

(Washington). Joe DiMaggio, Stan Musial and Ted Williams were heroes statesmen and generals could not rival.

Neighbourhoods cultivated their cultural styles. Desirable neighbourhoods had 'character' or were 'interesting'. Sometimes character took an ethnic form, but just as frequently it derived from neighbourhood history, from striking topographical features, or from stylised architecture: Beacon Hill in Boston, Pittsburgh's Mount Washington, Telegraph Hill in San Francisco, Rittenhouse Square or Germantown in Philadelphia, Washington, DC's Georgetown, Chicago's Gold Coast by Lake Michigan, Murray Hill and the 'Silk Stocking' district in New York City. Day-to-day life in an interesting neighbourhood was diverse and exciting. A walk of several blocks afforded glimpses into the intimacy of people's work, friendships or family squabbles. Flamboyant public behaviour was accepted and sometimes encouraged; observers could look on without fear or embarrassment. In the street and on the sidewalk, there was motion, colour, and drama. City people dressed to be seen in public, to make impressions, to appear fashionable. Many women in the 1950s would not go out without hat and gloves, even in the height of summer. Respectability mattered to rich and poor alike.

The joy of city life could be as simple as a pleasant, sunny apartment, a short walk to the bus connecting home and the office, a fruit and vegetable store at the corner, a butcher carrying good meat, newsstands, a Chinese or Italian restaurant, a hospitable bar with a large TV for baseball or the fights, the neighbourhood cinema, parks, hairdressers and barbers, jewellry stores, the bank, a dry cleaners for suits and dresses, and cigar stores for cigarettes, candy and chewing gum. Taxicab drivers talked your ears off about corrupt politicians, the lousy weather or their team losing the pennant. On holidays there were parades, sometimes familiar and sometimes unique: St. Patrick's Day for the Irish, although anyone could be Irish on March 17; Memorial Day for veterans; Fourth of July our Nation's Birthday; and also Macy's (the department store) Thanksgiving Day parade in New York; Mummer's Parade on New Year's Day in Philadelphia; Pasadena, California's Rose Parade and the Rose Bowl football game, also on New Year's Day.

In poor neighbourhoods, people lived as much in the streets and on corners as in their houses and apartments. They opened their doors and conducted household business on the stoop. Women hung out of windows conversing with neighbours, children ran up and down, mothers sliced vegetables for supper, teenage boys loitered down the block while someone's sister marched by across the street studiously ignoring them. In summertime, couples escape the heat on rooftops and children played in the water from fire hydrants opened with the city's unofficial consent. Flower shops or street runners sold numbers, for gambling was largely illegal. Men played cards and drank beer in the kitchen. The TV blared loudly in the living room, whether anyone was watching or not.

Life in the black community differed in part because blacks were segregated through the combined effects of white discrimination and their own desire for communal unity. Yet the black bourgeoisie or 'middle class' separated itself distinctly from working-class and impoverished blocks or neighbourhoods. The violent, angry hell described in Ralph Ellison's *Invisible Man* (1952) must not be taken for an accurate description of everyday life in Harlem. Closer to the common experience were Langston Hughes' tremendously popular newspaper columns on the life and times of Jesse B. Semple, better known as 'Simple'. 'What is it you love about Harlem?' Hughes cues Simple in the first person narrative:

'It's so full of Negroes,' said Simple. 'I feel like I got protection.' . . . 'I also like it because we've got subways and it does not take all day to get downtown, neither are you Jim Crowed on the way. Why, Negroes is running some of these subway trains. This morning I rode the A Train down to 34th Street. There were a Negro driving it, making ninety miles a hour. That cat *were really driving* that train! Every time he flew by one of them local stations looks like he was saying, "Look at me! This train is mine!" That cat were gone, ole man. Which is another reason why I like Harlem! Sometimes I run into Duke Ellington on 125th Street and I say, "What you know there, Duke?" Duke says, "Solid, ole man." He does not know me from Adam, but he speaks. One day I saw Lena Horne coming out of the Hotel Theresa and I said, "Huba! Huba!" Lena smiled. Folks is friendly in Harlem. I feel like I got the world in a jug and the stopper in my hand!'[23]

Sociologist Elliot Liebow's study of streetcorner life in black Washington, DC: *Tally's Corner*, captured the stability and routine of a kind of poverty that was unpleasant by working-class standards, yet fairly free of the horrors of poverty in Third World nations or depressed backwaters in the US. City life was rich in activity, resources and opportunities one could only dream about in rural Alabama.[24]

BEFORE THE DELUGE

Since the riots of the 1960s, the true tone of city life in the late 1940s and 1950s has become a moot question. I have argued in Chapter 5 that the riots were not the explosion of an anger pent up through years of discrimination, poverty and oppression. This is a controversial interpretation; many have asserted that bad conditions in the 1950s were an important cause of the rioting. Once the riots had occurred, however, it mattered little how affairs stood before July 1964 in Harlem or August 1965 in Watts, Los Angeles, California. The *stability* of city life in the 1950s was not artificial. However, a comparable stability could not be reimposed through policy and social action after the riots politicised race, ethnicity and poverty. For all the emphasis on an 'urban crisis' *after* the rioting, in 1968 and following, there was no mood of foreboding before the riots erupted.

The most important question about city life, race, ethnicity and poverty in the 1950s and early 1960s has not been adequately addressed: If the metropolitan central city and suburbs of the 1950s evolved through transformation of the turn-of-the-century industrial city, then what role did suburbanisation play in setting the scene for central city rioting in the 1960s? Having considered the suburbs in Chapter 2, and city life in the 1950s in this chapter, let us examine the second, more overtly dramatic, of the two social revolutions of the metropolitan era.

5. The Second Metropolitan Revolution: the Riots of the 1960s

On July 16 [1964], in New York City, several young Negroes walking to summer school classes became involved in a dispute with a white building superintendent. When an off-duty police lieutenant intervened, a 15-year-old boy attacked him with a knife. The officer shot and killed the boy.

In these terms, the Kerner Commission report described the incident sparking the first of the 1960s riots: Harlem, July 1964. Understanding the rioting and its significance requires an appreciation of its complexity, including this incident. The off-duty police officer was out of uniform; inquiries failed to establish that he had been in any sense 'attacked'; the boy, James Powell, was shot in the back at a distance of many yards while attempting to run away. To conclude that the Kerner Commission report presented a 'biased' accounting of this incident, or of the 'civil disorders' of the mid-1960s in general, would not resolve the problem. For a more accurate description would suggest that the Harlem riot erupted out of righteous indignation over James Powell's needless death.[1]

In their entirety, from small events preceding the 1964 Harlem riot, to rioting sparked by Martin Luther King's assassination in March 1968 and disturbances in 1969 and 1970, the riots of the 1960s constituted a national rebellion of metropolitan central city black communities. During the rebellion's course, every metropolitan city with a sizeable black community experienced a riot or 'civil disorder'.

The only exceptions were metropolitan areas in the South, some of which had minor incidents but no major disturbance. In addition, a number of small, non-metropolitan cities with sizeable black communities endured serious disturbances.

Most discussion of the riots has portrayed them as reactions to undesirable circumstances: pervasive racism throughout the society, lack of sufficient progress toward economic and social equality, or even evidence of backward movement toward a permanently separate and unequal society. In presenting the riots as a rebellion and a social revolution, I am counterposing to this portrait of revolt *against* circumstances an interpretation emphasising the purposefulness of the rioting. The specifically metropolitan character of the riots, and the systematic staging of a disturbance by each major central city black community, indicate that we should consider the rebellion an assault on the emerging post-war metropolitan community structure. The aspiring middle class used suburban community building to solidify its new position in national society. In related fashion, central city blacks used the riots to elevate their communities onto an equal footing with middle-class white suburbs, working-class white suburbs, and wealthy, middle-class and working-class central city neighbourhoods, as significant elements of the metropolitan community. The central city rebellion was more dramatic and violent than the middle-class suburban revolution, but similar in purpose.

The riots represented forces of settlement, they were attempts to alter the social status of central city black communities and their residents. Their impact on urban policy was considerable, although it was not acknowledged directly. The riots were a demand for attention, but not from government and urban policy primarily. Policy's response to the rioting took the form of controversy over an 'urban crisis', discussed in detail in Chapter 6. The impact of the riots as an aspect of settlement was very great. The rioting brought the racial factors in metropolitan structure out into full view, forcing whites to accept the right of blacks to control their own communities within metropolitan areas. The riots brought a new understanding of the two great migrations and the hopes that had drawn several million black people off the land to the big cities. The violence of the rioting was unfortunate, but it was not wanton or aimless. In so far as rioting can speak through actions, the riots of the 1960s were demands for equality and respect that perhaps could not have been communicated in any other manner.

One lesson learned from the riots was that historians had been ignoring the importance of violence in structuring city neighbourhoods in all periods of American development. This chapter begins with an illustration of the role of violence in the evolution of Chicago's Hyde Park–Kenwood area from the late nineteenth century to the 1960s. Particularly significant was the systematic eradication of violence and conflict from public accounts of the neighbourhood's past, such as the plans for a massive urban renewal effort in the 1950s.

The second section briefly surveys rioting and violence in large cities in the nineteenth century. Violence served an important political function in nineteenth-century cities and was understood as political action. Race was a factor in some nineteenth-century urban violence, but in the twentieth century cities began to experience 'race riots' of a new and extremely vicious sort. As a general phenomenon, race riots erupted in reaction to the Great Migration. Because the impact of black in-migration on a city was uncertain in its early stages however, the rioting lacked political and geographic focus. Lacking meaningful targets or purposes, white crowds frequently ended up venting their anger in sadistic beating and killing of unarmed, unresisting blacks, including children.

Between the early twentieth-century race riots and the pattern of nineteenth-century urban rioting, the riots of the 1960s had more in common with the older tradition of using violence to alter the neighbourhood social and political structure of cities. The third section places the riots in historical context, emphasising that they were not 'reverse race riots', with blacks rioting this time instead of whites.

The fourth section describes characteristic riot activities. Although the riots varied in size and level of violence, the way participants and crowds behaved followed certain patterns. By the summer of 1967 the course of a riot in a city had become fairly predictable, once it began. The significance of the rioting as a metropolitan revolution lies in this effort by every major central city black community to mount a riot involving the characteristic activities: massive crowds in the streets preventing police and firefighters from entering the area, looting of stores, setting fire to stores, and keeping the riot going for several days and nights.

Mayors and governors appointed official riot commissions to investigate and interpret the rioting. In the fourth year of rioting,

Lyndon Johnson acknowledged its national scale by forming a President's Commission to search for broad social causes. The commissions attempted to give a particular political meaning to the rioting, emphasising the racism inherent in American society, the black heritage of slavery, white hatred and discrimination, the economic and social distress of blacks in the central cities, the lack of economic opportunities and the failure of government to improve opportunities for blacks, and, as an immediate cause, bad relations between black communities and the police and other city officials and agencies.

The presidential commission, headed by Illinois Governor Otto Kerner, emphasised white racism as the cause of the riots, but proposed expansion of existing Johnson administration economic and social programmes, especially job training programmes, as the most appropriate federal response. Although the official investigations recognised that the riots were phenomena of large cities, none of the reports stressed factors relating to metropolitan area structure. The suburbs were virtually never mentioned.

In the last section, I have interpreted the rioting as a metropolitan revolution comparable to the suburban, middle-class revolution we considered in Chapter 2. This is a new interpretation, but in the context of our discussion of metropolitan settlement since the Depression it should not be controversial. From abroad, observers of the riots anticipated that the national government and its policies were the ultimate target. Most Americans, white as well as black, agreed with the official commission assertions that the rioting was a reaction against the racism inherent in American society. These interpretations revealed more about the people who held them than about the riot participants and their motivations. All creditable explanations of the riots argue that they had a purpose. Close attention to who rioted, and what they did when they rioted, strongly supports a metropolitan interpretation.

Chapter 6, on the urban crisis of the late 1960s and early 1970s, describes the controversy over the crisis as policy's response to the riots. Ultimately federal policy did not adopt the 'anti-urban crisis' orientation that many Congressmen, federal officials, mayors, activists and policy experts vigorously promoted. In part, their initiative failed because they discovered that the metropolitan aspects of the crisis were much more important than the factors that involved federal responsibilities. Their attempts to build a case for federal assumption of central city economic and social problems collapsed for lack of justification for federal involvement.

The urban crisis was a metropolitan crisis, made national only because national settlement was predominantly metropolitan. The riots of the 1960s were national in a similar sense; they were metropolitan phenomena, projected nationally because the nation was mostly metropolitan. As with the suburban revolution in the previous decade, Americans had to adjust not only to the events immediately before them, but also to the reality that the United States was no longer a society of farms, small towns and neighbourly relations.

THE ROLE OF VIOLENCE IN STRUCTURING URBAN NEIGHBOURHOODS: CHICAGO'S HYDE PARK–KENWOOD

Historians attempting to put the riots in context discovered that they had been greatly underemphasising the use of violence to alter the urban social structure. Comparing the 1960s riots with the major racial disturbances of the early twentieth century, the Detroit riot of 1943, the Chicago riot of 1919, and the 1917 East St. Louis riot, revealed striking differences. Broader consideration of urban rioting as a phenomenon suggested that characterising the 1960s riots primarily as racial confrontations obscured their continuity with a long history of rioting as a mechanism for altering the social balance between groups and neighbourhoods in American cities.

The history of Chicago's Hyde Park–Kenwood neighbourhood is an instructive example of the role violence has played in structuring the city. Hyde Park lies south-east of the 'Black Belt' neighbourhood where participants in the first Great Migration concentrated on arrival. As the Black Belt overflowed in their direction, Hyde Park reacted. Real estate men took control of the Kenwood and Hyde Park Property Owners' Association and used it to 'make Hyde Park white'. Calling up the First World War as metaphor, they launched a publicity campaign against a black 'invasion' endangering property values. While the Association pressured people not to sell or rent to blacks, and campaigned for loan money to assist blacks to buy homes in existing black neighbourhoods, others turned to violence. Analysis by the Commission on Race Relations appointed to investigate the 1919 Chicago riot confirmed fifty-eight instances in which houses were deliberately bombed between 1917 and 1921. Many of these bombings occurred in Hyde Park–Kenwood. Most cases involved houses and apartments on predominantly white blocks sold or rented to blacks, but the targets of bomb attacks also included the elegant Lake Shore Drive home of a white apartment houseowner who had been renting to blacks.[2]

White gangs and 'athletic clubs' supplemented the real estate mens' propaganda campaign and the selective bombings with street clashes and attacks that resulted in the deaths of blacks on several occasions. Arrivals of new black families on predominantly white blocks triggered white threats and rioting. Blacks and concerned whites pointed repeatedly to the 1917 riot in East St. Louis, warning that the accumulation of incidents was pushing Chicago inevitably toward a similar explosion. Finally a vicious white attack leading to the drowning of a black swimmer at a public beach did set off the massive 1919 riot. But the violent white defence of Hyde Park did not end with the riot. The bombing incidents escalated in 1920, and the Property Owner's Association attempted to establish impenetrable boundary streets for an all-white Hyde Park.[3]

By the next era of Hyde Park–Kenwood's history, the campaign of terror and violence against black incursion had vanished from memory, at least as far as whites were concerned. 'Only a minute fraction of the population was Negro until the end of World War II', University of Chicago sociologists Peter Rossi and Robert Dentler wrote in their 1961 study of Hyde Park–Kenwood urban renewal. They described Cottage Grove Avenue, the dividing line drawn in blood by the events of 1917–21, as a 'natural barrier to the expansion of the Negro "ghetto" to the west.'[4]

Harold Mayer and Richard Wade referred to the bombing incidents in their popular 1969 history of Chicago, but avoided identifying Hyde Park–Kenwood as the neighbourhood where most of them occurred. In a later chapter, after describing the neighbourhood as a favourite residential area for Chicago's leading business, political, intellectual and cultural figures, they reported that 'poor whites and Negroes' spread into Hyde Park–Kenwood from adjacent traditional slum areas 'during the Depression and in the post-war years' as a result of 'the normal processes of urban change'.[5]

Although it was not a slum, or even a seriously deteriorated area, Hyde Park–Kenwood became the site of one of the largest urban renewal efforts undertaken in any city. Fear that failing to stabilise the rapidly changing racial composition would eventually require the University of Chicago to abandon its mammoth campus in the centre of the neighbourhood played not a little part in this. Before 1950, Rossi and Dentler wrote, Hyde Park–Kenwood 'was predominantly upper middle class or better and almost entirely white'. Social changes beginning during the Second World War reached Hyde Park–Kenwood around 1950, threatening 'the maintenance of the area at its prewar level of living'. In blunt language, the social flood gates burst and approximately 23,000 blacks moved into the neighbourhood between 1950 and 1956. Concurrently, approximately 20,000 whites evacuated. Within six years the non-white proportion of the population increased from 6 to 37 per cent. Urban renewal could not be mobilised to drive back this second, extremely successful black invasion. Instead, in the name of inter-racialism, the renewal interests used eminent domain, condemnation, clearance, reuse preparation and new development to stabilise a checkerboard pattern of white and black blocks and subareas for the indefinite future.[6]

With the sole exception of the nationally prominent black Chicago *Defender*, the city's newspapers commended the renewal plan. The *Defender* branded the renewal effort 'segregationist'. Rossi and Dentler conceded the justice of the charge, but defended the plan on the grounds that limiting the black population to its 1957 level was essential for achieving long-term inter-racial stability. Except for upper- and middle-class blacks already settled within Hyde Park–Kenwood, the *Defender* accurately expressed prevailing black suspicion of unstated motives and goals. Many blacks saw renewal as a smokescreen for university ambitions to clear black residents from blocks adjacent to the campus and build a buffer zone of development defending it from black communities to the west and south. An even larger group regarded the plan simply as a white scheme to prevent any additional families from moving into a neighbourhood most Chicago blacks considered 'an almost ideal residential location'. Summarising results of an attitude survey of Hyde Park–Kenwood residents, Rossi and Dentler wrote:

For Negroes from every class level the unrenewed community was so much better than the 'ghetto' from which they had moved that the importance ascribed by whites to renewal seemed only a flimsy excuse. Except at the uppermost level of the Negro community, renewal plans were seen as directed specifically against Negroes.[7]

RIOTING AND VIOLENCE IN URBAN POLITICAL HISTORY

Nineteenth-century rioting served to create and maintain city neighbourhood divisions among national and religious groups, as well as between white and black. Brawling and rioting were such a familiar inheritance from the eighteenth century that Boston Mayor Josiah Quincy made little effort to stop them when he mobilised the city's first effective police force in the 1820s. Quincy did challenge the volunteer fire companies, which functioned more as associations for neighbourhood defence against immigrant and rival groups than as fire-fighting units. To the great satisfaction of the increasingly wealthy and powerful fire insurance companies, he forced the fire brigades to recognise mayoral authority and accept centralised professional supervision. Only after antagonism to the Irish climaxed in two unprecedented incidents, the burning of Charlestown Convent by a mob of several thousand in August 1834, and the Broad Street Riot between central city tenement Irish and numerous volunteer fire companies in June 1837, did the city create a police force strong enough to confront mass violence.[8]

Pre-Civil War Philadelphia displayed a complexity of rioting and violence approximating a system of social politics. Anti-black violence was endemic, punctuated occasionally by major incidents. White mobs invaded the black South Street community in coordinated attacks for three successive August nights in 1834, destroying two churches, several pubs, and more than thirty houses. Two black deaths were reported. Whites reputed to befriend or do business with blacks were also attacked. Irish handloom weavers were constantly engaged in violence in the 1840s, struggling along with other weavers against encroachments of the factory system, or standing alone defending themselves from the Native American riot of 1844. In the Kensington anti-railroad riot of 1840, an entire neighbourhood rose up and eventually succeeded in driving out the Philadelphia and Trenton Railroad, which the Pennsylvania legislature had granted a right-of-way down a main commercial street. Historian Bruce Laurie's description of the activities of fire companies and street gangs in conjunction with the 1844 Native American anti-Irish riot demonstrates that fighting, arson, crime and rioting had become institutionalised means of achieving and consolidating control of one's neighbourhood.[9]

In New York City, violence and rioting became so intricately intertwined with more conventional political practices that parties and factions took to employing them as a matter of course. The evolving police force, based on the London model, was little more than an additional factor in the political rough and tumble. The business class demanded 'order', meaning that the Irish must be effectively controlled. But the only practical basis for a lowered level of turmoil was to integrate the Irish into the social structure, and onto the police force. Fernando Wood, the mayor who finally perfected the art of controlling and using the police force in a political way, left his political opponents no recourse but to obtain a state legislative reassignment of the fundamental police power. The 1857 Metropolitan Police Act transferred all officers to a force controlled by a Metropolitan Police Board, appointed by the Governor, on which the mayors of New York City and Brooklyn sat merely as two of seven members. Wood's legal manoeuvrings to prevent the Act's going into effect led to a 'police riot' between officers loyal to the mayor and those committed to the new Metropolitan Force.

Although the Metropolitan Force eventually won out, the pent-up social and political antagonisms exploded six years later in the 'Draft Riot': four days of rampaging violence in which attackers burned a draft office, the Fifth Avenue Colored Orphan Asylum, a police station, and many houses and stores. Nominally, the riot consisted of mobs of Irish, angry over being conscripted to fight in the Civil War, attacking blacks. Eleven blacks were officially reported killed by rioters, including people lynched and burned to death. Later the police estimated that as many as 1,000 people might have been killed. Historian James Richardson's more dependable estimate of between 200 and 500 still makes the Draft Riot the most severe single riot incident of the nineteenth and twentieth centuries.[10]

The Civil War, the military draft that many considered blatantly unconstitutional, and the preceding history of violent competition between the Irish and black communities, have obscured the more important significance of the Draft Riot as an event in New York

City's continuous process of social and political development. Among the Metropolitan Police, the riot acquired a reputation as a moment when the City hovered on the brink of mob rule and was rescued only because a police force independent of the dominant Democratic political factions was available to suppress it. The Paris Commune uprising of 1871 made New Yorkers uncomfortably aware of the potentially revolutionary power of the city's masses. Joel Headley, a contemporary newspaper reporter, reinterpreted the Draft Riot as America's narrow escape from its own Commune uprising in his history of New York City's 'great riots' from 1712 to 1873. Given the events of 1877, when the Great Railroad Strike led to rioting in almost every major city, such fears were hardly unwarranted.[11]

TWENTIETH-CENTURY RACE RIOTS

The immediate background of the 1960s riots was the major race riots in northern cities earlier in the century. Two of these, the 1917 East St. Louis riot and the 1919 Chicago riot, were directly linked to the first Great Migration. Chicago and St. Louis were the two principal destinations for Great Migration participants, and these riots have customarily been explained as white reactions to the deluge of new arrivals. Both riots consisted of whites invading black neighbourhoods, beating blacks they came upon on the streets, shooting indiscriminately into houses, entering houses to seize and beat people, setting houses on fire, and in several cases shooting the people escaping the fires. Some blacks who had been beaten were then shot to death. Thirty-nine black deaths were officially recorded in the East St. Louis riot and twenty-three in the Chicago riot.[12]

The Detroit riot of 1943 has also customarily been explained as a reaction to the sudden large-scale influx of black migrants. As in Chicago and East St. Louis, most riot activity consisted of white mobs attacking blacks. Twenty-five blacks died, officially. In Detroit, however, blacks looted and burned stores in the black community and clashed with the police, mostly during the looting and burning. A number of the twenty-five blacks who died were shot and killed by the police. These aspects of the Detroit riot differed significantly from Chicago and East St. Louis, where police either systematically avoided riot areas, observed white attacks but refused to intervene or make arrests, or actually joined white mobs. August Meier and Elliot

Rudwick have suggested a transitional status for the Detroit riot, because it combined the white invasions of the black community characteristic of earlier race riots with the black rioting within the black community, accompanied by confrontations with the police, predominating in the riots of the 1960s.[13]

Two major Harlem riots, in 1935 and 1943, foreshadowed most aspects of the 1960s riots. In both cases, the rioting consisted of blacks massing in the streets, breaking store windows, looting and starting fires. Rioters attacked and beat whites they encountered. Riot activity was confined entirely to Harlem, and the only whites actively involved were police making arrests and attempting to suppress incidents. Except for some brick and bottle throwing, rioters did not attack the police. Although they were described as race riots when they occurred, and linked to the East St. Louis, Chicago, Detroit and other incidents, the Harlem riots lacked the one element crucial to a true racial incident: attacks on blacks by the dominant, white, racial group. Historian Robert Fogelson has suggested that together with the riots of the 1960s the Harlem riots represent a new type of incident, more akin to a mass protest than a racial confrontation.[14]

THE 1960s RIOTS IN HISTORICAL CONTEXT

From a long historical perspective, the riots of the 1960s have more in common with the tradition of purposeful rioting to alter the urban social structure than with the history of racism and racial violence. The similarities were not readily apparent while the 1960s riots were occurring, especially the role of the police in earlier violence. Despite their enthusiasm for comparing the post-war experience of blacks in cities with late nineteenth- and early twentieth-century immigrant struggles, historians had played down the use of violence and police repression to control immigrant neighbourhoods, as well as the resistance put up by immigrants in the form of gang activity, crime and illegal commercial enterprise. Post-war America is an advanced industrial society grounded on complex technology and scientific social analysis. Mass violence can erupt in such a society, it is assumed, only as a consequence of profound and fundamental dysfunction: the rise of Hitler and Nazism in Germany due to humiliating military defeat and hopeless depression, for example. For the United States in the 1960s, only the history of enslavement and racist oppression of blacks seemed a sufficiently drastic flaw in the social system to justify large-scale rioting. The possibility that the riots were not primarily racial in origin or intention was therefore rejected.

Yet attempts to explain the violence as a reaction to the racial situation proved very unsatisfactory. Most whites, and many blacks as well, had difficulty understanding what motivated the rioters to take to the streets, especially at that particular time: 1964–70. More progress had been made in establishing legal civil rights and dismantling institutionalised racism in the ten years from 1954 to 1964 than in the entire era from the end of Reconstruction in 1877 to the Supreme Court's 1954 outlawing of segregation. Wartime opportunities for industrial jobs, followed by continued improvement in economic opportunities since the war, meant that the black rioter of the 1960s enjoyed better material wellbeing and had brighter future prospects than blacks in any period in US history. The racial interpretation raised an unanswerable question: Why now? – just when the most rapid and impressive progress seemed to be unfolding.

Viewing the riots in relation to the social structure of the metropolitan community, however, rather than as black protests against racism, provides better answers to questions of motivation, purpose and timing. Seeing the 1960s riots as struggles to gain control of the central city black community, and to assert its political and social importance vis-à-vis other metropolitan area communities, neighbourhoods and groups, places them in continuity with rioting in previous eras. It also sets the stage for interpretations that correspond more accurately to the character of specific activities and rhetoric in the various riot incidents than arguments emphasising mass protest against society-wide racism.

The central city black communities that mounted the riots were socially cohesive, politically aware, and every bit as conscious of the economic and social processes of post-war metropolitan area development as white working-class central city neighbourhoods or white suburbs ten miles from downtown. Use of the term 'ghetto' to describe central city black communities, which began only a year or two before the riots erupted, was adopted and even encouraged by blacks themselves. 'Ghetto' meant oppression of Jews in Europe, but blacks perceived Jews as a powerful racial minority that had achieved tremendous social success in America precisely because of their solidarity and singleness of purpose. The fact that the black communities were quiescent in the 1950s must not be interpreted as a lack of awareness of the suburbanisation and central business district redevelopment going on all around them. Many aspects of the rioting parallel uses of rioting and violence by the Irish in the 1840s and 1850s, when their labour was essential to the city economy, but their culture, religion and political demands were repugnant. As with the Irish a century before, the police were an immediate object of much anger and attack in the 1960s riots, primarily because they treated the black community as enemy territory in need of pacification.

Urban rioting has occurred since 1970, but in quite different forms from the rebellion of the 1960s. Electric power blackouts sparked riots on two occasions in New York City in the mid 1970s. The contrast with the city-wide blackout of November 1965, when no violence or illegal activity of any kind occurred, was striking. If nothing else, the incidents and their differing outcomes taught sociologists to tread more cautiously when searching for explanations of rioting. The 1980 Liberty City riot in Miami represented yet another type of disturbance. Here riot activity was mounted directly in protest against failure to accuse and punish white police officers who had beaten a prominent black attorney to death. The rioting included several vicious murders of whites. Neither participants nor commentators have suggested continuity between the 1960s riots and these later riots. As they recede in time, the 1960s riots appear increasingly distinct as a rebellion against specific metropolitan circumstances in the mid 1960s. Let us examine details of several incidents and then consider effects the rebellion wrought on the metropolitan community's social structure.

WHAT HAPPENED IN THE RIOTS?

Almost without exception, activity in the 1960s riots was confined to the neighbourhoods where participants lived. Stages of many riot incidents resembled demonstrations or even spontaneous celebrations. Initially, investigators assumed they understood why participants were rioting, but wanted to discover who rioted as a key to the specific social discontents being expressed. Their studies revealed no differences between the typical rioter and the typical riot neighbourhood resident. Significant proportions of residents actively engaged in riot activities. Louis Harris' 1966 nation-wide black attitude survey showed 15 per cent of respondents prepared to join a riot occurring in their neighbourhood and 24 per cent unsure that they would not participate. How these attitudes might translate into actions becomes clearer from a survey in the two main neighbourhoods involved in the 1967 Detroit riot, where 11 per cent reported participating in rioting, 20 to 25 per cent described themselves as 'bystanders' and 16 per cent claimed to have worked to stop the violence. Most significant, perhaps, is that only 48 to 53 per cent said they had stayed at home or outside the riot areas. Given the nature of the Detroit incident, and the likelihood of being arrested simply for being outdoors in a riot area, it is difficult to imagine how someone could have been out on the street and yet believed they were mere observers of riot activity.[15]

Most riot incidents began with an immediate provocation. Harlem 1964 began with the killing of James Powell. Los Angeles' Watts riot of 1965, the first indication of the massive power and violence the rebellion often unleashed, stemmed from a confrontation between a crowd and the police over an arrest for drunken driving. Arrest of a taxicab driver, followed by rumours that he had been beaten or perhaps killed while in police custody, sparked the 1967 Newark riot. Many provoking incidents involved motor vehicles and the police, highlighting a bitter history of police-black community conflict as a source of anger and motivation.

Riot activity usually concentrated in the commercial centre of the neighbourhood. Major riots lasted several days, with peaks and cessations of activity each day. Intense activity in the Watts riot began on the day after the provoking confrontation with police. Masses of people congregated in the business section, two miles from the site of the original incident, and began smashing store windows, taking merchandise and setting fires. Thousands of people milled around in the streets, including many women and children. The National Guard arrived late in the day and helped the police arrest almost 4,000 people. Thirty-four deaths were officially reported and $35 million in property damage or loss during three days of severe rioting.[16]

Initial activity in the Newark riot consisted of a march protesting police mistreatment of John Smith, the arrested taxicab driver. Rocks were thrown at the police, police station windows were broken. Following police dispersal of the march, some looting and setting of fires occurred. Major rioting broke out the next evening following a second protest march. Activity concentrated along Springfield Avenue, a main commercial street. Store windows were broken and merchandise carried off. Fires were set. Due to the large number of participants, police could only cordon off the riot area; they lacked sufficient strength to move along the avenue and control activity. Participants were able to engage in 'shopping for free', carrying home the entire contents of furniture, clothing, appliance, food and liquor stores. State police and New Jersey National Guard troops arrived on the third day, Friday 14 July. Coordination of city police, state police and troops was very poor. Many incidents of uncontrolled shooting at supposed 'looters' occurred. Rumours of 'snipers' in high-rise housing projects led to several situations in which police and troops bombarded buildings with gun and rifle fire. Later investigation failed to establish firm evidence of anyone firing shots from the buildings. Approximately 1,400 rioters were arrested. Despite media publicity concerning fires and destructive violence in the Newark riot, estimated loss from damage was only $2 million, compared with $8 million estimated losses in store merchandise.[17]

New Haven's riot in August 1967 typified the national character of the rebellion. The provoking incident, the shooting of a Puerto Rican by a white restaurant owner who claimed he had been threatened with a knife, served more as an excuse for rioting to begin than as a deeply resented community grievance. Excitement had been building in the black community all summer, and especially since the Detroit riot three weeks previously. The Kerner Commission classified the incident 'serious' on grounds of the scale and duration of activity, the mayor's state of emergency declaration, and the use of state police. Official reports insisted that no shots were fired by police during the six days the incident lasted. Several people reported being shot at by police, but in general official claims of good police conduct were justified. Numerous whites volunteering to assist the police were arrested when they would not leave the riot area. There were no deaths, even the initial shooting was not fatal. Rock and bottle throwing began in the neighbourhood where the shooting occurred and only sometime later broke out in the central black neighbourhood. At the height of the violence, on the third evening, there was activity in four black neighbourhoods, including breaking windows, looting and setting fires. Liquor stores were the principal targets. No 'sniper' incidents occurred.[18]

Comparing the number arrested, 353, with their analytic formula for participation in 1967 incidents, Kerner Commission researchers estimated that 35 per cent of New Haven's black community residents between the ages of 10 and 59 took part in the rioting, approximately 1,800 out of 5,246. The high participation rate, in conjunction with the relative minimum of extreme violence, suggests the black community believed it was demonstrating solidarity with rioting communities in other cities. The absence of demands arising from specific local grievances indicates that New Haven blacks expected to benefit from rioting by way of a national response to a national rebellion, not through concessions or special programmes obtained from New Haven whites. The black community leader most actively demanding city support for activities and programmes, Fred Harris, became immobilised between the rioters and the police in his efforts to calm the violence. Afterward he found his attempts to act as intermediary had destroyed his credibility as a community leader. He became entangled in legal complexities involving drugs and eventually left New Haven entirely. Mayor Richard Lee insisted both during the riot and after that it was not about New Haven specifically: 'what happened here is part of urban America, 1967. It can happen regardless of the city or state, anywhere in the nation.' Although such a statement was self-serving in the extreme, the riot participants did not challenge Lee's interpretation of why New Haven was having a disturbance.[19]

Detroit experienced the most serious riot. The post-riot participation survey, and the 5,642 people arrested, led researchers to estimate that approximately 17,000 had participated actively in riot activities. The survey suggested that another 34,000 'by-standers' were out in the streets during the incident but did not engage in volence or looting, and approximately 25,000 others were working to calm or counter the rioting. From a historical perspective all three types of behaviour must be considered participation in the incident, raising the absolute total to 76,000 people.

The rioting stemmed from police arrests of more than eighty people attending a party at the United Community and Civic League, a private social club known for gambling and after-hours drinking. Suspicion that officials and the media were attempting to cover up the murder of Danny Thomas, a black veteran, by a white gang several weeks before had generated rising anger. Initial riot activity centred on 12th Street, a major commercial district in the black community. By the evening of the second day, 23 July 1967, looting and widespread setting of fires had begun that continued throughout three succceeding days and nights. State police and Michigan National Guard troops were unable to control the situation. Governor George Romney delayed asking the President to send federal troops because a declaration of a 'state of insurrection' would have been required that would have released insurance companies from commitments to reimburse fire damage and property loss. Later, on the advice of former Deputy Secretary of Defense Cyrus Vance, his personal observer at the scene, President Johnson committed army paratroopers.[20]

Despite numbers in the tens of thousands, riot participants did not carry their activities outside black neighbourhoods. Only a handful of incidents came to light in which whites were attacked. White participation in riot activity, especially cooperative black-white looting of stores, was common. The Kerner Commission researchers concluded from their analysis of riot arrests in twenty-two 1967 incidents that 15 per cent of people arrested were white. A large proportion of this 15 per cent consisted of whites arrested in the Detroit riot. In their determination to portray the riots as Negro rage against society-wide lack of economic and social opportunity, the Commission relegated this data to footnotes and cast all description and analysis to suggest that no white participation had occurred. Two of seventeen looters killed in the Detroit riot were white. Forty-three deaths were officially reported. Police, the National Guard and the army were directly or inadvertently responsible for thirty-one; only three died as the result of actions by riot participants.[21]

Most riot activity involved thousands of people milling around in the streets while the more bold broke store windows and carried merchandise home. Once empty, a store would often be set afire with a 'Molotov cocktail', petrol in a glass bottle with a rag for a wick. In Detroit 683 structures burned, one-third of them residential. The burning of residences was probably accidental, with strong winds and the closeness of buildings causing store fires to spread. Detroit was the only riot in which there was significant damage to residential structures. The Fire Chief later reported that he did not believe residential fires were intentionally set. Firefighters attempting to extinguish fires were frequently assaulted with rocks, bottles and, less frequently, gunfire. Constant repetition of the expression 'Burn, baby, burn!' suggested to some that rioters regarded the fires as symbolic purification of the ghetto neighbourhood. A more straightforward interpretation would be that setting fires demonstrated residents' power to control events in their community, and preventing firefighters from extinguishing the fires further underscored community power.[22]

As in previous riots, firing of guns was pejoratively characterised as 'sniper' activity, conjuring images of fanatical lone Japanese riflemen on South Pacific islands in the Second World War. While some firing on police, firefighters and troops undoubtedly occurred, responding to gunfire soon turned into an excuse for uncontrolled violence by the police and especially by the National Guard. National Guard troops had no training for civil disorders or even for crowd control in peaceful situations. As rumours spread among the troops that snipers depended on streetlights to see their targets, they took to systematically shooting out all streetlights with their rifles in any area to which they were assigned. Official telephone numbers for public reporting of 'sniper' fire brought in hundreds of calls, most of them undoubtedly the result of inappropriate firing by National Guard and police. To stop the problem, army paratroopers were ordered to remove all ammunition from their weapons. National Guard troops were also ordered to remove their ammunition, but the order was widely disobeyed. Post-riot investigation revealed that by the later days of the incident the most dangerous elements were not rioters but police and National Guard troops either rendered uncontrollable by anger and fear or simply taking advantage of the confusion to exert violence against the rioters. Detroit tragically underscored the lesson of previous riots, that the strongest possible efforts should be exerted to prevent police or troops from discharging their weapons.[23]

Most significant of all was the effort by virtually every metropolitan black community, in cities large and small, to participate in the national rebellion by initiating riot activity. This aspect of the riots was obvious to officials in cities experiencing riot activity and to the Kerner Commission and other investigating bodies. In carrying out the President's charge to discover 'What happened?' specifically during the first nine months of 1967, the Kerner Commission found that controversy over the definition of a 'civil disorder' made it difficult to determine the exact number of incidents. By one definition, there had been 217 disorders, by a more severe standard only 51. Finally the Commission settled upon a list of 164 incidents in 128 different cities: 8 'major disorders', 33 'serious disorders', and 123 'minor disorders'. Controversy centred on whether various lesser incidents were worthy of attention. The Commission commented that the minor disorders 'would not have been classified as "riots" or received wide press attention without national conditioning to a "riot climate" '.[24]

UNDERSTANDING THE RIOTING: OFFICIAL INTERPRETATIONS

Disagreement about certain implications of the riots obscured the strong consensus on several fundamental issues. Above all, it was believed that the racial element was of primary importance. Since whites had not been active participants in confrontation with blacks, as in the race riots of the past, the racial aspect was interpreted as black protest. Contrast between the violence of the riots and the non-violent methods so forcefully emphasised in the civil rights marches of the early 1960s and the 1963 March on Washington suggested that blacks had turned to violent protest out of frustration. The rioting was therefore an indicator that racism was becoming more entrenched in American institutions. The implication of this train of logic was that unless dramatic positive measures were initiated immediately, conditions would worsen further and blacks would be driven to even more violent rioting in order to communicate their protest message.[25]

The strongest expression of this interpretation came from the Kerner Commission, officially known as the National Advisory Commission on Civil Disorders, appointed by President Johnson in the summer of 1967. The Commission's 'basic conclusion' was that 'Our nation is moving toward two societies, one black, one white – separate and unequal.' In addition, they warned:

Reaction to last summer's [1967] disorders has quickened the movement and deepened the division. Discrimination and segregation have long permeated much of American life; they now threaten the future of every American. This deepening racial division is not inevitable. The movement apart can be reversed. Choice is still possible. Our principal task is to define that choice and to press for a national resolution. To pursue our present course will involve the continuing polarization of the American community and, ultimately, the destruction of basic democratic values.

The Commission went on to call for 'a commitment to national action – compassionate, massive and sustained'.[26]

The Commission members were aware that they were putting forward the same interpretation as other investigating bodies, and for that matter the same type of interpretation that official commissions investigating earlier riots had espoused. Following their recommendations, they gave special recognition to the testimony of black psychologist Kenneth Clark, who had reminded them they were rehashing the warnings and promises of official commissions for the 1919 Chicago riot, the 1935 Harlem riot, the 1943 Harlem riot, and the 1965 Watts riot. 'It is a kind of Alice in Wonderland –' Clark told them, 'with the same moving picture shown over and over again, the same analysis, the same recommendations, and the same inaction.' This time, the Kerner Commission promised in rhetorical response to Clark, the outcome would be different.[27]

Official investigating commissions do not have the luxury of examining violence on its own terms. Once large-scale violence has occurred, the political system must grant it a retroactive legitimacy in order to neutralise future incitements to violent protest. The major conclusion proclaimed by the Kerner Commission had no factual basis, nor did the strange social and economic history of the American Negro making up the bulk of their final report succeed in substantiating the claim that racial divisions were widening. In discussing unemployment, for example, a topic of primary concern as a source of black discontent, the report noted in its discussion of data that differences between black and white workers were not as great as in the past. Yet in its recommendations the Commission simply ignored the data and their implications and argued that a major policy response to the riots should be training programmes to increase and improve black employment.[28]

The main source of discontent treated by the Kerner Commission that was in fact directly relevant to the rioting was police behaviour toward the black community. The research staff alerted Commission members to the adverse consequences of the McCone Commission's attempts to whitewash inexcusable police actions in the Watts riot, and they were determined to deal with the police issue more appropriately. Police relations with the black community in Los Angeles had been very bad and police repressiveness during the Watts riot was extreme. Coroner's inquests determined that police officers had been responsible for sixteen 'justifiable' homicides, a legal term providing protection from civil and criminal prosecution by the victims' families.

The McCone Commission, officially designated the Governor's Commission on the Los Angeles riots, believed it was essential to exonerate the police from blame. They were particularly concerned to protect Chief William H. Parker, because of his national reputation as a model professional. In addition to renown stemming from his work, Parker had become immortalised as the beloved chief of Sergeant Joe Friday on the popular radio and television show *Dragnet*. The Commission conceded that there was 'a deep and long standing schism' between the police and 'a substantial portion of the Negro community'. Regarding Parker, however, they concluded:

> Chief of Police Parker appears to be the focal point of the criticism within the Negro community. He is a man distrusted by most Negroes and they carefully analyze for possible anti-Negro meaning almost every action he takes and every statement he makes. Many Negroes feel that he carries a deep hatred of the Negro community. However, Chief Parker's statements to us and collateral evidence such as his record of fairness to Negro officers are inconsistent with his having such an attitude. Despite the depth of the feeling against Chief Parker expressed to us by so many witnesses, he is recognized, even by many of his most vocal critics, as a capable Chief who directs an efficient police force that serves well this entire community.[29]

The Kerner Commission final report spoke in dispassionate tones, but presented example after example of unacceptable actions by police and the National Guard. They appended to their recommendations a lengthy chapter of special recommendations concerning 'control of disorder', much of which represented criticism of methods police and National Guard units had been using. Although the reality of most riot incidents was that official violence was considerably more dangerous, especially to people, than the actions of riot participants, the prevailing response to the Commission's harsh judgments of official behaviour was strongly negative. Many whites believed in 'conspiracy' or 'riff-raff' theories, instigation of rioting by politically subversive and criminal elements. To them, the Kerner Commission's procedural refusal to seriously consider the presence of organised instigators was reprehensible.

The Commission's own racial attitude survey in fifteen cities revealed that 34 per cent of whites spontaneously identified 'looters and other undesirables' as the 'main cause' of the riots, about 24 per cent identified 'Black Power and other "radicals" ', and about 7 per cent mentioned 'Communists'. (Respondents were free to name several causes.) The most frequent black response to the same question was 'discrimination and unfair treatment', given by 49 per cent. Unemployment and bad housing were each mentioned by about 22 per cent of blacks. Only 25 per cent of whites mentioned discrimination as a main cause. Almost 50 per cent of whites surveyed believed that large disturbances such as Detroit or Newark were planned in advance, compared with only 18 per cent of black respondents. When asked what was the most important way a city government could prevent a Detroit-style riot from occurring in its own city, about 47 per cent of whites mentioned more police control. The most common response by blacks, given by about 25 per cent of respondents, was 'better employment'.[30]

THE RIOTS AND METROPOLITAN COMMUNITY STRUCTURE

The Kerner Commission's accusation that American society was becoming more divided ignored the one great post-war change without which the 1960s riots would never have occurred: the migratory transformation that had made black Americans more predominantly metropolitan than American whites. The Commission used the rhetoric of separation because they believed that black economic and social improvement must involve leaving the central city 'ghetto' neighbourhoods and dispersing throughout the metropolitan area. Because they regarded white racism as the underlying cause of the Negro's problem, the Commission advocated integration of blacks, pepper and salt fashion, among the majority white population as the fundamental first step toward reform in all areas: education, employment, housing, and so on. Neither established black leaders, nor the black community residents who had brought the riots about, were certain how to respond to the Commission's classic liberal ideology and reasoning. Although the riots were being universally interpreted as a form of protest, in fact even riot participants looked back on the events of 1967 or 1968 with amazement at the scale and pervasiveness of what had transpired. Only after it was over, was anyone in a position to say what six years' rebellion might mean.

The Commission focused attention on distress in central city black neighbourhoods, using the term 'ghetto' over and over, as evidence of racial separation. Its report considered the great migrations out of the old South to the cities as only one of several factors in the 'formation' of the ghettos. The monumental progress already achieved through rural-to-city migration was not acknowledged. In defining conditions in the central city ghetto as the negative pole against which future progress should be measured, the Commission was at least giving recognition to the metropolitan context of the rioting. The Commission apparently did not consider the possibility that the riots were an attempt to use the strengths of central city black community life to make further progress.

The Commission's recommendations emerged as a confused mixture of national anti-discrimination measures and specifically urban employment, housing and education integration schemes. The proposals for action began with a reference to 'the continuing social and economic decay of our major cities'. As with our discussion of race, poverty and ethnicity in Chapter 4, it is difficult to determine whether the Commission believed blacks were the victims of urban decay, or its cause. The Commission contrasted its advocacy of integration to 'a policy of "enrichment" aimed at improving dramatically the quality of ghetto life', but without efforts to promote integration. Without substantial integration, they concluded, enrichment programmes would accomplish little. 'Programs must be developed which will permit substantial Negro movement out of the ghettos', the Commission argued, otherwise true equality between black and white would never be achieved. 'In a country where the economy, and particularly the resources of employment, are predominantly white, a policy of separation [such as allowing concentration in 'ghettos' to continue] can only relegate Negroes to a permanently inferior economic status.'[31]

Was this how riot participants wanted their actions translated into political demands? The character of the riots, what did and did not happen, suggests that they were not expressions of discontent with ghetto life, or protests demanding more integration and equality of opportunity. The confinement of riot activity to black neighbourhoods, the absence of attacks on governments and institutions, the lack of anger against specific white individuals such as exploitative merchants, landlords or officials, are starkly inconsistent with interpretations emphasising discontent or protest. Looting was particularly difficult to reinterpret as a form of legitimate protest, especially when characterised as 'shopping for free'. Setting fire to stores made some sense if it could be shown that hated white merchants were specifically targeted, while stores owned by blacks were spared. Unfortunately no such systematic procedures were followed. While residences were conscientiously spared, any store was apparently fair game. The individuals throwing the Molotov cocktails did not care who owned the store they were setting ablaze.

More significance can be extracted from the riots by treating them as a national attempt by central city blacks to achieve recognition as a major social and political force in the metropolitan community. Having migrated to most metropolitan areas in substantial numbers, blacks now seized an opportunity to show their unity and their power. Above all, the rioting demonstrated the ability of black community residents to control their neighbourhoods. 'Shopping for free', while crowds of people in the streets rendered the police ineffective, was a way of proving that community residents possessed the ultimate power when they chose to assert it. By midsummer 1967 creating a riot in one's own community had become a matter of pride to many, a means of joining a national rebellion and heightening its intensity.

The riots succeeded immensely in gaining central city black communities national political attention. In so far as rioting can convey an articulate message, the extent and fury of the rebellion demonstrated a powerful unity and determination among urban black community residents nation-wide. The demand by central city black communities for appropriate recognition had much in common with the suburban revolution mounted by aspiring whites over the preceding twenty years. Changing the social structure of metropolitan areas eventually transformed the basis and character of social classes nationally. The national significance of the riots must also be interpreted by way of their impact on the metropolitan community. Blacks rioted for national recognition, but the increased recognition they eventually received would be as one entity among others within metropolitan social and political structures.

Many derived a strong sense of pride and accomplishment from the rioting. The rebellion resolved much ambivalence about the standing of blacks in the metropolitan community by creating a positive image for central city black neighbourhoods. Big city black communities might be poor, but they had demonstrated their power to control their own affairs. Interpretations emphasising protest, and demands for social and economic change as the purpose of the rioting had the drawback of constantly re-emphasising white control of the socio-economic system. To many blacks, however, the riots represented a fundamental rejection of the tradition of demanding change from whites in favour of demonstrating black self-confidence and power.

Establishing the standing and power of the black community within the metropolitan social structure provided blacks with a rough equality with the central city white working class, the suburban middle class and other metropolitan classes and groups. Policy discussion underwent a profound change as a consequence of the rioting, as we will see in Chapter 6. Electoral and bureaucratic politics in cities made room, however grudgingly, for black participation. Integrating white suburbs proved of less interest to blacks than the Kerner Commission and many policy experts expected. White fears that the riots represented black demands to live in middle-class suburbs and send their children to suburban public schools proved unfounded. Perhaps most valuable of all to blacks themselves was the new freedom the rioting opened up for black people to express their pride and their emotions publicly. The differences in dress, hairstyles, movement, expressiveness, and interaction with whites in public, from before 1964 to after 1970 were extraordinary.

Within our discussion of settlement patterns on the one hand and urban policy on the other, the riots of the 1960s represent an aspect of settlement patterns to which policy later had to adjust. The riots shocked the world. In Europe or Asia, observers naturally wondered whether nation-wide outbreaks of violence represented some form of revolutionary discontent with the American political system. When the rioting is examined in detail, its characteristic forms reveal that it was a distinctly urban, metropolitan phenomenon. The spread of rioting nation-wide related more to the similar metropolitan form of local community in all parts of the country than to direct links between the violence and the national social or economic system. It is in this sense that the 1960s riots have more in common with nineteenth-century city riots than with 'race riots' as conventionally understood. What we will find as we turn to examining the policy reaction to the riots is that they were treated as an urban and metropolitan issue rather than a national racial crisis. Policy focused on the notion of a national crisis, but emphasised its urban, metropolitan character. Eventually this approach to the crisis led to reconsideration of the metropolitan aspect of American society. Americans' doubts about a metropolitan America intensified.

6. Urban Crisis

Policy controversy about the riots quickly reached a consensus that the nation was experiencing an urban crisis. No rioters carried their activities into the suburbs, nor did suburbanites feel specifically implicated by the rioting. But as discussion of the crisis evolved, the realities of race, class and metropolitan structure became sharply delineated. The suburban fringes were predominantly white and increasingly middle class. The metropolitan poor were largely concentrated in central cities, poor blacks almost exclusively so. And because the crisis was perceived as an urban crisis, the metropolitan area became the appropriate community within which social disparities should be equilibrated. If events had not sufficiently connected the riots with the suburbs, policy bound them together inextricably.

The urban crisis debate confronted race, class and metropolitan structure by constructing a stylised discussion of metropolitan political organisation and its economic and social implications. Three topics came to dominate this discussion: central city fiscal crisis, suburban exploitation of the central city, and racial school, housing and employment integration as a solution to the crisis. The sense that the metropolitan community, central city and suburbs together, bore ethical responsibility for resolving the crisis ran very strong. Behind the notion of suburban exploitation lay the presumption that the suburban middle class was enjoying its comforts at the expense of black central city education, health and services. Levying salary (payroll) taxes on people who worked in the city became a popular remedy for central city fiscal problems because it would capture revenue from suburban commuters to offset costs of services for blacks and the poor. Most proposals for housing and school integration throughout central city and suburbs were put forward as a means of forcing middle-class suburban whites to share the burden of black poverty and inequality.

The urban crisis was most acutely a crisis of the large central city governments. Although much discussion elaborated needs of blacks and poor people in cities, central city governments were always the most urgent candidates for assistance. In so far as the crisis demanded a national realignment of races and classes, central city governments endured the shocks and pressures. The federal government enthusiastically debated how best to aid the central cities with their plight, while carefully avoiding admission of direct federal responsibility. What was in fact a social crisis became transformed into a city government crisis that various social programmes might or might not alleviate. Mayors absorbed the heat of protest, many even welcomed the accompanying national publicity. President Lyndon Johnson publicly championed the misfortunate, while privately fearing that backlash from the rioting would terminate his political career. Ironically, it was mishandling of the Vietnam War, rather than the urban situation, that forced him to resign from politics in March 1968.

The regulars of urban policy controversy: the Congressmen, social service professionals, economists, demographers, mayors, sociologists, civil rights leaders, planners, housing industry lobbyists, commentators and others, had not anticipated the riots. As policy's response to the rioting, the urban crisis was something of a diversion. A great deal had been accomplished since the late 1940s in the name of 'saving the central cities'. Shifting the theme of policy discussion to urban crisis did not mean that efforts to save the city had failed. Rather, as the influential policy journal *Daedalus* suggested in its autumn 1968 issue, the 'conscience of the city' had expanded to embrace new concerns. The urban crisis involved problems and issues not addressed by the 'saving the central cities' debate of the 1950s. After some progress along lines laid out through debating the urban crisis, policy shifted back to its older concerns: the importance of metropolitan development to national economic growth; public encouragement of urban investment, especially in housing; the appropriate objectives of federal involvement in urban affairs. The shift can be attributed only in part to Richard Nixon's election as President in 1968, and re-election in 1972. By 1976, when they recaptured the White House, the Democrats had conceded Nixon's approach to urban issues a grudging approval.

This chapter singles out the urban crisis for special attention in order to illustrate the importance of research, logical argument, and informed debate in determining the course of urban policy. In Chapter 7 we will return to our ongoing discussion of policy, picking up from where we left it at the end of Chapter 3. The urban crisis controversy deserves the close analysis it receives here for several reasons. For one, it elicited the most sophisticated policy-oriented research of any incident in the evolution of metropolitan urban policy. Second, it was the most prominent situation in which Congress and federal officials looked to social science researchers for guidance in deciding whether or not to adopt a proposed new orientation for federal urban policy and programmes. Ultimately they rejected a 'combat the urban crisis' orientation, in considerable part because research, and assertions based on research data, had failed to devise compelling reasons why the federal government should take responsibility for confronting the crisis. Researchers laboured mightily to make a case for anti-crisis policy. They served decision-makers just as well by failing as they would have if their efforts had succeeded, however. Presumably, the negative research outcome meant that federal anti-crisis programmes would have proved misguided and ineffective if they had been undertaken.

The first three sections of this chapter explain the major ways the urban crisis was characterised. The first, central city fiscal crisis, was a pressing problem in its own right. Controversy over the urban crisis attempted to explain central city fiscal problems in terms of broad social causes that linked city finances to poverty, distress, and the concerns of central city black communities.

The next section describes characterisations of the urban crisis in terms of 'exploitation' of central cities by their suburbs. These approaches came closest to blaming suburban whites for central city poverty and distress, and by implication for the riots as well. By avoiding central city taxation on the one hand, and by excluding blacks and low-income people from living and working in the suburbs on the other, suburban whites were enjoying all the benefits of metropolitan living without bearing responsibility for metropolitan poverty and distress. Economists concocted very ingenious manipulations of data in their efforts to demonstrate that this sort of argument had validity. However, none of the data projects convincingly established white suburban responsibility for resolving the urban crisis.

Third comes discussion of a lively debate that grew out of the suburban exploitation research, the controversy between 'opening up the suburbs' to allow central city blacks and low-income people to live and work there, and 'gilding the ghetto', a moderately pejorative title for job training and industrial development incentives in central city black and low-income neighbourhoods. Setting aside the discussion of responsibility for the urban crisis, this confrontation attempted to evaluate the relative merits of the two strategies for alleviating central city poverty and distress. The principal conclusion of numerous research studies and comparisons was that the issues involved, discrimination, unemployment, and the potential impact of job opportunities on problems of poverty, were too multi-faceted to be significantly affected by *either* strategy.

The uninspiring outcome of these attempts to build a rationale for an 'anti-urban crisis' policy led policy researchers to terminate the controversy abruptly in the mid 1970s. This had unfortunate consequences for civil rights and poverty activists who had been using the urban crisis to justify their campaign against suburban housing and job discrimination. Two approaches to the crisis, 'suburban exploitation' and 'opening up the suburbs', had identified suburban discrimination as the principal cause of central city distress. Suburban integration activists had joined the policy controversy in hopes of promoting their campaign, and for a time it brought them publicity and assistance. When the research effort collapsed, many suburban integrationists felt betrayed. Urban policy experts lost interest in testifying before the courts in suburban discrimination cases, and judges quickly perceived that suburban integration was no longer considered a promising strategy for helping the cities. The metropolitan area-wide housing, job and school integration movement lost its momentum.

As the urban crisis controversy was concluding, there was a nasty incident. The final section describes research and confrontation over 'white flight', an argument asserting that court-ordered racial integration of central city schools was accelerating white middle-class out-migration from city to suburbs. The white flight confrontation revived several of the urban crisis approaches, suburban exploitation primarily, but with a reversal of their logical progression. Proponents of the white flight argument attempted to suggest that central city school integration did nothing to alleviate poverty and distress, and in addition had the indirect effect of driving white middle-class taxpayers out of the city and thus exacerbating central city fiscal problems. The white flight confrontation is of interest as a flagrant example of misuse of research methods and data in policy controversy. For researchers it confirmed the wisdom of abandoning the urban crisis approach.

Central city distress had not been alleviated, and policy had not adopted a significant response to the riots, but the urban crisis, as it had been defined and debated, had come to an end. President Nixon proclaimed its end somewhat prematurely in 1973; by 1977 virtually everyone involved in urban policy agreed. President Carter was simply accepting their judgment when he decided against an anti-crisis orientation for his urban policy. Much of the general public, and many Democratic voters in central cities, were surprised by Carter's behaviour once he was in the White House. Those who were aware of what had transpired in the urban crisis controversy were not surprised.

Was there a *real* urban crisis that policy examined, debated, and then chose to ignore? Certainly the riots, and the poverty and social problems in central cities, suggested that something was drastically wrong. Policy, we must remember, is an *orientation* for governmental action, not a set of solutions for social problems. When government acts to confront problems such as central city poverty, policy provides guidance for designing strategies and running programmes. The 'saving the central cities' policy led the federal government to undertake urban renewal. But urban renewal did not 'save' the central cities by any commonsense meaning of that word; nor would a federal 'anti-urban crisis' policy have necessarily gone further toward alleviating central city distress than the programmes implemented under the new federalist community development policy adopted in its stead by the Nixon administration and continued under Presidents Ford, Carter and Reagan. We will consider new federalism and community development in Chapter 7.

The point of this special examination of a policy that was rejected is to emphasise the difference between conditions in urban communities, our *settlement* forces and characteristics, and the conceptualisation of urban conditions by government when it is preparing to act. To the federal government, accepting the notion of 'crisis' would most likely have led to assuming responsibility for the fiscal problems of central city governments. Ultimately an anti-crisis policy was declined not because central city governments were not experiencing severe fiscal crisis, but because policy experts were not able to demonstrate why the federal government had an obligation to help central city governments with their financial problems. Policy experts tried their best to make this case, but by their own admission they failed. In terms of the way we have defined policy, the urban crisis controversy is an example of the policy process working as it should and of the federal government drawing the appropriate conclusion from the outcome. Along the way, many researchers and activists learned a hard lesson.

CENTRAL CITY FISCAL CRISIS

Mayors experienced the urban crisis as a very tangible problem of difficulty in balancing their budgets. Expenditure demands grew more rapidly than revenues. This was paradoxical from one perspective because federal programmes were channelling increasing amounts of money to cities. By 1971, when the Model Cities programme was coming into high gear, when welfare benefits were improving and a host of renewal programmes were all flourishing, most large cities were receiving one-quarter or more of their revenue from the federal government. However, federal programmes may have contributed to the budget problem by generating expectations they could not satisfy. The causes of large-city budget crisis were not simple or obvious.

Most discussion of budgetary crisis tried to suggest that a national urban crisis was the underlying cause. Some argued that central city fiscal crisis was the manifestation of the urban crisis, the crisis itself consisting of economic and social problems in the cities. Economic and social problems generated service needs that drove large-city expenditures beyond revenue capabilities. Constraining expenditures within revenue limits, according to this argument, would only exacerbate misery and suffering in the city.

Others argued that fiscal crisis stemmed from weakening of the cities' commercial and industrial viability. Large cities seemed to be losing their power to spawn businesses and create jobs. Thousands of acres cleared under urban renewal awaited new development that stubbornly failed to materialise. Property taxes and other revenues stagnated or declined; even raising the rate of taxation brought only small increases in total revenue. Whether flagging economic viability derived from social disorder was a controversial question.

Explanations that failed to link the budget problems of central city governments to causes implying an urban crisis were of little policy interest, however accurate they might be. Conservative political scientist Edward Banfield provoked controversy and even anger by arguing that blacks and what he called the 'lower class' were no more in need than they had ever been, perhaps less. Rather, Banfield suggested, they were using the urban crisis as an opportunity to make demands. Whatever they won in terms of federal programmes, expanded city services, or political visibility would be pure gain. Banfield did not blink at accusing his policy opponents of arguing from social guilt, or weakness of political will. Apart from the crisis of conscience many were experiencing, Banfield believed the urban crisis had little material substance. If city budgets were out of balance, expenditures could, and should, be trimmed to match revenue capabilities.[1]

In practice, the moral or political legitimacy inherent in pressures driving up city government expenditures mattered little. The pressures were real and mayors had to deal with them. One major source of rising expenditures involved city agencies receiving requests from people who had never before attempted to obtain services. Federal Medicaid, for example, began to provide rights to free medical care for participants in the welfare system in the late 1960s. State governments bore responsibility for 50 per cent of Medicaid costs. Some cities, particularly New York City, experienced rising expenditures because their state governments passed along part of the Medicaid burden. A broader consequence, experienced by all central cities to some extent, was that as welfare clients became accustomed to having a right to demand medical care at hospitals and clinics, their new boldness carried over to other public services.

Policy researchers recognised that they had to tread carefully in explaining central city fiscal crisis. One promising line of argument was to associate budgetary problems with poverty among the city's population, implying that poverty was therefore at the heart of the urban crisis. Those who followed this avenue became aware of crucial problems in logic, however. Nationally, the most severe poverty was not urban but rural. In addition, migration studies showed that poor rural people experienced significant improvement in income, health and wellbeing when they moved to central cities. Central cities contained only about 30 per cent of the nation's substandard housing in 1966; more than 50 per cent of substandard housing was outside metropolitan areas. To a policy researcher this meant that identifying poverty as the essence of central city problems opened the door to responses that rural poverty was much worse, and that the urban crisis was not as pressing as a rural crisis that was not even being publicised.[2]

President Johnson initiated his War on Poverty in 1964, before the riots began. The majority of poor people, like the majority of the population as a whole, lived in metropolitan areas; but War on Poverty rhetoric did not try to suggest that poverty was predominantly an urban problem. As policy controversy fashioned the urban crisis, the relationship of the War on Poverty to urban policy became problematic. Identifying poverty as a major source of the urban crisis would allow new urban programmes to emerge as expansions of the War on Poverty. But the contradictory implications of explaining the urban crisis in terms of poverty aroused doubts about the policy enterprise. Mayors and many others took the pragmatic view that the urban crisis was real, regardless of social researchers' difficulties in explaining it, and cities welcomed assistance from any source. Learning that rural poverty was more severe than central city poverty did not help meet demands on city government for services and aid. Mayors wondered whose side the urban policy experts were on.

SUBURBAN EXPLOITATION OF THE CENTRAL CITIES

Metropolitan community interdependence offered a possible solution to the dilemma of explaining central city crisis. Nationally, the metropolitan sector was wealthier than the non-metropolitan. If assistance was going to be provided to the central cities, the concentration of wealth and resources in metropolitan areas made them perhaps the most appropriate source, preferable even to federal assistance. In so far as metropolitan areas could be described as economically and socially unified, central city poverty and fiscal distress could be delineated as problems internal to a larger, healthy community fully capable of alleviating them. Following this logic, arguments evolved grounded on various assertions that the suburbs bore responsibility for central city crisis. To a lesser or greater degree, all these arguments implied that central city crisis resulted from exploitation by the suburban fringe.

Identifying suburban wellbeing as the source of central city distress proved no less problematic than efforts to implicate poverty as the underlying cause of the urban crisis. Policy writers frequently neglected to recognise that they were accusing the suburbs of exploitation without establishing grounds for suburban responsibility. Alice Rivlin, Charles Schultze and associates at the prestigious, politically liberal Brookings Institution wrote in describing the central city fiscal crisis as of 1973: 'Although cities may not be able to do much by themselves, most metropolitan areas as a whole do have the capability for dealing with the growing imbalance between the resources and needs of their core cities.' Suburban tax capacity was growing while many central city tax bases were deteriorating, and expenditure levels were higher in central cities and rising more rapidly than suburban expenditures. Yet Rivlin and Schultze's analysis of relative revenue-raising capability showed that central cities had greater taxable resources per resident than their suburbs. Readers came away believing the suburbs should help alleviate central city crisis, when in fact the research evidence failed to establish either suburban responsibility for central city problems, or greater suburban capability to fund central city expenditures.[3]

Eluding central city problems loomed large in suburban exploitation arguments. Central cities were purportedly victims of white middle-class 'flight' to the suburbs, not so much to escape crime, decline and distress as to avoid being taxed to underwrite escalating central city expenditures. The fact that fleeing whites continued to work, shop and enjoy themselves in the city demonstrated their dependence upon it. Many Marxist and radical writers adopted the white middle-class flight argument in the mistaken belief that successfully blaming the middle class for central city poverty somehow demonstrated the bankruptcy of US capitalism. No one could explain how to tell an aspiring working-class city family skimping and saving to join the suburban middle class from a fleeing, potentially bigoted middle-class family escaping central city property taxes in order to keep more of its income for itself.

Middle-class flight arguments often warned of cumulative worsening of the central city crisis. As a central city lost more and more of its middle class, the tax burden on those remaining would have to increase, giving them an incentive to flee as well. In short order only the rich and the poor would be left. Businesses would follow their middle-class customers to the suburbs and further undermine central city revenue capacity. Black commentators frequently attacked middle-class flight on grounds that it portrayed central city blacks and poor people as if they were a social plague. A sizeable white middle-class majority in the central city could tolerate a moderate minority of blacks and the poor, but when the proportions tipped too far the snowballing exodus would inevitably begin.

Exploitation that seemed so straightforward to many proved impossible to demonstrate in research studies. Researchers were particularly distressed by the policy implications of social ecologist Amos Hawley's discovery of suburban exploitation as early as 1940. Hawley had shown not that middle-income families were escaping central city costs arising from poverty and social distress, but rather that suburbanites were benefiting personally from central city services without paying for them. Hawley postulated that the suburban population of a metropolitan area must generate costs for central city governments through use of the central city for work, shopping and pleasure. Using data from 76 metropolitan areas, he estimated that every additional suburban resident cost the central city $2.77 in added service expenditures. Since there was every reason to assume that this kind of suburban exploitation was still in effect in 1970, exploitation researchers feared that their argument would blow up in their faces. Rising central city costs might prove to be caused not by the city poor and their problems, but by middle-class suburbanites taking a free ride on city services.[4]

Economist William Neenan showed that Hawley's argument applied to the 1960s as well. Neenan succeeded in estimating the dollar value of central city services received by residents of six Detroit suburbs in 1966 and the amount of revenue they paid to the city. Although residents of the exclusive suburb of Gross Pointe Park were paying Detroit $1.84 more in revenue than they received in services, residents of the five other suburbs were benefiting in amounts ranging as high as $7.24 per person. The excess would have been considerably higher if Detroit had not had a city income tax. Detroit receipts from Grosse Pointe Park amounted to $7.82 per resident. Neenan concluded that with the exception of the very wealthy suburbs, Detroit's tax on suburbanites earning income through central city payrolls was too low to cover the cost of services it was providing to suburban residents.[5]

Neenan's study offered encouragement to advocates of city payroll taxes that would collect revenue from the middle class regardless of residence: central city or suburb. Whether suburbanites were bearing their fair share of the central city's costs for services to the poor remained in dispute. Julius Margolis and others pointed out that large suburban populations enhanced the value of central city real estate and the profitability of commercial businesses. The chief exploiters of the central city poor might therefore be central city real estate owners and commercial businessmen, not the suburban middle class. Margolis' argument suggested that the plaintive wails of distress from central city landlords and store owners about excessive property and retail sales taxes might be discounted as self-serving. Also monopoly corporations with central city corporate headquarters might be paying far less than their appropriate share of city costs.[6]

Believers in suburban exploitation retreated from these methodological complexities to the simple charge of disparity in fiscal resources. Suburbanites were richer in income and wealth than central city residents, but paying less proportionately in taxes because of the political fragmentation of the metropolitan community. Suburban-central city fiscal disparity arguments suggested that a metropolitan-wide tax system would overcome this inequity and provide the funds to alleviate central city expenditure crisis.

But fiscal disparities also succumbed to insurmountable conceptual difficulties. Proponents were unable to explain how their charges differed from arguing that higher income suburbanites should allow taxes to redistribute their income and wealth to the central city poor. Discussion of metropolitan political unification usually accompanied the fiscal disparities debate. If the entire metropolitan community were under one government, wealthy suburbanites could not escape taxation to underwrite the health, education and social costs of adequately serving the poor. But critics pointed out that under a metropolitan government the upper majority of the income distribution might just as easily overwhelm the lower minority politically and refuse demands for service rather than agree to higher taxes. Middle- and upper-income whites might choose to send their children to private schools and use their political clout to trim public school expenditures drastically. Margolis speculated that total public spending by a unified metropolitan government could well be considerably lower than current spending by a large central city government and numerous fragmented suburban jurisdictions. There was no guarantee that the central city poor would be better off under metropolitan-wide government.[7]

OPENING UP THE SUBURBS VERSUS GILDING THE GHETTO

Even if the suburbs were not the source of central city problems, perhaps they could contribute to effective solutions. Closely allied to the exploitation debate were arguments based on the assumption that suburban opportunities for social improvement were superior to central city conditions. Suburban schools were better; suburban neighbourhoods were not plagued by crime, blight, deterioration and social pathology. Most importantly, while the central cities were losing manufacturing and other jobs, the best job opportunities for people with minimal education and skills were with new or expanding companies tending to locate toward the edges of the suburban fringe. The suburbs might not have caused the social problems of central city residents, but through systematic discrimination against blacks and poor people they were walling off access to suburban housing, education and employment. Suburban exclusion was blocking the path to the metropolitan community's best opportunities for social advancement. Causes were not as important to this line of argument as comparing improvement strategies. Could a campaign against suburban discrimination produce more effective results at less cost with fewer drawbacks than expensive direct investment in central city poverty and economic development programmes?

Overcoming suburban racial and income discrimination gained popularity as an 'alternative' to job training, housing and community anti-poverty programmes in central city black and poor neighbourhoods. These were labelled 'ghetto gilding', after a controversial 1969 article by economists John Kain and Joe Persky: 'Alternatives to the Gilded Ghetto'. Anthony Downs, a highly respected expert in housing market economics, prominently associated himself with a strategy of 'opening up the suburbs'. Jobs were the key to this debate. Job training programmes, usually involving subsidies to participating employers, had been the most hopeful War on Poverty strategy. The search for alternatives began when five years' experience with job training showed few lasting results. Lack of success was explained in part by the reality that central city employers were more likely to close and move away than to create new jobs, despite the availability of willing, newly trained black workers. It was not enough to train central city workers for jobs, they had to have access as well. If most new jobs were being created in the suburban fringe, black workers needed *entrée* to the suburbs.[8]

Proponents of opening up the suburbs did not suggest that job opportunities tended to locate in the suburbs for racist or discriminatory reasons, they simply asserted it as a reality with unfortunate consequences for central cities. 'Approximately three-quarters of all new industrial plants in metropolitan areas were located in suburbs during the 1960s', Michael Danielson recited in his study of exclusionary suburban politics; 'In the fifteen largest metropolitan areas, suburban employment increased by 3.1 million between 1960 and 1970, while the number of jobs in the central cities dropped by 836,000.'[9]

Less frequently mentioned was the back-commuting phenomenon, the predominance of black workers commuting from central city homes to suburban jobs against the flow of white suburbanites commuting to the city. Statistics on place of residence and place of work suggested that blacks were adapting to metropolitan structure in a different fashion from whites. In 1960, Chicago had 4,069 non-white workers commuting from suburban home to central city job, compared with 323,374 white workers. But while 76,247 white workers engaged in back commuting from city home to suburban job, about one-third of the suburb-to-city flow, 12,394 non-white workers were back commuting from city home to suburban job, more than three times the number of traditional commuters. By 1970, when the ghetto gilding alternatives debate was heating up, Chicago's non-white suburb-to-city commuters had increased 89 per cent to 7,702. Traditional white suburb-to-city commuters increased only 6 per cent to 341,749. White back commuters increased substantially, 90 per cent, to 145,167. But black back commuters, non-white central city residents commuting to suburban jobs, increased more than threefold, over 200 per cent, to 39,731. It is also interesting to observe that in 1960 there were 20,690 non-whites both living and working in Chicago's suburbs, considerably more than the number of commuters from the city. Yet by 1970 the number of non-whites living and working in the suburbs had only increased to 35,567, about 4,000 less than the number of black commuters.

Data for nine selected metropolitan areas suggest that blacks aggressively pursued job opportunities in both central city and suburb during the 1960s, but were slower to move to the suburban fringe to live. Table III shows figures on the four permutations of work and residence and increases from 1960 to 1970. The increase in employment of non-white workers living in the nine central cities was 265,277, of which 160,710 new jobs were in central cities and only 104,567 were in the suburbs. The total increase in employment of non-white workers living in the suburbs was 105,118, of which 45,816 new jobs were in the central cities and 59,302 were in the suburbs. Thus non-white workers living in the central cities entered almost twice as many new suburban jobs as non-white workers who were living in the suburbs by 1970. It is also significant that the largest number of new jobs were found in the central cities during a decade when the total number of jobs located in the central cities was declining significantly in all nine cities studied.

TABLE III   Employment of non-white workers by place of residence and place of work in nine selected metropolitan areas, 1960 and 1970, and increases 1960–70

	1960	1970	Increase 1960–70
Non-white workers living in central cities and working in central cities	1,104,210	1,264,920	160,710
Non-white workers living in suburbs and working in central cities	27,760	73,576	45,816
Non-white workers living in central cities and working in suburbs	89,779	194,346	104,567
Non-white workers living in suburbs and working in suburbs	152,343	211,645	59,302

Sources: U.S. Census Journey To Work Survey, 1960 and 1970; Kenneth Fox and Ray Harris, 'Racial Differences in Metropolitan Commuting Patterns, Changing Trends 1960 and 1970', unpublished study, 1981. The nine metropolitan areas are Cleveland, New York, Washington, Denver, New Haven, Chicago, Boston, Detroit and Philadelphia.

The figures imply that blacks with suburban jobs may have preferred central city to suburban living. The kinds of data available did not permit differentiation between phenomena caused by suburban housing discrimination excluding black residents and phenomena resulting from black preferences for living in the central city. Once again, methodological problems cast doubt on the assertions central to the debate. There was no evidence that discrimination against black or minimally educated, low-skill workers differed in severity among suburban employers compared with central city firms. Charlotte Fremon concluded from a study of central city and suburban employment by occupation in eight major metropolitan areas in the mid 1960s that as far as employment discrimination was concerned, central city black and low-skill workers were experiencing considerable loss of employment due to discrimination by central city employers who were filling low-skill jobs with white workers commuting from suburban residences. She warned that the focus on potentially inaccessible jobs in the suburbs was distracting attention from the more serious problem of similar employer discrimination in *both* central cities and suburbs.[10]

All other factors aside, a black worker seemed equally likely, or unlikely, to be hired for a suburban job opening as for a central city opening, providing he succeeded in learning about the job and applying for it in time. Proponents of the ghetto gilding alternatives argument suggested that information and access were the key problems, that the chief obstacles preventing blacks and the poor from finding and holding good jobs were distance between the central city ghetto and suburban jobs, lack of information about suburban jobs, and difficulty in suburban job searching. Proponents assumed that central city workers wanted to overcome these obstacles by moving to the suburban fringe, but that they were prevented from doing so by suburban housing discrimination.

The National Committee Against Discrimination in Housing, a civil rights organisation with a long-standing concern over residential discrimination of all varieties, seized the opportunity presented by the alternatives debate to prepare a major comparison between employment and housing discrimination in suburbs. Their report purported to show that suburban jobs could be relatively available to blacks and other minorities, but that suburban refusal to build appropriate low-cost or low-rental housing, and racial discrimination in the rental and sale of existing housing, were preventing them from living in close enough proximity to get and hold the jobs. Showing that residential discrimination in the suburban fringe was severe was easy. Proving that redistributing the black and minority population throughout the metropolitan area, rather than concentrating them in certain central city neighbourhoods and a few older suburbs, would improve their employment status and incomes was not within the Committee's statistical capabilities. The Committee was not able to show that improving geographic access to suburban jobs, if it could be achieved, would result in more blacks and minorities obtaining those jobs.[11]

Economist Bennett Harrison succeeded in at least suggesting that the opposite was the case, that for one or a combination of reasons black workers found better employment opportunities in the central city. 'Non-white underemployment, in all of its many manifestations', Harrison showed,

> is pervasive *throughout* the metropolitan area. On the average, central city men living in nonpoverty neighborhoods (i.e. outside the 'ghetto' but inside the city limits) appear to enjoy a slight advantage over other urban non-whites. They receive somewhat higher earnings, are unemployed less often, find their way into slightly higher status occupations, and enjoy higher family incomes than either ghetto or suburban non-whites.

Harrison's findings suggested that employment discrimination was more severe in the suburbs than in the central city, something proponents of the alternatives argument had assumed was not the case.[12]

Finally, arguments appeared corresponding to our discussion in Chapter 2 of ways aspiring white families used the suburbs to advance their social standing. Political scientist Michael Danielson marshalled compelling evidence that suburban whites actively excluded blacks and low-income people as a strategy for protecting and enhancing their own superior standing in the national social structure. He reminded everyone involved in the alternatives debate that the advantages suburban residence provided for whites were based, in considerable part, on discouraging blacks and minimally educated, low-skill central city residents of all races and ethnicities, from aspiring to middle-class jobs and careers and from living in middle-class communities. 'Middle-class families commonly equate personal security, good schools, maintenance of property values, and the general desirability of a residential area with the absence of lower-income groups', Danielson contended.

Given these concerns, residents of middle-class areas rarely are content to rely solely on economic factors to separate them from the poor. Instead, they seek to use the local political system to exclude those whose presence threatens to undermine the quality of life in their neighborhood.

His arguments helped explain why Harrison had found that non-ghetto central city blacks were more successful socially and economically than suburban blacks. Potentially, an aspiring black family had a better chance of succeeding if it moved to a black middle-class city neighbourhood than if it attempted to integrate itself into a predominantly white suburb.[13]

Somewhat later, in 1979, when data on the considerable increase in black suburbanisation during the 1970s were available, Thomas Clark showed that the converse of Danielson's argument was also true. Clark demonstrated that suburban residence was beneficial for black families that had already achieved middle-class status, but less advantageous to poor and working-class blacks than remaining in the central city. In other words, blacks could live in the suburbs if they preferred them to city living, but residential integration did not mean that the occupational and status mobility mechanisms operative for aspiring white families would begin to function for blacks as well. Clark's conclusions paralleled William Wilson's controversial assertion that the pervasive racial forces in the national social structure were impacting different classes of blacks in different ways as a sizeable black middle class emerged. Clark suggested that the same could be said for the impact of metropolitan area structure on black social standing, mobility and opportunities.[14]

THE STRUGGLE FOR METROPOLITAN INTEGRATION

Policy experts can be fickle allies, as social activists have learned again and again. If the logic of the relevant social analysis cannot be consistently aligned with the objective activists want to pursue, social scientists and policy researchers will often abandon an issue abruptly.

Such was the outcome of the urban crisis as a policy enterprise. The 'alternatives to the gilded ghetto-opening up the suburbs' debate was the last defensible basis on which researchers believed they could argue that something should be requested, or demanded, from the suburban middle class because it would benefit blacks and the poor in central cities. When research evidence suggested that integrating blacks and the poor into the suburbs was not likely to be of much benefit in improving their occupational status or incomes, the alternatives debate petered out. And for all intents and purposes that was the end of the urban crisis as well, at least as far as policy controversy was concerned. None of the lines of argument had been very compelling, not poverty as a cause of central city fiscal crisis, not suburban exploitation, and not even opening up the suburbs. A valiant rhetorical and research effort had come to naught; the only thing to do was to shift to another controversy, redefine the issues and terms of debate and hope for better results. We will be following these new policy directions in the next two chapters.

The activists who had become involved in the urban crisis controversy felt abandoned at the altar. Civil rights organisations, especially those concerned with school and housing integration, had hoped research would demonstrate that fiscal crisis in the central city could be most effectively alleviated by programmes to break suburban racial exclusion and promote integration throughout the metropolitan area. When the research effort failed most social scientists withdrew, leaving the civil rights activists promoting urban crisis arguments before public forums, television interview shows and Congressional hearings without benefit of expert evidence and support. Metropolitan school and housing integration continued to be desirable, but suddenly their relevance to urban policy was in doubt.

Several prominent metropolitan integration campaigns lost momentum in mid-course: city-suburban school integration, metropolitan-wide siting of public housing, and non-exclusionary zoning. Activists and civil rights organisations pursued metropolitan-wide integration as a strategy for obtaining better quality education and housing. Integration has value as a social objective, but its primary importance is as an assurance that blacks have access to resources or amenities on an equal basis with whites. The philosophy adopted by the Supreme Court in its landmark school integration decision, the 1954 Brown versus Board of Education case, has been central to black struggle for equality through integration: separate is inherently unequal.

Civil rights activity had been concentrated in the South in the late 1950s and early 1960s. The major organisations, especially the National Association for the Advancement of Colored People (NAACP), used their urban strength in the North and West to support the Southern effort. The fury and extent of the riots took them by surprise. The urban crisis debate, with its clear concern for racial issues raised by the rioting, encouraged campaigns for metropolitan integration in progressive Northern states: Massachusetts, Connecticut, New York, New Jersey, Michigan. The alliance between urban policy and civil rights activism stirred expectations of significant achievements.

Little racial integration had occurred in northern and western suburbs up to this time, even in the politically progressive states. Individual middle-class black families had moved to suburban homes, but their intuition about white racism made them fearful that clusters of black suburban residents would arouse white antagonism. An imaginative attempt to overcome this danger was the cooperative community of Village Creek, founded in Norwalk, Connecticut, at the far edge of the New York metropolitan area in the 1950s. The community bylaws called for proportions of white and black residents, and even mandated that any house coming up for sale between two houses owned by families of the same race had to be purchased by a family of the opposite race. The cooperative board, elected by the residents, reserved the right to intervene in sales and purchases if the bylaws were being violated. Village Creek attracted middle- and upper-middle income families, many of them political progressives. The effort to achieve a racial balance with a significant proportion of black families was a success. Yet Village Creek failed to spawn any other cooperative multi-racial communities.

Given the extremely limited black participation in post-war suburban development, metropolitan area-wide school integration seemed more promising to civil rights activists, as a first initiative, than a metropolitan housing or employment campaign. Metropolitan school integration would benefit poor black central city children primarily, by providing them access to suburban schools. In part, activists expected the city children to benefit because suburban schools had better equipment, better trained teachers and more special services, but also they hoped that bringing suburban children to city schools would lead white suburban parents to demand that central cities raise their schools to suburban standards.

Education has always been a state government responsibility, not a local responsibility, and suburban resistance to integration with central city school systems was on very weak legal grounds. Yet an antagonistic Supreme Court chose to side with the suburbs and undermine the metropolitan school integration campaign. Disintegration of policy concern for the urban crisis contributed to the legal defeat by diffusing support for metropolitan school integration as a solution to urban problems. Suburban opposition to integration with central city school systems was low-keyed in tone but extremely intense. Without strong arguments that a broad range of social objectives would be advanced, the court had little reason to provoke suburban middle-class wrath.

The Supreme Court established its position on segregation and appropriate remedies within a city school system in the 1973 Keyes decision involving Denver, Colorado. The court ruled that decisions and actions by school authorities which increased racial segregation, particularly when accompanied by rejection of alternatives that would better integrate the schools, constituted *de jure* segregation, that is they were equivalent to passing laws and regulations segregating the schools. Victims of such practices were entitled to the same remedies as victims of formal segregation laws. This put many northern and western cities on the same footing as southern states and cities where segregation had been written out in black and white. The Court ordered Denver to rearrange the students so as to achieve an integrated pattern throughout the school system.[15]

The Keyes decision had its most significant impact in the case against the Boston school system. Federal judge W. Arthur Garrity applied the Keyes criteria and found Boston guilty of segregating its schools. He rejected all claims that the racially segregated distribution of students was an unintended consequence of housing patterns and a policy of neighbourhood schools, pointing to school board actions facilitating and encouraging a racially dual system. Garrity ordered preparation of an integration plan and personally supervised its implementation year by year. The Boston remedy became notorious as a supposed example of 'forced busing to achieve racial balance'. What opponents of the integration plan concealed was that Judge Garrity's remedy involved busing of fewer children shorter distances than the busing of white children through black and

Hispanic neighbourhoods to all-white schools that the Boston school committee had been willingly arranging and financing. Garrity's court had found that 30,000 students were being bused, many of them to overcrowded all-white schools, while predominantly black schools had hundreds of empty places. As in many, many cases where remedies involving busing were ordered, the question in Boston was not whether students would be bused, because students were already being bused to maintain segregation. The issue was where the buses would go.[16]

City-wide integration was not of much value however, if black, poor and minority students predominated throughout the school system. The only hope of assuring high-quality education lay in integration patterns incorporating a majority of white students. If the white middle class were not dependent upon the public schools for their own children's education, entire central city school systems might be allowed to deteriorate, rendering integration an exercise in futility. Metropolitan-wide, central city-suburban integration was the appropriate solution and civil rights activists did their utmost to persuade the courts to mandate metropolitan integration plans.

The relevant law and precedent were absolutely straightforward: because education is a state responsibility, there was no legal basis for confining segregation remedies within central city boundaries. Despite the constitutional and legal circumstances however, the pressure on the Supreme Court to rule against metropolitan remedies was extreme. In the face of enormous white suburban political power massed against integration with city schools, a court dominated by conservatives had little incentive to impose programmes that neither Congress nor any state legislature had been willing to mandate. The first test case, involving Richmond, Virginia ended in a 4-4 tie, defeating a proposed city-suburban integration remedy but not resolving the question conclusively.

Finally, in 1974, the court decided against metropolitan integration in a case involving Detroit. Detroit had been found guilty of segregating its schools, but because two-thirds of all pupils were black the lower court reasoned that an integration scheme confined to the city alone was insufficient. It ordered a plan integrating Detroit city schools with those of fifty-three surrounding suburbs. The Supreme Court was asked to block the integration plan on the grounds that the suburbs were not responsible for the segregation problem in Detroit and therefore should not be compelled to participate in the remedy.

The Supreme Court devised an argument to justify agreeing with this reasoning and passed it by a 5-4 vote. The pressure upon them included a strong campaign in the House of Representatives to legislate away court powers to order school integration plans, President Nixon's vocal opposition to forceful integration remedies in the 1972 election campaign, and popular and Congressional agitation for a constitutional amendment against busing for racial balance. Perhaps most influential on the justices were briefs from attorneys general in a number of states urging them not to assert that state responsibility for education implied a black child's right to remedies across school district or city boundaries.[17]

Metropolitan-wide housing integration fared better at the hands of the Supreme Court, but made little progress for lack of implementation. A black Chicago woman named Gautreaux charged the Chicago Housing Authority and the federal Department of Housing and Urban Development (HUD) with systematically segregating Chicago's black population by locating the vast majority of all public housing 'within the areas known as the Negro ghetto'. As in the Detroit school case, the lower courts confirmed the charge of segregation and ordered a 'comprehensive metropolitan area plan' for the siting of public housing projects and allocation of federal rent subsidies. HUD defended itself by pointing to the Detroit school decision and arguing by analogy that Chicago's suburbs had not participated in causing the segregation, therefore they should not be burdened with the remedy. The Supreme Court rejected this reasoning, but not because they had changed their minds about the Detroit case. Rather the justices affirmed by an 8-0 vote that HUD, not the suburbs, was responsible for carrying out the remedy, and therefore the suburbs had no grounds for objecting. The court tempered the implications somewhat by rejecting the metropolitan-wide plan as excessive. Only enough suburbs need be included in the remedy to appropriately balance Chicago's black population.[18]

Unfortunately it was extremely unlikely that the Gautreaux remedy would increase the number of black or poor central city families moving to the suburbs. For despite the combined city-suburban plan, no low-income housing would be built in the suburbs, or existing rental housing subsidised, unless the local suburbs agreed to become involved. Voluntary local participation had been a cornerstone of federal public housing programmes from their beginning in 1937. Nothing short of a 'political revolution' could change this.[19]

Ultimately little suburban integration was achieved through construction of public housing in suburbs, but some progress occurred under the Section 8 rent subsidy programme. Section 8 paid approved landlords the difference between 25 per cent of the participating tenants' income and the 'fair market rent' on the apartment. Plans setting aside a proportion of suburban Section 8 apartments for poor and black tenants did eventually generate some integration of Chicago suburbs. Section 8 was not a large programme however, and with the winding down of concern over the urban crisis the pressure to expand it dissipated.[20]

Suburban exclusion of blacks and the poor also came under challenge. Suburbs achieved effective exclusion by two methods: adopting zoning codes barring multi-unit structures and small house lots, and avoiding participating in subsidised housing programmes. The National Committee Against Discrimination in Housing told the Supreme Court that the barrier of all-white suburbs confining blacks and poor people in the central cities would not be breached 'until local governments have been deprived of the power to exclude subsidized housing and to manipulate zoning and other controls to screen out families on the basis of income and, implicitly, of race.'[21]

A favoured legal interpretation was the New Jersey Supreme Court declaration in the 1975 Mt. Laurel case that under the constitutional proviso to promote the general welfare, suburbs such as Mt. Laurel had a

> presumptive obligation . . . affirmatively to plan and provide, by its land use regulations, the reasonable opportunity for an appropriate variety and choice of housing, including, of course, low- and moderate-cost housing, to meet the needs, desires and resources of all categories of people who may desire to live within its boundaries.

Another potentially effective strategy lay in the success the Suburban Action Institute and the City of Hartford, Connecticut achieved in getting the courts to prevent seven suburbs from receiving $4.4 million in federal community development grants because of their exclusionary housing and land use policies.[22]

Judges could sweep away legal barriers, but they could not build low-cost housing or settle black and low-income families in suburbs where they were not wanted. The regional planning agency for

Dayton, Ohio, metropolitan area achieved some success with a 'fair-share' plan to spread subsidised housing among all communities, city and suburbs, in approximate inverse to their current proportion of poor residents. Only 1,700 of 14,000 units were sited in Dayton, while Kettering and Oakwood, two well-to-do suburbs, were each allocated more than 600 units. There was strong resistance from some blacks and many whites, but carefully built alliances prevailed and the plan went into effect late in 1970. Fair-share schemes did not catch on in other metropolitan areas, however.[23]

Construction of subsidised housing in suburbs by a metropolitan, state or federal agency was a direct way of surmounting practical and political obstacles. But the first attempt at direct construction by New York State's Urban Development Corporation (UDC) triggered the demise of the entire campaign against suburban exclusion. UDC enjoyed one notable success in the Rochester metropolitan area. Its 'Nine Towns Program' for affluent Westchester County in the New York City suburban fringe ignited not just resistance but a legislative campaign that eventually denied UDC its powers and mandate to make suburban life accessible to low-income central city residents. UDC director Edward Logue eulogised: 'There is no constituency in the United States today of any consequence for opening up the suburbs.'[24]

WHITE FLIGHT: THE END OF THE URBAN CRISIS

Abandoning the activists at the height of their struggle for metropolitan integration was not the final scene policy researchers played in the urban crisis melodrama. There was a nasty epilogue. In 1975 the politically influential Urban Institute, a semi-public research centre or 'think tank' founded by HUD during the Johnson administration, promoted claims by sociologist James Coleman that court-ordered busing was causing 'white flight', loss of white students from the public schools of central cities where integration schemes were imposed and acceleration of white migration from those central cities to their suburban fringes. Coleman had been principal author of the multi-million dollar study of racial differences in educational opportunity mandated by the Civil Rights Act of 1964 and on the basis of the findings he became a vocal proponent of the educational advantages of integration. Now, when he changed his position, his assertions made headlines all over the country.

Coleman's message was that activists should terminate their campaign to integrate central city schools through court action because it was instigating disruption without achieving significant improvements for black pupils. In the context of the urban crisis controversy as a whole, Coleman and the Urban Institute seemed to be signalling activists to give up integration as a strategy for black advancement not just metropolis-wide but even within the confines of central cities. Coleman hinted that the central city crisis was winding down, that growth was about to resume, and that social stability would be the best inducement to progress for blacks.

> Now, when the black population in central cities is stabilizing due to reduced rural-urban migration and reduced birth rates, and when many older cities have major inner-city rebuilding plans, is a time which brings an opportunity to create of our large cities stably integrated urban centers. For some cities, this is a last opportunity, because stabilization can occur only if there is a sufficiently racially-mixed population base in the cities. Affirmative integration policies in schools (for that is what the current court remedies have become, despite the protest that it is only *de jure* segregation that is being eliminated) should be directed to strengthening and stabilizing that racial mix – not toward destroying it, as many existing desegregation plans are doing.[25]

The Coleman–Urban Institute offensive aroused controversy not because its objectives were undesirable, but because it endangered the credibility of social science research on policy questions. As education researchers Thomas Pettigrew and Robert Green emphasised, it was 'an unprecedented campaign ... to influence public policy'. Coleman did more than present research results and hold press conferences, he appeared on TV shows, wrote popular media articles, pressed his conclusions on the US Civil Rights Commission and testified in the Boston desegregation case on behalf of the anti-busing Boston Home and School Association. When his aggressiveness was questioned on professional grounds, Coleman retorted with personal attacks on his critics.

The problem was that Coleman's research was seriously flawed. Coleman revised his analysis several times in mid-course but never satisfied his critics; in the end they had to perform their own analyses of the data in order to put the debate on an acceptable footing. The research results were complex. The term 'white flight' had no unambiguous interpretation, whether court-ordered school integration was contributing to it or not. At most, racial factors were one among many reasons why white central city families moved to the suburbs. For small and medium-sized cities there was no meaningful change associated with desegregation that could be characterised as 'white flight'. For large cities, white flight very clearly *did not* occur where there were metropolitan school systems: Miami, Jacksonville, Tampa, and Fort Lauderdale in Florida, Nashville, Tennessee and Charlotte, North Carolina among cities studied. In large cities without metropolitan school systems, white flight did seem to occur in the first year of desegregation, especially in the South, but abated significantly after the first year. Also, this large-city white flight was no greater in cities enduring court-ordered desegregation than in cities instituting their own voluntary integration schemes.[26]

Pettigrew and Green argued that the results strongly favoured the policy position they and many others had been supporting all along: metropolitan-wide integration. The policy implication of Coleman's research discoveries was that desegregation schemes applied to large cities alone, without involvement of their suburbs, worked badly. This was no basis for terminating court-ordered desegregation; instead it was yet another argument favouring metropolitan-wide remedies. But Coleman refused to soften his policy recommendations, even after criticism of his research forced him to concede to the US Civil Rights Commission that he had not demonstrated a strong causative relationship between court-ordered desegregation and white flight.[27]

When the dust settled, researchers recognised that the urban crisis was over, at least as a policy issue. Fear of causing white flight represented an assessment that sufficient concern had been tendered to race and poverty in the central cities. One way of interpreting the urban crisis controversy is to see it as the testing of various responses to the riots and to central city problems. The controversy openly invited the federal government to devise new forms of aid or development for central cities, for example. This invitation was declined; although federal relations with central cities changed considerably in the early 1970s, the changes were not conceived or implemented as responses to urban crisis.

The urban crisis controversy very pointedly encouraged industrial employers building plants and creating jobs in metropolitan suburbs to demand easy access to black and low-wage workers. Researchers at the Urban Institute, interestingly enough, put forward an updated version of new town planning from the 1920s and 1930s in which industrial employers and the federal government would jointly build 'industrial manpower communities' in the suburbs. Industrial manpower communities would overcome the suburban exclusion dilemma by concentrating black and low-income families in their own suburban town. Unfortunately, the crux of the scheme: large corporate interest in bringing black and low-wage central city workers to suburban plants, failed to materialise.[28]

Without encouraging responses from either the federal government or large industry, it is not surprising that central city blacks and poor people showed little enthusiasm for moving to the suburbs. For the urban crisis debate also raised the possibility that ambitious black central city workers and families might mobilise a suburban exodus and try to replicate for themselves the white working-class advances of twenty years previous. Both the conservative 'opening up the suburbs' proposals and the civil rights organisations' struggle to crack exclusion and build low-rent suburban housing fell flat politically. In addition to the lack of corporate enthusiasm, a plausible explanation for these failures is that central city blacks and low-income people preferred to stay in large cities and continue their struggle with city governments and economic interests for services, housing, education, jobs and political power. Strategically, this was probably a better course to follow.

Chapter 7 will take up the evolution of policy from the point we left it at the end of Chapter 3, the height of urban renewal in the mid 1960s. This discussion of the urban crisis has been an interlude in that history. The story of the crisis controversy is important for what it illustrates about the interaction between policy and settlement forces. If one, or several, of the options put forward had been taken up enthusiastically, the subsequent evolution of both policy and settlement would have been different. In Chapter 8 we shall consider further why some urban policy initiatives succeeded and others failed.

7. New Federalism: from Urban Renewal to Community Development

From Lyndon Johnson's initiation of the War on Poverty in 1964 to Richard Nixon's establishment of community development revenue sharing in 1974, urban policy replaced its commitment to saving the central cities with a concern for political process in cities and among the levels of government: federal, state and local. While the transition was occurring, the Johnson administration's desire for participation by blacks, poor people and other politically uninvolved groups seemed to differ profoundly from the Nixon administration's determination to return power from government to the people. Yet after 1974 ideological and partisan disagreement subsided. Even the most socially concerned Democrats conceded that large federal programmes targeted at specific urban problems were no longer appropriate. No one proposed to resume large-scale building of subsidised housing after the Nixon administration terminated most federal construction programmes. And unexpectedly the community development programme facilitated a reorientation of city politics that approximated the War on Poverty's ideal of 'maximum feasible participation' by neighbourhoods and groups.

Urban policy preceded and guided settlement forces in the first decades of the metropolitan era. Now in the latter years policy followed the lead of migration and settlement dynamics. Saving the central cities was a policy founded on expectations that national growth would conform to a metropolitan pattern. By the mid 1960s the national constellation of metropolitan areas was fully established. Even inter-regional population shifts took the form of more and less rapid metropolitan area growth in particular regions, not of differing settlement patterns from region to region. National population was approaching 200 million and expected to reach 300 million in the 1990s. Yet policy proposals such as channelling growth to new metropolitan areas, combating suburban sprawl, or anticipating the flowing together of metropolitan areas to form consolidated urban regions, failed to galvanise enthusiasm for reordering the settlement pattern.

The shift in urban policy began under the guise of concern for poverty. Lyndon Johnson declared his War on Poverty in 1964 with the conviction that a growing economy offered the material resources to eradicate all problems of insufficient income. The poor lacked means and income because they did not participate fully in the economy for various reasons. Johnson proposed to identify faulty participation in its diverse forms and overcome it. Poverty was not a distinctly urban issue, but very quickly participation emerged as the main policy question and the shift to concern for political process in city politics began. By 1966 the Johnson administration had pinned its best hopes on a 'model cities' programme, a large-city social and political development strategy incorporating the major elements of the original poverty programme within a metropolitan policy framework.

The first three sections of this chapter consider the War on Poverty, Model Cities, and also Johnson's success in establishing a cabinet department for urban affairs. This would seem a logical step, given the increasing size and importance of federal urban programmes. In practice, coordinating diverse programmes proved troublesome and acrimonious. The Department of Housing and Urban Development's difficulties in implementing complicated strategies raised concern that government's ability to generate social improvement might have severe limits. These doubts are elaborated in the fourth section.

If the urban crisis had emerged as policy's main concern, very different federal programmes would have been initiated. Policy based on the urban crisis debate would have attempted to *guide* settlement forces, primarily by encouraging black and poor migration from central cities to suburbs. As we saw in Chapter 6, none of the essential players for such a transformation of metropolitan area structure responded strongly to the debate. The urban crisis episode is a very enlightening illustration of a policy initiative that failed because its expectations about changing settlement forces proved inaccurate.

The policy that *did* take shape, community development based on expanded participation, went through stages of being combined with, and then separated from, issues of social welfare, education and training, employment and family structure. For in addition to redirecting urban policy, the War on Poverty initiated political concern about the social and psychological effects of federal programmes upon their beneficiaries. Was federal welfare undermining the two-parent nuclear family? Were anti-poverty and job training programmes encouraging young workers to depend entirely on public employment for their livelihood? Johnson's years in the White House were not favourable to careful evaluation of long-term policy implications of this kind. As he escalated the Vietnam War it overshadowed and then eclipsed domestic issues. Ultimately the great *Tet* offensive of January and February 1968 forced him to decline re-election, an act equivalent to resigning from office in its practical implications. It fell to the Nixon administration to sort out differing policy areas and propose appropriate programmes for consideration.

A 'new' federalism on the one hand, and a separate social policy on the other, was the Nixon administration's resolution of the definition problem. Proponents of an anti-urban crisis policy attacked Nixon's proposals as disguised attempts to dismantle federal welfare, public housing, urban renewal and Model Cities by any available means. Slowly but relentlessly, Nixon's policy initiatives prevailed, largely because proponents of a comprehensive social and redevelopment policy to combat the urban crisis were not able to marshal a convincing case for their perspective. Following description of the transition in policy from Johnson to Nixon, I have emphasised the significance of the Nixon administration's creation of a social policy separate from urban policy.

The next two sections deal with the impact of Nixon's new federalism on existing urban programmes. The administration systematically re-evaluated urban renewal, public housing and Model Cities in light of the federalist, decentralising approach to participation and process. Their conclusion was to terminate urban renewal and public housing construction, and most other targeted or 'categorical' urban programmes as well, and replace them with unconstrained grants to city governments for community development. This 'sharing' of federal revenue for urban community development followed the model of 'general revenue sharing' with states and localities that the administration had devised as the principal strategy for putting its new federalist philosophy into practice. In place of the housing subsidies provided through federally constructed public housing, the Nixon administration introduced 'Section 8', a subsidy programme for low-income families renting housing on the private market. The second of these two sections describes the community development 'block grant' programme and the Section 8 rental subsidy programme in detail.

City planners working with the community development block grant programme came to favour the separation of urban settlement objectives from social welfare strategies. The next section describes changes in planning and politics in cities following the introduction of block grants and Section 8 rent subsidies. In the past, mayors had favoured economic development strategies to attract and hold industry and retail business, using the prospect of new jobs to answer demands for neighbourhood and social programmes. Indiscriminate campaigns to attract jobs made for bad planning however, and rarely brought direct benefits to the people in greatest distress. Separating social policy concerns from community development strategy freed local planners to argue against badly conceived economic development projects on the basis of their potentially destructive impact on neighbourhoods and community groups. Plans making community progress entirely dependent upon attracting manufacturing, corporate headquarters, shopping malls, conventions and tourism to a central city, regardless of the cost in housing destroyed, neighbourhoods disrupted or families dislocated, seemed increasingly inappropriate, whether they fulfilled their promises of economic growth and job creation or not.

Policy controversy and programme development did not advance as smoothly in these years of metropolitan stabilisation as in the late 1940s and the 1950s. Important lessons were learned about differentiating between good intentions and appropriate policies. The Nixon administration initially appeared strongly anti-urban. Yet new federalism's programme for large cities, community development block grants, proved adaptable to neighbourhood and group demands in ways that urban renewal and other restricted, 'categorical', programmes would not have permitted. The final section evaluates charges that the federal government *abandoned* the cities when it declined to adopt an 'anti-urban crisis' policy. Although liberal Democrats pressed this charge while Nixon, and then Gerald

Ford, remained in office, they were unable to persuade Jimmy Carter, the Democratic President elected in 1976, to reverse the new federalist orientation of urban policy. Chapter 8 continues the policy theme through the Carter administration.

Policy's regular participants became increasingly cautious through the 1970s, awaiting clear signs of the new direction settlement forces might be taking. Was metropolitan growth coming to an end? Had migration reversed in favour of towns and rural areas not economically and socially subordinate to metropolitan central cities? In the absence of a federal policy response, would central city distress worsen to the point that federal intervention became unavoidable? Our discussion in this chapter will set the stage for a final consideration of settlement forces and settlement policy in Chapter 8.

PRESIDENT JOHNSON'S WAR ON POVERTY

Few federal initiatives have sparked as great a change in local politics as Lyndon Johnson's War on Poverty. Its impact was out of all proportion to the expenditures involved; in many respects, the effects achieved were not dependent upon its infusion of federal money into local affairs. President Johnson's original conception was that successful management of the economy had rendered poverty unnecessary. If some of the population continued to suffer from insufficient employment and income, the problem was more one of lost opportunities than lack of wealth or resources. The Economic Opportunity Act of 1964 implemented this strategy by emphasising job training for young people with insufficient education and skills as the type of programme most likely to show meaningful results. When research revealed that a large proportion of the poor were elderly, the Johnson administration added a second strategy of increasing benefit levels under Social Security and initiating the Medicare and Medicaid health subsidy programmes. Yet the most significant changes wrought by the War on Poverty were not associated with either of these strategies.

The power of the War on Poverty derived from its theory that insufficient participation in local politics by the poor, and other excluded groups, was a major cause of economic poverty and social distress. Nominally, this was no more than a revision in federal rhetoric, as many critics have pointed out. Not even the authors of the original legislation could later determine who injected the fatal phrase over which so much controversy raged. Carrying the title 'Economic Opportunity Act' and a subtitle announcing that its goal was 'to mobilize the human and financial resources of the nation to combat poverty in the United States', the law proposed to operate through 'community action agencies', legally and politically free standing local organisations to be formed and administered with the *maximum feasible participation of the residents of the areas and the members of the groups served*. The community action agencies were intended to overcome government's failure to coordinate services at the local level in such a way as to effectively meet the needs of poor people. The phrase 'maximum feasible participation' was interpreted to mean that only organisations independent of the existing governmental system, with significant proportions of poor people on their governing boards, could achieve such an objective.

Maximising participation struck a responsive chord among those who believed that poverty was in large part a political problem. In combination with the civil rights act the Johnson administration was moving through Congress at the same time, the participation aspect of the poverty programme became the basis for attacking the exclusion of blacks from city partisan politics, from city government employment, and from federal urban policy controversy. The community action programme also had a major impact in towns and rural areas, especially in the South in conjunction with the Voting Rights Act of 1965. To blacks trying to become involved in community action, 'poor' meant 'black', and 'participation' represented a federal mandate to demand influence in local decisions. In some cases, Hispanic, native American and other minority communities were able to make similar use of community action programmes.[1]

In large cities, community action opened the door to black influence and black government employment equivalent to their numbers in the city population. Although the rigid structures of 'parallel institutions' within political parties for blacks who became active in city politics had begun to break down as early as the New Deal, it was community action that finally ushered in a new state of affairs. Community elections for governing boards of community action agencies, and opportunities to become agency directors and employees, brought forward a new class of black leaders determined to challenge white politicians and bureaucrats as equals. The fact that many of these new leaders were not themselves poor, but frequently middle-class and professionally educated, was sometimes used to argue that the new black participation was little more than opportunistic exploitation of the true black urban poor. To white ethnic party leaders and their followers these distinctions between poor and professional blacks meant little. Most white politicians regarded community action primarily as a threat to advantages they had long enjoyed from racist party structures and government employment practices.[2]

The relation of the riots to the new black participation sparked by the War on Poverty has been difficult to assess. Political scientist Frances Piven and social theorist Richard Cloward have argued that Johnson and other national Democratic Party leaders sensed the rising discontent and initiated the new approach to participation as a strategy for absorbing and directing black activism to their own advantage.[3]

Paul Peterson and J. David Greenstone, both political scientists, suggest it was more a case of coincidence: the Office of Economic Opportunity (OEO), the agency responsible for overseeing community action, was attempting to increase its power within the federal government at the same moment black activism in cities escalated on several fronts, including both demands for participation and rioting. Peterson and Greenstone have demonstrated in detail that OEO initially planned the community action programme with little emphasis on participation, but quickly altered strategy when it sensed the possibilities for building its own power base among large-city blacks discontented with local officials and politicians.[4]

A problem with both of these explanations for the new concern over participation is that they explain a major shift in policy as if it were little more than a reaction to black pressure and disruption. Federal encouragement of participation at the local level of government was not necessarily the most appropriate political response to black activism or to the riots. Peterson and Greenstone, John Donovan, Daniel Moynihan and others have all underscored the drawback that the participation strategy intensely antagonised city Democratic party leaders such as Mayor Richard Daley of Chicago. While working to the immediate advantage of OEO, it probably harmed Lyndon Johnson's larger political interests.[5]

More significant to the long-term evolution of urban policy was the linking of participation with poverty, unemployment, education and social welfare. As debate on these issues continued, strategies grounded in participation emerged increasingly as an *alternative* to confronting central city poverty and distress by expanding urban renewal into a massive federal urban development programme, including housing construction and rehabilitation, mass transit, public works replacement, hospital and health centre expansion, industrial development, and so on. Given a choice between these two approaches, few black activists would have preferred the participation strategy to direct federal investment in central city development.

A CABINET DEPARTMENT FOR URBAN AFFAIRS

The relationship between urban policy and the structural arrangement of urban programmes within the federal bureaucracy has never been straightforward. Lyndon Johnson's success in persuading Congress to authorise a cabinet department dealing with urban affairs in 1965 was no exception to this rule. When the Urbanism Committee proposed a federal urban affairs bureau in the draft of *Our Cities*, its parent National Resources Committee mandated there be no mention of creating a permanent bureau in the final report. They feared antagonism to further proliferation of New Deal agencies might sink the whole effort to initiate federal urban policy. Better to keep policy and structure separate for the time being.[6]

In the 1940s competition between an agency emphasising housing and one emphasising urban affairs or development ran parallel to controversy between housing objectives and development objectives in the design of federal programmes. President Truman's compromise on a free standing Housing and Home Finance Agency, below cabinet level but not under the control of any cabinet department, resolved little.

Following the 1954 reform of urban renewal, Senator Joe Clark of Pennsylvania led a campaign for a department of 'housing and urban affairs'. Clark had risen to prominence by defeating the corrupt Republican machine that had controlled Philadelphia city politics since the 1880s. It made no administrative sense, he insisted, for a mid-twentieth-century urban nation to have a powerful Department of Agriculture representing its constantly diminishing farmers but no department responsible for the affairs of its vast urban population. Again, however, substance prevailed over form. Interests concerned first and foremost with defending the housing and renewal programmes were reluctant to spare any of their resources to help Clark win his fight for organisational recognition of the importance of cities.[7]

John Kennedy was strongly committed to a cabinet-level agency. His bill to create a 'Department of Urban Affairs and Housing' also featured a prominent 'declaration' of established urban policy. Kennedy's proposal foundered for myriad reasons, among them the prospect that the black director of the Housing and Home Finance Agency, Robert Weaver, would probably become the secretary. A new cabinet department and the first black cabinet officer in US history both in the same stroke was apparently too much for a number of Congressmen.[8]

Lyndon Johnson's 'Department of Housing and Urban Development' passed Congress almost effortlessly, and Robert Weaver did become history's first black cabinet member. Yet success in finally establishing a cabinet department in 1965 did little either to strengthen federal urban policy or to end the ambivalence about whether urban affairs deserved a cabinet department. One of the first things the Nixon administration investigated upon coming to power in 1969 was whether Congress could be persuaded to abolish HUD and demote urban affairs back to their previous secondary status. Jockeying for control between the old Housing and Home Finance Agency, the Federal Housing Administration, and the Public Housing Administration virtually paralysed the department in its first years. And while Congress allowed the executive branch to upgrade urban affairs, it did nothing to alter its own arrangements for considering urban policy. Both the House of Representatives and the Senate continued to send urban and housing matters to committees concerned primarily with banking.

MODEL CITIES

Two immediate policy problems confronted the new Department of Housing and Urban Development: citizen participation demands inspired by the War on Poverty, and the beginnings of the riots. The

Watts riot erupted as Congress was in the final stages of passing HUD's establishing legislation. No one could foresee the years of rioting still to come, but even on its own terms Watts was profoundly disturbing. A new policy initiative by the new Department would help draw national attention in a positive direction. A task force of prominent figures in urban policy, headed by HUD Assistant Secretary Robert Wood, put together a programme that Johnson rushed to present to Congress in a special message in January 1966. Past efforts to meet the needs of urban Americans had been 'inadequate', Johnson proclaimed, hence the appropriateness of a 'demonstration cities program' funding innovative approaches in selected cities. Experiences with the demonstration projects could become the basis for new and more effective national programmes.[9]

Connotations of protest and dissent made the word 'demonstration' in the programme's formal title unpopular with HUD and local officials. It became familiar instead as 'Model Cities'. The conception of the HUD task force was to aid the poorest, most deteriorated city neighbourhoods, in a context of metropolitan area-wide efforts to coordinate all federal programmes under a metropolitan development strategy. Their theory was that a combination of action from above, at the metropolitan level, and from within, in the worst slum areas, would increase participation by blacks and the poor, and at the same time encourage central city and suburban governments to take a positive attitude toward the new participants. The task force hoped the improvement generated by federal funds would eventually become self-sustaining as corporations and private developers absorbed central city blacks and poor people into their metropolitan development projects as workers, consumers and residents.

To initiate this sophisticated scheme, the HUD task force proposed two kinds of activity in the draft legislation. The targeting of slum areas was to consist of very large grants to 'city demonstration agencies' in about sixty cities, to plan and coordinate programmes for specifically designated 'model city neighborhoods'. The task force expected applicants to target their city's worst neighbourhood. Projects had to promote both physical and social development, increase the supply of low and moderate cost housing, and 'make marked progress in reducing social and educational disadvantages, ill health, and underemployment and enforced idleness.'[10]

To promote metropolitan planning, the legislation authorised supplemental grants to be added to numerous existing federal programmes, on the condition that the programmes be coordinated with a metropolitan area strategy. Coordination would be provided by metropolitan planning agencies, which would be funded largely out of the supplemental grant monies. To receive the supplemental grants, local governments in the metropolitan areas would have to submit their proposals to review by the designated metropolitan planning agency. An important task force objective in this metropolitan part of the legislation was to further creation of metropolitan area 'councils of governments' (COGs), a promising reform movement of the 1950s and early 1960s. The metropolitan planning agencies reviewing the Model Cities supplemental grants would provide staff and substance for the metropolitan councils and work to expand their role in the politics of metropolitan areas.

An important factor in shaping Model Cities strategy was the influence of Walter Reuther, president of the United Auto Workers (UAW) union, and Jerome Kavanaugh, mayor of Detroit. The UAW had its international headquarters in Detroit and was very concerned about the city's future. The HUD task force was created, in considerable part, in response to their request, and both became task force members. Reuther and Kavanaugh were intent on persuading President Johnson to create a programme that would provide a city like Detroit both sufficient funds, and sufficient administrative freedom, to experiment with innovative approaches to central city deterioration and poverty.

One function of the 'demonstration' aspect of the task force's design was to limit the number of cities in order to channel large amounts of money to each city's target neighbourhood. Johnson let it be known that he planned to spend $6 billion on new domestic programmes, of which $2.5 billion would go to Model Cities. Congress disliked the limited number of cities originally proposed, eventually increasing it to 150. This aided the bill's passage; 150 projects would spread the benefits across a larger number of states and Congressional districts than 60 projects. Increasing the number of participating cities diluted the potential impact of projects, but even the revised Model Cities programme was far more efficient than the War on Povery pro- grammes for channelling federal funds to a distressed city neigh- bourhood. Depending upon where the Model City neighbourhood boundaries were drawn, the programme could become an effective mechanism for aiding a central city's black community. For example,

Seattle, Washington, one of the first group of 63 cities awarded funds, designed its programme for a neighbourhood that included only 10 per cent of the city's total population, but 85 per cent of the black population.[11]

Model Cities was the first stage of the transition in federal urban programme design from urban renewal to community development. Its focus on neighbourhoods and their development responded to the demands for participation aroused by the War on Poverty by attempting to coordinate federal programmes and city agencies in a comprehensive attack on all the problems of a distressed area. 'Seattle's five year program aims at a turn-around of all aspects of life' in the target neighbourhood, the Seattle plans' authors announced. 'We need altered ways of life as well as altered lives.'[12]

However, Model Cities learned its lessons about rampant participation from the War on Poverty. Citizen participation in Model Cities programmes was carefully structured and controlled. Local Model City agencies, (CDAs), were designed to be created, staffed and monitored by the mayor's office. Citizen participation could not include veto power over the mayor's choice of agency director. President Johnson, HUD officials, and Congressional Democrats were determined not to repeat the mistake of the War on Poverty's community action programme in allowing local programme agencies independence to attack Democratic mayors and their political supporters. HUD Assistant Secretary Ralph Taylor, the first head of the programme, laid down a cardinal administrative principle that Model Cities was to be a 'mayor's program'.[13]

THE LIMITS OF SOCIAL TECHNOLOGY

Model Cities did its best to grapple with the dilemma national governments face whenever they attempt to reform themselves from the grassroots upward. How can a governmental programme orchestrate participation in social improvement by the intended beneficiaries without controlling them so much that reform becomes a staged and manipulated puppet show? As the Congressional Research Service explained in its 1973 evaluation of Model Cities, CDAs were mandated to administer the programme 'in such a way as to obtain the widest possible distribution of citizen participation and the maximum degree of local initiative in demonstrating new approaches to problem solving.' Above all, the 'demonstration' aspect of the legislation demanded that cities receiving funds should not treat Model Cities as 'just another Federal program'.[14]

Many Johnson administration 'Poverty warriors' earnestly believed that well-conceived, well-run programmes could effect major changes in a neighbourhood, and perhaps in a whole city. City planners promoted comprehensive planning, especially as revised under the influence of Jane Jacobs' concepts of neighbourhoods, as the appropriate technology to employ. Eight years' experience with Model Cities tested these beliefs and expectations. There is always considerable lag between the emergence of a consensus about the best strategy for pursuing social objectives and the point when federal programmes based on the new strategy begin to function. Enthusiasm for comprehensive planning peaked in the early 1960s. But in the chronology of programme evolution, the early 1960s were seeing only the earliest completions of urban renewal projects, all based on techniques in vogue ten or more years previously. Programme design and implementation moved more quickly after the creation of HUD in 1965. By 1970 a number of Model Cities neighbourhood development projects were under way.

Model Cities demonstrated the limited capability of even the best coordinated physical, economic and social programme to generate improvement in a neighbourhood. Programme evaluations described the problem in terms of conflict between 'service delivery' objectives and 'strategic planning' objectives. If a city chose to utilise all available funds and show tangible results, the service delivery option, it usually ended up paying the majority of the money to outside service providers. The providers' programmes, in turn, would generate some immediate effects in the Model Cities neighbourhood, but the economic and social improvement would dissipate soon after the programmes terminated. Many target neighbourhoods appeared capable of absorbing vast inputs of service through job training, special education, housing rehabilitation, health services or recreational programmes, without significantly evolving toward economic self-sufficiency and social stability.

Strategic planning objectives might involve developing capabilities of the target neighbourhood's skilled workers to undertake housing rehabilitation. The mayor's Model Cities oversight agency would grant rehabilitation contracts to black carpenters or handymen and train them on the job in business management. In the first few years, quality suffered and costs ran high. Newly minted contractors sometimes absconded with tools and materials, never to be seen again. Eventually, persevering cities built up a corps of reliable firms. By competing successfully against established contractors, they assured that a growing share of Model Cities rehabilitation spending went to neighbourhood companies and workers. Evaluation of such a contractor development strategy in its first year, or even its third or fourth year, tended to be disappointing from a service delivery perspective. Often struggling homeowners questioned why they had to endure insufferable delays and marginal workmanship while their contractor learned the mysteries of business and bureaucracy by trial and error.[15]

The service delivery strategy produced physical changes: rehabilitated houses, graduates of crash reading-skill programmes, concrete and glass health and social service centres; but it changed the people of the Model Cities neighbourhoods little. The strategic planning strategy could develop capabilities in people, but only with tireless effort and saintly patience. And in the interim service needs had to wait. Meeting them temporarily with outside contractors would undermine the whole purpose of the self-help approach. Unfortunately HUD's Model Cities guidelines demanded both short-run delivery and long-term development immediately. It was not enough for the professional planners supervising a Model Cities programme to show that services were effectively produced, targeted and delivered; by some magical process they had to transform the people of the target neighbourhood into the service producers and providers at the very same time.

City planners involved with Model Cities recognised almost from the outset that the participatory approach to neighbourhood development placed them, as white middle-class professionals and cultural and poltical outsiders, in an untenable position. Model Cities not only identified the problem of poverty neighbourhoods as social underdevelopment of the neighbourhood population, it also postulated in its basic assumptions that bricks and mortar were not the means to social goals. Planners had listened to Jane Jacobs' criticisms of professional planning because, for all her vituperation against bad plans, she seemed to agree that good physical coordination of streets, parks, open space, diverse uses and public facilities could assure social order and neighbourhood harmony. Model Cities neither emphasised physical city planning and redevelopment, nor suggested that professional planners and technical expertise should play the central role in making its strategy work at the neighbourhood level.

The bureaucratic design of Model Cities involved intricate technical supervision at HUD in Washington and expert professional planning skills at the metropolitan and city levels. Only projects conceived and drafted by experienced planning and redevelopment officials or consultants had a chance of receiving funding. For all intents and purposes, citizen participation by Model Cities neighbourhood groups never extended to the actual design of programmes. Because the everyday interactions consisted almost entirely of professionals in Washington dealing with professionals in metropolitan and city agencies, the planning profession experienced the failings of Model Cities as a crisis of knowledge, theory and technical ability.

Model Cities' metropolitan strategy failed rather completely. Metropolitan regional planning agencies were designated, and they performed their mandated review functions (so-called A-95 reviews, after the Bureau of the Budget document establishing the procedures), but no progress toward true metropolitan planning resulted. Many metropolitan councils of governments suddenly sprang into existence, but even well established COGs found that the A-95 review powers and the supplemental grant monies did little to increase their political influence over city and suburban politics.[16]

Above all, the metropolitan strategy failed because industrial corporations and real estate developers showed no enthusiasm for drawing central city blacks and low-income people into the suburbs. If corporate interest had been strong, both the metropolitan council of governments movement and metropolitan planning would have progressed brilliantly. Without it, there was little the COGs and planning agencies could achieve on their own initiative, even with the clout provided by the supplemental grants. To some extent, the Model Cities strategy was a prototype for the kind of federal strategy contemplated by proponents of an anti-urban crisis policy in the early 1970s. Lack of corporate and private developer interest had a similarly depressing impact on both situations. Far more needs to be learned about why corporate and real estate capital turned away from metropolitan development in the late 1960s. I will offer some tentative propositions in Chapter 8.

Failings highlighted by the Model Cities experience, combined with concern that the profession included virtually no one who was not male, Caucasian, and of middle-class background, brought on a crisis in planning. Students and faculty of planning schools called for a fundamental reassessment of the planning enterprise, and of the working planner's role in society. One interpretation of planning's failings was that planners had been insufficiently political. Political scientist Alan Altschuler had criticised the politically inept way planners approached urban renewal as early as 1965. He recommended they learn to play the political game. Another manifestation of crisis in the planning profession was the rise of 'advocacy planning', a strategy for planners to present themselves as expert representatives of distinct groups or interests: non-whites, poverty neighbourhood residents, the politically powerless. Advocacy planners attacked the profession on ethical grounds for catering to wealth and power when it should have been championing social equity and economic redistribution.[17]

Yet even the most radical planning proposals involved further institutionalising planning as a professional activity within urban government. This conflicted with urban policy's emerging long-term objective of expanding participation. In so far as the War on Poverty and Model Cities strategies for participation succeeded, the city's problem populations were supposed to become capable of formulating their needs and desires in political terms. As they strengthened their political self-confidence, they would be able to negotiate for resources and benefits on an equal footing with businesses, banks, real estate owners, and the middle class. Expanding urban renewal into a comprehensive social and economic development enterprise, carried out by massive planning and redevelopment agencies in the cities, was an approach the federal government might have pursued, but it was not what Lyndon Johnson favoured as federal urban policy. Rather he believed that social problems derived from the reluctance of blacks and other groups to jump into the mainstream of economic, social and political action: to acquire viable skills in school, to compete for high-paying industrial and public sector jobs, to demand better health care and social services, to desire suburban homes and cars and the life style of the middle class. Professional planners or administrators working through bureaucratic organisations were not the appropriate agents for reversing this sort of deficiency.

FROM JOHNSON TO NIXON

Johnson was not able to carry his initiatives very far. Much as he might have wanted to win a second full term as President, dramatic military setbacks in Vietnam compelled him to announce in March 1968, that he would not seek re-election. This was the practical equivalent of resigning from office because it instantly rendered him a lame duck President. Hubert Humphrey, Johnson's Vice-President and favoured successor, had begun his political career as Mayor of Minneapolis and was strongly committed to helping the large cities. Robert Kennedy, who probably would have captured the Democratic nomination and won the election if he had not been tragically assassinated in June 1968, was even more sympathetic to urban and poverty problems than Humphrey.

In contrast, the federal urban policy community considered Richard Nixon, the Republican presidential candidate, anti-urban. Nixon's strident condemnation of 'crime in the streets', in combination with his encouragement of white ethnic pride, implied that gains made by blacks and poor people during the Kennedy and Johnson years were going to be rolled back if he became President. 'Crime in the streets' was a rhetorical way of suggesting that both the riots and urban crime were perpetrated by a black criminal class in need of the strong discipline promised by another Nixon campaign theme: restoring 'law and order' in local communities.

Once in office, the Nixon administration proved a curious amalgam of innovation, obstinacy, and perversity. Nixon's overarching approach to domestic policy: 'new federalism', differed profoundly from the liberal philosophy espoused by Johnson and most Democrats, and also by most social scientists involved in policy controversy. Liberals assumed the object of policy was social progress and individual wellbeing. Nixon and his followers objected that liberal assumptions failed to define the appropriate role of government in society. Pursuing social progress therefore degenerated into uncontrolled expansion of federal spending and excessive federal interference in state and local affairs. New federalism proposed to restore a more appropriate balance among federal, state and local governments, and to lessen the prominence of government in all its forms in American life. When Nixon talked about 'returning power to the people', he meant that government should divest itself completely of a portion of its coercive strength.

The Nixon administration began by studiously examining federal urban involvement from a new federalist perspective. Most regular participants in urban policy controversy assumed this was a delaying tactic while the new administration mobilised a frontal assault on the federal commitment to cities. When Daniel Moynihan, one of the authors of the War on Poverty and a strong supporter of Johnson's urban initiatives, became Nixon's chief domestic policy adviser, many urban policy people reacted as if a traitor had defected to the enemy.

The Nixon administration continued some programmes and moved to terminate others. More importantly however, their new federalist perspective eventually prevailed. George McGovern, the 1972 Democratic presidential candidate, sank like a stone in the opinion polls with his liberal policy orientation. Nixon's impact on urban policy was multi-faceted. Eventually community development emerged as the focus, but several intermediate steps were essential.

A SEPARATE SOCIAL POLICY

Before it began putting its new federalist philosophy into practice, the Nixon administration altered policy in another fundamental way by reorganising the various areas of 'domestic' policy. Urban policy and poverty issues had become badly entangled during the Johnson administration. The HUD task force that designed Model Cities proposed to resolve much confusion by transferring the Community Action Program, the main citizen participation aspect of the War on Poverty, to the new Department of Housing and Urban Development. The White House declined the suggestion for political reasons, necessitating creation of a second, often conflicting, citizen participation apparatus within the Model Cities programme. The Nixon administration set aside poverty entirely and began discussing a new set of issues that came to be referred to as 'social policy'. The effect on urban policy was to narrow and more clearly delineate which questions should be considered 'urban' and how they should be addressed.[18]

Welfare, family structure, and employment incentives were the issues that became the core of social policy. The Nixon administration committed itself to a total reform of the welfare system. Their 1969 Family Assistance Plan attempted to eliminate contradictions between welfare for the non-working poor and disincentives in the income tax system discouraging people trying to earn enough by working to stay off welfare. Described as a 'negative income tax', and also as a 'guaranteed income' or 'income maintenance' system, the objective of the Family Assistance Plan was to structure the new policy discussion around incentives strengthening the two-parent family and encouraging work, while reducing and discouraging dependence on government programmes. The administration even proposed a major expansion of day care for pre-school children as a means of freeing their mothers to work.[19]

The Nixon administration's motives for creating a social policy separate from urban policy may have been partly negative. They put forward their Family Assistance Plan at a time when the urban crisis controversy we discussed in Chapter 6 was at its height. There is little question that Nixon and his urban advisers wanted to prevent 'crisis' from becoming the central concern of urban policy and programmes. Crisis implied urgency, and also strengthening the governments at the front line of the emergency. Allowing urban policy to become 'anti-urban crisis' policy would have led to central city development programmes favouring blacks, the big city white working class, and older cities in the north-east and Great Lakes regions where the crisis was most severe. All three constituencies had strong Democratic political loyalties. If it were a direct question of where to promote development, the Nixon administration favoured suburbs over cities, and among regions, the part of the country beginning to be known as the Sunbelt: the south-east, especially Florida, the south-west and California.

Whether a Democratic Humphrey or Kennedy administration in 1969–73 would have battled the urban crisis head-on, where the Nixon administration charted another course, is not an appropriate question to ask. The concerns grouped under the umbrella of social policy were all highly deserving of national attention on their own merits, apart from their contribution to the problems of cities. The Democratic-led Congress spoiled Nixon's welfare reform crusade. The Family Assistance Plan passed the House of Representatives twice and twice was prevented from coming to a vote in the Senate, despite heroic administration efforts. If a grave mistake was made in not rallying policy to confront an urban crisis, the Democrats must share the blame equally with Nixon and his followers.[20]

It is more important to assess the *effects* of creating a social policy separate from urban policy than to evaluate the Nixon administration's motives. Their strongest motivation, a desire to revamp the federal bureaucracy, did not derive from urban concerns at all. The principal impact on urban policy was to separate out all issues involving redistributing or subsidising income, and transfer them to the social policy area. The results were enlightening.

A particularly striking demonstration of the value of the Nixon administration's social policy perspective was its application to federal financing of construction of low-rent housing. The previously prevailing explanation for why the federal government should pay to construct low-rent housing was that the private market failed to create enough low-rent units of acceptable quality. Virtually all low-rent units came into existence as older housing 'filtered down' to low-income people. The number of filtered-down units of adequate quality and size was always far too small. Private new construction could not be undertaken profitably, hence the need for federally-financed construction.

The Nixon administration's separating out of subsidy and redistribution issues divided the problem into two parts. One, the question of whether there would be an adequate supply of low-rent housing without federal intervention, they agreed might be an appropriate issue for urban policy. But whether low-income people should receive subsidies associated with their housing needs, the Nixon administration regarded as a question of social policy, to be evaluated together with other questions of income, taxation, subsidy and redistribution.

Research undertaken from the new perspective brought to light two powerful findings. Inadequate low-rent housing was not primarily a big city problem; only a minority of the nation's low-income people with substandard housing lived in metropolitan areas. As to whose housing was being subsidised, the largest federal subsidies for metropolitan area housing were going by way of income tax deductions to middle-class and wealthy homeowners. Clearly, treating low-income housing problems as an urban policy question had not produced good results. Subsidising middle- and upper-income people more than the poor proved to be a failing of urban renewal as well, when evaluated from a social policy perspective.[21]

TERMINATING URBAN RENEWAL AND PUBLIC HOUSING CONSTRUCTION

The Nixon administration's urban programme agenda seemed as dramatic a break with the existing state of affairs as its policy perspective. Rumours leaked from the White House that HUD was to be stripped of cabinet status. Nixon's cabinet-level Council for Urban Affairs, formed during his first week in office to assist in developing a national urban policy, got an indifferent reception. The press attributed greater significance to the appointment of the black mayor of Fresno, California as Assistant HUD Secretary in charge of Model Cities. While the re-examination of current strategies was under way, programmes were continued, often with increased funding. Eventually, the Nixon administration did initiate two very great changes: termination of urban renewal and cessation of federally-financed housing construction.

Much of the controversy over Nixon's initiatives revolved around whether they constituted abandonment of long-established commitments. Lyndon Johnson had called for significant increases in urban renewal, housing, and Model Cities in a February 1968 message to Congress on the crisis of the cities. He highlighted lack of employment and inadequate housing as the principal components of the city crisis and called for establishment of a ten-year national housing goal: market production of 20 million new units and federally-assisted rehabilitation or replacement of 6 million substandard units by 1978. Congress approved the housing goal, but Johnson's resignation from politics in March threw everything into confusion. As Nixon's presidency began, proponents of the urban crisis approach insisted that a commitment to resolving the crisis was firmly in place and had to be honoured; others discounted such claims as propaganda for one of several directions policy might take.

Rationales for ending urban renewal and federally-financed housing construction derived from new federalism and the new social policy. The major practical application of new federalism was revenue sharing. Beginning early in his administration, Nixon fought to replace grant programmes involving strict control by the federal bureaucracy with unrestricted transfers of federal tax revenues to state and local governments, to be spent at their discretion. Both Democratic and Republican economic advisers recognised that federal tax revenues expanded rapidly as the economy grew, while state and local taxes lagged. But why, new federalism asked, did the greater efficiency of federal revenue collection inevitably turn spending into an exclusive federal privilege? The grant-in-aid system used for most domestic programmes shifted decision-making and power upward to the federal level, Nixon argued. Revenue sharing would retain the advantages of federal revenue collection while allowing state and local governments to control programmes and be accountable for their effectiveness.

Nixon proposed revenue sharing in August 1969 as an alternative to creating new programmes or expanding current grants-in-aid to state and local governments. Early in 1971 he sent Congress a message calling for 'special revenue sharing for community development'. Urban renewal, Model Cities, and most small physical development grant programmes would be lumped into single community development 'block' grants paid to cities according to a formula involving population size, poverty problems, and housing overcrowding. 'Block', meaning 'undifferentiated lump', was an antonym to 'categorical', the technical adjective describing grants for specified uses: urban renewal or Model Cities for example.[22]

The administration decided to terminate federal financing for housing construction after getting favourable results from social policy analysis of housing subsidies. Implementing the research we considered above as our illustration of the social policy approach, they addressed housing as an income and resource problem of low-income people. The main difficulty, they argued, was not lack of adequate housing but rents higher than poor people could be expected to bear. Solution: a housing allowance programme for qualifying low-income families that would pay the difference between 'fair market' rent and 25 per cent of the family's income. HUD legislation for 1970 authorised the Secretary to conduct housing allowance experiments, which proved quite successful. Nevertheless, many Congressional Democrats and most housing experts continued to resist Nixon's reforms, insisting that the supply of adequate low-rent housing units was insufficient and that a full-scale housing allowance programme without continued construction subsidies would simply produce massive rent inflation.[23]

Controversy also ensued over whether urban renewal had outlasted its usefulness. Nixon and his closest advisers probably decided at an early stage that they wanted both public housing construction and urban renewal terminated. When it became clear that Britain was moving to terminate state construction of housing, resolve strengthened. Housing allowances became the focus of the campaign to end construction. As for urban renewal, HUD officials appointed by Nixon argued that renewal had lost its momentum at the local level, bogged down in red tape, political deal-making and real estate manipulation.

Proponents of an urban crisis approach to policy did not deny urban renewal's problems, they simply feared that assistance lost when renewal was closed out would never be replaced. Intimations of dark administration purposes heightened their apprehension. In 1973, when controversy was far advanced, HUD Secretary George Romney told an important Congressional subcommittee he was considering cutting off all federal funds to badly deteriorated neighbourhoods in twenty central cities. Continuing to operate programmes in areas where they had no chance of working was wasteful, Romney argued. Urban crisis proponents jumped on Romney's statement as an indication he was preparing to abandon the cities. Romney denied that his testimony implied such a drastic conclusion, but his critics came away believing they had witnessed a trial presentation of the administration's true anti-city strategy.[24]

General revenue sharing passed Congress in October 1972. The following month Nixon overwhelmingly defeated George McGovern in the presidential election. Illegal activities later exposed in the Watergate inquiry aided the campaign effort. Emboldened by the magnitude of his victory, Nixon impounded new spending on all housing subsidy programmes and on some community development programmes as of 5 January 1973, and made preparations to suspend new urban renewal and Model Cities spending on 30 June. Funds would not be released until the administration had completely reassessed federal involvement with housing. Nixon pressed Congress strongly to enact a special revenue-sharing programme for urban community development and threatened not to release impounded community development funds until such a programme was in place.[25]

Impounding funds already appropriated was unconstitutional and Congress screamed in outrage. This and other wilful actions early in Nixon's second term put Congress in the angry righteous mood that eventually led them to force his resignation over the Watergate break-in and cover-up. Contrary to what might be expected in such a situation, however, Congress cooperated fully with Nixon's efforts to replace urban renewal and housing construction subsidies with new approaches. Week by week, Congress moved closer to realising the truth about Watergate: the crimes the President had personally authorised, and the subterfuges he was devising to obstruct the judicial process from uncovering what he had done. Yet the most important transition in federal urban programmes since the 1949–54 initiation of urban renewal went forward as if Congress and the President were friendly political allies.

Nixon presented findings and recommendations from the housing policy re-evaluation to Congress in September 1973. Almost $90 billion had been allocated since 1937 for construction and subsidisation of housing, he reported, yet in the process the federal government had become 'the biggest slumlord in history'. Federally subsidised construction was a cumbersome, inefficient and inequitable way to solve the housing problem of low-income people. Only a portion of all low-income families benefited from construction subsidies, many others were compelled either to live in substandard housing or to spend excessive proportions of their income to obtain decent housing. Nixon called upon Congress to shift from construction subsidies and emphasis on public housing to a housing allowance scheme assisting low-income people to live in private market housing. In so far as construction needed to be stimulated, Nixon proposed incentives for private industry to construct new units specifically for the allowance programme.[26]

COMMUNITY DEVELOPMENT AND SECTION 8: CONGRESS ACCEPTS NEW FEDERALISM AND SOCIAL POLICY

Congress did not act on Nixon's initiatives in 1973, but in the Housing and Community Development Act of 1974 they terminated urban renewal, established community development revenue sharing as the principal strategy for federal assistance to cities, and created a housing allowance programme. They even included new construction incentives in the housing allowance scheme. Nixon's personal influence may have aided passage of his programme, but not in any readily understood fashion. Spring and summer 1974 were the months of confrontation about the White House tapes, leading finally to discovery of the metaphorical 'smoking gun' implicating Nixon in criminal conspiracy over the Watergate break-in. The policy analyst is hard pressed to explain how Congress could threaten a President with impeachment to the point of forcing his resignation, and then approve his fundamental revisions of urban policy and programmes the following week. Yet that is what happened.

Of the $11 billion allocated under the 1974 Act $8.6 billion went to community development revenue sharing. Most of the money was to be distributed by right or 'entitlement' to cities of over 50,000 population, based on a formula taking account of population size, housing overcrowding, and poverty. Grants would be made over three years. Unlike grant-in-aid programmes that paid their federal dollars to an independent local authority, community development block grants would go directly to the mayor or other chief executive officer. Cities were required to submit a three-year plan. In revenue sharing's spirit of eliminating federal control over local actions however, HUD was denied power to withhold a city's grant on the basis of inadequacies in its plan. Grants could only be held up if planning data describing community needs were grossly inaccurate.

While the act brought urban renewal to an end as a programme, cities were expected to spend most of their block grant money continuing urban renewal style activities: land acquisition, slum clearance, demolition, housing rehabilitation, and neighbourhood redevelopment. The Congressional conference committee underscored the emphasis on physical development by warning that social service spending ought not to exceed 20 per cent of a city's grant. The act stated that a city's activities should 'principally' benefit people of low and moderate income, and cities were required to assure citizen participation. Again, however, HUD received no specific powers to withhold funds from cities that did not conform.[27]

Of the $1.2 billion allocated for housing assistance $1 billion went into 'Section 8', the new housing allowance programme. Rather than making payments directly to needy tenants, the programme was to consist of long-term contracts between HUD and private developers, landlords or public housing agencies, designating specific apartments for Section 8 subsidies. Approved apartments could be existing units, or units to be constructed or rehabilitated. A family meeting the programme's income guidelines could actually obtain a subsidy only by being accepted as a tenant in a designated Section 8 unit. Housing owners were given the power to select tenants for their approved units. Once in a unit, however, a tenant could be evicted only by the supervising local public housing authority. At least 30 per cent of tenants assisted in a locality had to be low-income, others could have moderate incomes ranging as high as 80 per cent of area median family income.[28]

For tenants, Section 8 rental payments were similar to payments for public housing: they paid between 15 and 25 per cent of their total income in rent. Housing owners then received from the Section 8 monies the difference between the tenant's contribution and a pre-determined 'fair market' rent based on prevailing private rents in the locality. HUD controlled total programme expenditures by limiting the number of units each local housing authority could authorise for participation in the Section 8 programme. In all, it was an ingenious combination of subsidies for deserving families with incentives for private owners and developers.

COMMUNITY DEVELOPMENT PLANNING AND POLITICS

Nixon's new federalist and social policy reforms completed the transition away from an urban policy oriented around saving the central cities. Critics remained sceptical about community development block grants and Section 8 housing assistance as they got under way, but when Jimmy Carter emerged as the Democratic candidate in 1976 and then won the presidency, block grants and Section 8 became the favoured programmatic strategies of Democrats as well as Republicans. The sceptics found themselves isolated.

The saving the central cities policy, and its principal strategy, urban renewal, wrought the profound changes in city politics described in Chapter 3. New federalism, and its principal strategy, community development, worked a comparably significant transformation on political processes in cities. Aspects of the transformation approximated Johnson's War on Poverty vision of what increased participation by poor people, blacks, and neighbourhood groups might accomplish. With urban renewal's complex planning requirements removed, neighbourhood, racial and ethnic competition for city development money flourished. The drawbacks critics anticipated, corruption and sloppy management, did not materialise. Local contracting practices and project execution standards did not deteriorate with the elimination of strict HUD supervision. City planning rose to a new level of sophistication in response to the loosening of control over the kinds of projects and activities eligible for federal funding.

Community development block grants effected changes primarily because they injected the federal assistance for revitalisation directly into the city's budgetary politics. CD monies were up for grabs in the same arena with regular city capital and operating expenditures. This was exactly the opposite of urban renewal's cardinal rule that project planning, management and spending must be structurally independent of regular city agencies and finances. Urban renewal offered cities large sums of money to undertake major clearance and redevelopment projects, but demanded they carry out the projects through an independent redevelopment agency insulated from political influence. Redevelopment agencies shunned cooperative projects involving regular city departments. Regional and Washington urban renewal administrators preferred to see personnel of regular departments transferred to the redevelopment agency payroll, rather than have to supervise complicated department-agency inter-relationships.

Community development encouraged cities to phase out their independent redevelopment agencies, integrate redevelopment employees into the regular personnel system, and blend their block grant dollars into the general fund budget process. Wards and neighbourhoods, blacks, Hispanics, and other ethnic and minority groups began demanding their fair share of community development funds along with their share of regular capital projects and departmental services. A new community development politics emerged from this increasing competition. Where urban renewal involved planning and rationalising redevelopment in terms of discrete projects promising specific benefits, usually in the form of physical changes in a chosen neighbourhood, community development block grants encouraged cities to combine federal and local funds in broad strategies affecting many neighbourhoods and groups.

Mayors felt compelled to discover the development scheme that would trigger an economic renaissance. The Nixon and Ford administrations strongly emphasised public/private cooperation as the key to successful community development and President Carter concurred wholeheartedly. Urban Development Action Grants (UDAGs), devised by the Carter administration, made federal funds available to help cities overcome obstacles hindering private developers from going ahead with major projects. A sophisticated economic development planning rhetoric evolved, explaining how community development block grant funds could be combined with special grants such as UDAGs to 'leverage' private investment. New jobs created by the new investment, plus expanded employment in existing industries and businesses as a secondary effect of new investment, would in turn reduce unemployment, poverty and social distress.

From the new federalist perspective, it did not matter whether these economic development strategies stimulated investment and job creation or not. New federalism's objective was to shift responsibility for city conditions and prospects as completely as possible to the cities themselves. Federal assistance might continue to be necessary because of the greater efficiency of federal revenue collection, the rationale for revenue sharing, or on social policy grounds involving welfare, education, health or job training. But a policy designed to focus and encourage national development of cities, such as the save the central cities policy underlying urban renewal, no longer seemed appropriate as far as new federalism was concerned.

Community development politics put industry, retail and wholesale business, real estate owners and developers, bankers and investors on the spot about central city development. In the late 1940s most cities lacked the political dynamism and planning expertise to assemble and carry out large projects. By 1974, however, they had twenty-five years of urban renewal experience behind them. The worst slums and antiquated industrial areas were long since cleared, commuter highways and suburban beltways were in place, and central business district projects were functioning profitably in most metropolitan central cities. If business was concerned about the future of large cities, city governments stood anxiously ready to cooperate with their proposals.

From the perspective of large city blacks and Hispanics, Chicanos, elderly, and other racial, ethnic, low-income and neighbourhood groups, new federalist community development policy could work because of social solidarity and political experience built up over the decade since Johnson proclaimed his War on Poverty. The riots did as much to develop pride and unity within city neighbourhoods as community action programs or Model Cities demonstration projects, but Johnson and his advisers must be credited for identifying weak political participation by low-income and minority groups as a fundamental problem. As community development got under way in 1975 and after, groups and neighbourhoods recognised the opportunities block grants afforded and came forward with proposals and demands.[29]

Professional planners found the role of economic development promoter uncomfortable and tried to devise models of city development balanced between the grandiose schemes of big companies and real estate investors, and residents' demands to preserve and stabilise neighbourhoods. While cities needed new jobs, it was obvious that large industrial and commercial projects involved detriments as well as advantages. Few planners saw playing willing handmaiden to big corporations, banks and real estate men as the all-purpose solution to urban ills.

Often a large project meant beneficial jobs for some and neighbourhood destruction for others, offering the professional planner an impossible dilemma. An especially difficult example arose in 1980 when General Motors demanded that the city of Detroit clear the stable inter-racial neighbourhood of Poletown to build a parking lot as part of more than $200 million in federal, state and city assistance toward a new Cadillac assembly plant. The *New York Times* posed the issue in crude terms: 'Detroiters Confronting a Choice: New Jobs or Old Neighborhoods'. Consumer advocate Ralph Nader rushed in, expecting to win public sympathy against GM by defending the Poletown residents. Coleman Young, Detroit's liberal black mayor, attacked Nader as a 'carpetbagger' and most political leaders and groups involved agreed with Young that this was not the confrontation between the good people and the evil corporation Nader was trying to portray. Saving the Poletown neighbourhood by losing the Cadillac plant to another city was not an alternative most Detroit residents felt the city could afford, given its distressed condition.[30]

Cleveland city planning director Norman Krumholz and his associates dramatised the issues for the planning profession by emphasising that almost all large central cities were losing population, including many that were aggressively pursuing economic development. No perfectly coordinated industrial, commercial, office, tourism and housing development strategy could magically reverse decline at one stroke. Krumholz and associates called upon planners to employ a sophisticated political pragmatism that quickly became known as 'no growth planning'. 'It may be heresy of the highest order,' they wrote, 'but for those of us who labor in central cities, it might be appropriate to reinscribe the motto on the escutcheon of our profession to read: "Make No Big Plans. . ." ' The old motto, coined at the turn of the century by the City Beautiful planners, had been 'Make No Little Plans'.[31]

DID THE FEDERAL GOVERNMENT ABANDON THE CITIES?

A notorious story of the Vietnam War concerned the military public relations officer who explained that it had been necessary to bomb a village to destruction 'in order to save it'. Urban policy people sometimes reworded the story to describe how urban renewal fulfilled the federal commitment to save the central cities. Housing abandonment and arson throughout entire neighbourhoods, such as the South Bronx in New York City, implied the central city problem was worsening in the mid 1970s. Expert evaluations of the prospects for large cities turned increasingly pessimistic. However, only a few policy participants blamed the deepening distress on mistaken federal policy.[32]

As we have seen, the shift in urban policy toward participation and process resulted from initiatives arising at both ends of the political spectrum. Many liberal Democrats rushed to oppose revenue sharing because they feared incompetent city administrations would squander the money on anti-riot equipment for their police or reductions in property taxes benefiting retail businesses and middle-class homeowners. After several years' success with community development block grants however, it became clear that cities had achieved much of the political maturity Johnson hoped for when he proclaimed increased participation the best anti-poverty strategy.

In crude money terms, large cities received the strongest federal assistance under the supposedly anti-urban Nixon administration. Jimmy Carter, a Democrat, was the first President to try to restrain federal dollar flows to cities. Nixon's new federalist and social policy approaches successfully separated issues of individual wellbeing from questions of city development. Community development revenue sharing had a great advantage over programmes such as Model Cities because it posed funding issues directly about cities as communities, not as surrogates for economic and social problems of individuals, races and groups. As we shall see in Chapter 8, having the federal commitment to cities refined down to exact dollars and cents inspired Carter to try his hardest to cut the commitment in half.[33]

The clearest choice of the late 1960s and early 1970s was against adopting the urban crisis as the focus of urban policy. Those who accused Nixon or Ford or Carter of 'abandoning' the cities really meant that they were steering policy away from head-on federal confrontation with central city distress. But as we saw in Chapter 6, proponents of an anti-urban crisis policy never successfully defined causes of the crisis that were amenable to federal remedies. Within our framework of settlement forces on the one hand and policy on the other, the urban crisis represents forces of settlement, primarily blacks recently migrated to central cities making demands for neighbourhood control, city services and political recognition. Urban policy's evolution toward participation and process is perhaps most significant in so far as it draws the conclusion that these forces and demands were being presented to city governments and city political systems, not to the federal government. Among the books about the riots was one on Washington, DC, entitled *Ten Blocks from the White House*. Perhaps we have not sufficiently underscored the curious fact that no rioter took the trouble to walk those ten blocks and try to throw a stone at the President's window.

8.   Goodbye to Metropolis

Urban affairs experts awaited the 1980 Census figures on metropolitan growth with unusual anticipation. Estimates compiled in the mid 1970s had shown faster population growth in the nation's non-metropolitan counties than in metropolitan areas. Economic crises in 1969 and again in 1974–5 made demographers hesitant to proclaim an absolute reversal in the direction of settlement forces on the basis of sample studies. Better to wait for the complete 1980 enumeration to reveal whether the non-metropolitan trend had swelled later in the decade. The full Census would also help explain the new trend's significance.

The 1980 figures confirmed some expectations. Based on 1974 Census designations of metropolitan areas, the metropolitan population had grown at a rate of 9.1 per cent during the 1970s, while the non-metropolitan population grew at a 15.4 per cent rate. Although vulnerable to serious criticisms, this difference was significant. It meant the 1970s were the first decade since the 1810s in which established urban centres failed to grow more rapidly than rural areas and small towns. The non-metropolitan population increased from 54.4 million to 62.8 million, including net migration from metropolitan areas and from abroad of approximately 4 million. In terms of 1974 metropolitan area designations and boundaries, metropolitan population grew from 148.9 million to 162.5 million, a larger absolute increase but a slower rate of growth. Calvin Beale, demography expert for the federal Department of Agriculture, did his best to suggest that the higher non-metropolitan growth rate represented the cessation of urbanising settlement forces. The 1970s had been a great turning point in US history, if Beale's claims were accurate.[1]

Differences in interpretation arise because much 'non-metropolitan' population growth is due either to expansion of existing metropolitan areas into the territory at their edges, or to small urban areas pushing over the threshold into metropolitan status. Until all counties and urban areas had been appropriately reclassified on the basis of their 1980 population, the significance of the apparent shift remained questionable. In November 1981, the Census Bureau designated 36 new metropolitan areas and 1 area, Rapid City, South Dakota, that lost its metropolitan standing, for a total of 316 in the continental states and 2 in Hawaii and Alaska, plus 5 in Puerto Rico. In 1970, there were 242 metropolitan areas in the continental states and 1 in Hawaii. The new differentiation between metropolitan and non-metropolitan increased the metropolitan population to 169.4 million and reduced the non-metropolitan total to 57.1 million. Revised changes since 1970 were 30.0 million in metropolitan growth, a rate of 21.5 per cent, and a decline of 6.7 million in non-metropolitan population from the official 1970 figure of 63.8 million.[2]

Beale's hints that metropolitan expansion had come to an end proved inaccurate. The proportion of the national population living in metropolitan communities took a considerable jump from 69 per cent in 1970 to 75 per cent in 1980. What Beale had correctly identified was faster population growth at the rural edges of metropolitan areas, in small cities, and in some rural areas and small towns quite distant from cities, than within the boundaries of existing metropolitan communities. This *was* a new phenomenon, although not as great a transformation as Beale had implied. Before 1970 the fastest population growth had been occurring in established metropolitan suburban fringes, accompanied by a net loss of population from non-metropolitan to metropolitan areas. During the 1970s net national population growth continued to be metropolitan in character, but it differed from metropolitan expansion before 1970 in that it occurred primarily in territory that was non-metropolitan. New settlement forces appeared to be mobilising in the non-metropolitan parts of the country, but they were not yet independent of metropolitan influence.

In this concluding chapter I argue that the metropolitan era of US urban settlement and policy began drawing to a close in the late 1970s. The first section describes attempts during the metropolitan period to discover whether settlement forces were generating new kinds of communities. This is an essential activity for good policy-making. Neither of the two leading proposals, the Census Bureau's experiments with the 'consolidated urban region' concept and Jean Gottman's notion of 'Megalopolis', won strong acceptance.

The stagnation of the two largest consolidated regions, New York and Chicago, and also of Gottman's megalopolitan region from Maine to Virginia, in the 1970s, suggests that these concepts had not accurately captured the trend in national settlement forces.

Instead, the 1980 Census data revealed that the trend of the 1970s was the cessation of national population concentration into metropolitan areas. It is this stopping of metropolitan-oriented settlement forces, and their anticipated reversal in the 1980s and 1990s, that justifies delineating 1980 as the end of a metropolitan era. For the moment, the principal focus of national population concentration is the circular boundary where metropolitan fringes meet non-metropolitan territory. People continue to move *in* from non-metropolitan areas, and *out* from central cities and older suburbs, to new suburban-style developments at the outermost edges of metropolitan areas. Few of these people commute all the way to the central city to work, however. Their use of space is changing existing metropolitan areas into new community forms that are not yet clearly perceptible.

The prevailing form communities will assume in the post-metropolitan era will depend upon the kind of urban life Americans forge for themselves. It is clear that the new urbanism will be 'post-industrial', as analysts have been proclaiming for almost twenty years. The third section of the chapter attempts to give some substance to the entirely negative concept of post-industrialism. I introduce here the notion of 'diffuse' racial, gender and class forces that are constructing a new relationship among labour, capital, production and consumption. This new construction, taking shape within the existing Keynesian multinational capitalist market economy, cannot be more clearly defined for the moment than by calling it the 'diffuse economy'.

The fourth section explains some major trends of the 1960s and 1970s in terms of the diffuse economy. Application of the concept of diffusion to racial forces suggests that variations in behaviour associated uniquely with racial distinctions are disappearing. For example, Census data show that during the 1970s middle-class blacks in metropolitan areas began using the suburbs for residence and work in ways similar to middle-class whites. This was a profound change from before 1970, when data indicated middle-class blacks approached suburban living very differently from whites.

Meanwhile, below the middle class, black teenagers and white single mothers appeared to be joining black single mothers in a 'diffuse' style of manipulating employment, household formation, family structure, and government support programmes and social services. Social scientists have described these changes as a black teenage unemployment crisis on the one hand, and as the 'feminization of poverty' on the other. The diffuse economy approach suggests that what has been happening is that middle-class blacks are incorporating themselves into the mainstream socio-economic system, while young working-class blacks and single white women, many with children, are devising new ways of obtaining a livelihood that may eventually save them from succumbing to the degrading work, marriages, social service dependence, and unhappy family life their parents endured in the 1950s and 1960s.

Policy also shed its metropolitan orientation in the mid 1970s. This occurred not as a considered response to the cessation of settlement concentration in metropolitan areas, but as an expansion of emergency measures adopted to save the national banking and finance system from the catastrophe of New York City bankruptcy. Rather than attempting to force New York State to devise a metropolitan solution to New York City's 1974–5 fiscal crisis, which would undoubtedly have resulted only in driving the state government into bankruptcy along with the city, Congress agreed to a federal 'bail-out' for New York City. There was no discussion of involving New York's suburbs. In debating general guidelines for federal emergency assistance, Congress again neglected metropolitan approaches.

In the aftermath of the New York City crisis, Congress backed itself into a role of 'lender of last resort' for central cities with severe fiscal problems, in order to assure the banking and finance community that it was safe to continue investing in big-city municipal bonds and real estate. The new policy orientation described in these two sections involved direct relations between the federal government and central cities. In contrast to the urban crisis controversy of the early 1970s, the discussion of federal guarantees for central cities did not define central city problems in metropolitan terms, and did not expect the suburbs to become involved in alleviating those problems.

The final policy section briefly describes President Carter's urban policy. Central to the Carter policy was a characterisation of the nation's urban problem as 'the deterioration of urban life'. Carter intended this gloomy phrase to capture the essence of the transition to post-industrial society, arguing in policy reports that cities would play a different role in the post-industrial economy and that current urban distress was only the unpleasant consequence of an important national transformation. Carter strengthened the direct federal-central city relationship that had emerged under the Ford administration, making no attempt to reintroduce metropolitan issues. The Carter policy defined federal relations with suburbs primarily in terms of protecting them from the spread of central city deterioration.

The last section offers generalisations about policy and settlement at the close of the metropolitan era. I have suggested throughout the book that policy should not be judged as if it were strategy for solving urban problems. The 'saving the central cities' policy of the late 1940s, 1950s, and early 1960s did not free the large cities of deteriorating neighbourhoods and blighting influences. Nor did the participation and community development policies of the late 1960s and 1970s eliminate poverty and completely revitalise neighbourhood political and social organisation. Yet neither policy was a failure.

We should evaluate our urban policies in relation to settlement forces and trends. To some extent, policy can encourage or reinforce trends in migration or community formation. Using policy to redirect or oppose settlement forces arising from fundamental social and culture changes is almost always futile. What policy can do best is define and clarify settlement trends and emerging forms of communities, so that government programmes can coordinate with social, economic and cultural forces.

Good policy will also lay the foundations for optimism about urban life. Of all the policy orientations we have considered, I have criticised the Carter administration's policy approach most harshly. My reason is that they gave the people of older, declining central cities no basis for surviving the transition to post-industrial urbanism with hope, or even guarded enthusiasm. When the Urbanism Committee issued its *Our Cities* report in 1937, there was no prospect of significant federal spending on the cities. There *was* good reason to believe that urban economic and social change would slowly absorb unemployment and poverty, and stabilise city life at an acceptable standard. The Urbanism Committee encouraged this possibility. In contrast to these beginnings of metropolitan policy, the Carter administration concluded the metropolitan era of urban policy-making by describing conditions in large cities in the late 1970s as 'deterioration', and explaining that the demise of the city life and culture of the metropolitan era was inevitable. Settlement trends had turned against the dense compact metropolitan central city, and policy, as the Carter administration chose to pursue it, could do no more than ease the worst distress and work to prevent its spread to 'communities that are not yet distressed'. For city life in the next era of urban settlement and policy, in the 1980s and beyond, they had no encouragement to offer.

Policy should be straightforward about unpleasant conditions and difficult problems. But whether or not government, and the people government policies will serve, can address the future with optimism is not determined by circumstances. We defined policy at the outset as *how government chooses to act*. What it does when it finally takes action is not policy-making, but the implementation of policy. Surely even in dark times for our cities, policy can point us toward something better and prepare us to make the most of the resources we commit to urban improvement.

NEW COMMUNITIES IN THE MAKING

Changing non-metropolitan population becomes especially significant if it consists of settlement forces oriented toward alternatives to the metropolitan community. New community forms do not suddenly become prominent. Metropolitanisation was apparent as early as 1910, but it took until 1940 for the metropolis to become the dominant community type, the form of community in which most Americans lived. The non-metropolitan figures for the 1970s do not fully reveal the type of new community toward which settlement forces are shifting, but they do show the metropolitan community has begun to wane. The metropolitan era is concluding.

Most of what we can say about emerging new communities derives from projecting our analysis into the future. Our method has been to distinguish settlement forces from urban policies and programmes; only at a second stage have we considered interaction between them. From 1910 to 1940, metropolitanisation increased in force. Federal policy began to encourage even more rapid metropolitan growth in the 1940s by defining metropolitan communities very, very broadly. The popular response was positive, which has led us to forget that policy definitions and statistics are sometimes ignored or rejected.

During the metropolitan era, experts presented various arguments that metropolitan communities were being superseded by larger urban units. The Census Bureau introduced the 'standard consolidated area' concept in the 1960 Census to describe situations where a very large metropolitan area and several near-by smaller metropolitan areas had flowed together and become one continuous urbanised area. They designated only two such areas: New York and Chicago, but anticipated more in future decades.

In 1968 geographer Brian Berry reconsidered metropolitan area definitions at the Bureau's request. Emphasising the importance of commuting patterns as evidence of people's true notions of their community, Berry criticised the standard consolidated area concept for implying that the entire urban entity being described was a 'super' or 'greater' metropolitan area dominated by the large city at its purported centre.

Detailed data on commuting origins and destinations collected in the 1960 Census revealed what Berry called 'commuting fields': central locations to which a surplus of people travelled for work, plus the surrounding areas where the commuting workers resided. Berry's national map of commuting fields closely resembled the pattern of metropolitan areas. Where two or more metropolitan central cities had overlapping commuting fields, however, Berry showed that commuting to the largest of the cities from the smaller central cities and their fields was not in any sense 'dominant' over the smaller city's own commuting pattern.

In other words, the Census Bureau's New York and Chicago consolidated areas were legitimately a new form of urban area, but the suggestion that they were metropolitan areas of super size was inaccurate. Berry proposed instead that contiguous commuting fields with at least 5 per cent commuting from the central county of each field to the central county of the other, or others, be designated a 'consolidated urban region'. The term 'region' avoided the inappropriate implication that the largest city exerted dominance over the whole area, or that there was a hierarchical relationship among the area's cities from larger to smaller. Berry delineated 34 consolidated urban regions, including a New York region with 16 million population, a Chicago region with almost 9 million, and a Los Angeles region with almost 8 million.[3]

The most interesting proposal for an evolving community type was the French geographer Jean Gottman's description of the urbanised region along the Atlantic coast from southern New Hampshire to northern Virginia as a 'megalopolis'. Gottman laboured hard to dispel the impression he was calling this 600-mile long, 30–100-mile wide conglomeration of 37 million people (in 1960) a 'city', 'metropolis', or 'super-metropolis'. As with any form taken by concentrating settlement, Megalopolis deserved to be called a community because it was a single unit of dense and increasing population. The urbanised US north-east appeared most significant in relation to world population and its pattern of concentrating units. Density throughout Megalopolis averaged almost 700 persons per square mile, more than three times the density of the Pacific coastal region including San Francisco, Los Angeles and San Diego. Elsewhere, only south-eastern England, the urbanised region through Belgium and Holland, the dense regions of West Germany and northern Italy, Egypt's Nile Valley, and some regions in India, China and Japan approximated Megalopolis in scale and average density.[4]

Lewis Mumford attacked Gottman's proposal that the urbanised US north-east and megalopolitan conurbations elsewhere on the globe were living communities. Rather he associated them with Rome at the decline of the empire, for which he coined the term 'necropolis': the urbanism of civilisation disintegrating and dying. Mumford had begun his career full of optimism as a leader of the American garden city movement in the 1920s. His monumental commentary, *The City in History*, appearing the same year as Gottman's book, was optimistic about certain city types and historical eras, but declined through the nineteenth and twentieth centuries into pessimism and foreboding. Two world wars and the escalating nuclear arms race indicated to Mumford that industrial urbanisation and culture were nearing the end of their life cycle, as other productive technologies and their cultures had weakened and collapsed in past eras.[5]

Gottman's and Mumford's disagreements turned on their definitions of urbanism. If a megalopolitan region was to be acknowledged as a type of community, in the manner that the metropolitan area weathered controversy between 1910 and 1940 and finally gained acceptance as a community, what did megalopolitan communities imply about the course of urban development? Megalopolis differed most from a city or metropolis in its lack of centrality. Suburban-style land uses and residential patterns predominated; commuting from suburban residence to suburban job rivalled commuting flows from suburbs to central cities. 1970 and 1980 Census data on metropolitan areas within the urbanised north-eastern region showed central city populations declining. Older suburban areas stabilised or lost population as well in the 1970s. Most population growth in the north-eastern coastal region from 1970 to 1980 occurred in areas that were non-metropolitan in 1970. Already in 1961, and increasingly since, Megalopolis resembles a vast suburban expanse within which cities persist as the historical foci of specialised activities favouring high density. The cities do not dominate, nor does the expanse depend upon them for its wealth and wellbeing.

BEYOND METROPOLITAN CONCENTRATION

Megalopolitan regionalism has often been condemned as 'urban sprawl', not a new community type but a formless proliferation, without social coherence or cultural integrity. Cynical detractors adapted from map abbreviations the title 'BosNYWash' (Boston–New York–Washington) as a derogatory name for the 600 × 100 mile geographic monstrosity. However, disdain for the looks of new patterns tells little about their social purposes. The dynamism of metropolitan concentration in the 1940s, 1950s and 1960s derived from two great migratory struggles: white working-class suburbanisation, and black exodus from the rural South to metropolitan cities. Social forces and cultural preferences were the primary determinants of community forms according to this interpretation. Production, transportation and communication technology played a secondary role.

The settlement forces we have emphasised represented struggles to transform the class and racial structure of US society. Gottman's Megalopolis, the merging of metropolitan areas to form a broad urbanised region, implied a subsiding of the class and racial settlement forces we have linked to metropolitan concentration since 1940. Gottman suggested that the large cities within Megalopolis did not exert dominance over the region, as they had over their suburbs when they were central cities of freestanding metropolitan areas. He anticipated that national population would continue to concentrate in the region from Maine to Virginia and that Megalopolis would grow larger into the 1970s and beyond. However, without dominant central cities functioning as magnets to draw migration and economic activity, and without major social forces elsewhere pushing migration into the Megalopolitan region, Gottman's analysis lacked a strong explanation for why growth should continue.

In fact, the population of the Maine to Virginia region stabilised in the 1970s. On these and other grounds, most analysts concluded that Megalopolis was not an accurate delineation of the settlement forces and trends at work. Population had stopped concentrating in most of the metropolitan areas of the region, and in many other older metropolitan areas as well, but not because the concentrating settlement trends had shifted to a higher order of urban areas such as Gottman's Megalopolis.[6]

The 1980 Census data support assertions that metropolitan concentration has ceased. The Census portrait of settlement changes in the 1970s shows metropolitan growth, but an end to non-metropolitan decline and out-migration. In part, the data look this way because the non-metropolitan classification is no longer meaningful. Berry's 1968 reconsideration of Census definitions strongly suggested that dividing national settlements between metropolitan and non-metropolitan patterns had reached the limits of its significance. He demonstrated in one presentation of his analysis that 87 per cent of the national population lived within the commuting field of a metropolitan central city in 1960. Another 9 per cent lived in the commuting fields of smaller cities, many of which grew to metropolitan size by 1980. The obverse of these percentages conveys their significance best: Berry estimated that only 4 per cent of the population in 1960 lived in communities originating from non-metropolitan settlement forces such as agriculture, mining, or resort industries based on natural attractions. If commuting field analysis was relevant, non-metropolitan settlement had become little more than a repository of exceptions within the complete metropolitanisation of US society.[7]

Metropolitan concentration in the form of central city growth has subsided, but population outside established metropolitan areas continues to concentrate into suburban fringes. Part of this concentration occurs in the territory adjacent to existing metropolitan suburban fringes, and part condenses as suburbs around small cities. Metropolitan central cities, especially the largest and oldest cities, lost population at a considerable rate during the

1970s. The composite picture suggests that urban areas continue to expand, but within areas a levelling process is operating. If these trends continue, settlement throughout the US will consist of large expanses of population with a common suburban appearance, varying in size from a north-eastern coastal region of 50 million or more to small regions of 1 or 2 million in Colorado or Utah. Very dense cities will persist within the regions, but primarily as centres for specialised economic functions. People living in the very large regions will have little, if any, sense that the region as a whole is a community.

POST-INDUSTRIAL URBANISM: THE DIFFUSE ECONOMY

The racial and class forces behind the new settlement trends can best be described as 'diffuse', and the socio-economic system associating the labour, capital, production and consumption involved as the 'diffuse economy'. 'Diffuse' is a preferable term to 'post-industrial', which acknowledges new phenomena but fails to characterise them. Calling the new forces 'diffuse' emphasises the ways they are contributing to the disintegration of rigid institutional structures: the loosening of paternal dominance over the family; the increase in 'career changes' over the span of individuals' work lives; the acceptance of both genders in highly sex-stereotyped occupations: male nurses and female firefighters for example; the rise of unemployment and layoffs as employer strategies for controlling professional and middle-class workers, measures previously confined to working-class occupations.

Class forces in the diffuse economy are in the process of disassembling rigid class structures, groupings and dividing lines. The continuing reluctance to 'reindustrialise' US heavy industry as a cure for stagnation and recession stems in large part from monopoly corporation managers' perceptions that young people will not submit to the extreme productivity demands by which profit was extracted in heavy manufacturing during the 1950s and 1960s. Young people are not attracted to a reconstituted industrial working class based on advancement only by seniority, harsh workplace discipline, political submission to large bureaucratic unions, and reduction of all aspirations to crude questions of wages, working conditions and fringe benefits.

The diffuse economy involves new styles of work that reduce the disjunction between worktime and leisure time, and the geographic separation of the workplace from the home. 'Cottage' industry in homes or small shops using computer technology has been a recent experiment to discover whether a sizeable class of people will present themselves as an enthusiastic new workforce. Insurance companies, the banking and credit industry, mail distributors, and other employers of millions of clerical workers in large offices are considering farming out their information-processing to young mothers and teenagers working at home terminals according to their own rhythms, day or night, for long hours or in intermittent spurts.

Grim warnings that home computer work will expose those who accept it to pittance wages and extreme exploitation are inappropriate, for they incorrectly assume that workers' solidarity and strength can only be sustained in large offices where hundreds work face to face eight hours a day. Contrary to Harry Braverman's insistence that technology has been used to 'degrade' work and workers in the twentieth century, the prevailing lesson of industrial history is that technological revolutions benefit both capital and labour. The assembly line proved useless when Henry Ford first introduced it in auto production; as quickly as workers acquired the minimal training necessary, they became disgusted and quit. The assembly line only began to function profitably when the $5 a day wage was introduced, allowing line workers to earn more than the skilled handcraft workers they were displacing. Similarly, home computer work will probably flourish only after its workers are satisfied they have made substantial gains over large office conditions and remuneration.[8]

METROPOLITAN DECONCENTRATION, THE DIFFUSE ECONOMY AND RACE

Metropolitan deconcentration characterised black population growth and migration in the 1970s as well as white. Net black migration out of the South ceased; the proportion of the nation's black population living in the South increased very slightly from 51.9 per cent in 1970 to 52.2 per cent in 1980. Cessation of migration out of the South was the main factor contributing to a decline in the proportion of the black population living in metropolitan central cities from 58.2

per cent in 1970 to 57.8 per cent in 1980. The big increase was in black suburban population, which grew from 3.6 million in 1970 to 6.2 million in 1980. This 2.6 million increase constituted two-thirds of the entire national increase in black population from 22.6 million in 1970 to 26.5 million in 1980. The proportion of the nation's black population living in metropolitan suburban fringes increased from 15.9 to 23.3 per cent. The proportion living in non-metropolitan areas declined from 25.9 per cent in 1970 to 18.9 per cent in 1980.[9]

The similarity in black and white settlement trends in the 1970s was quite a change from the 1960s and previous decades. Black suburbanisation consisted in large part of middle-class central city residents moving to suburbs. Blacks did not generate rapid non-metropolitan growth, as the white population did, primarily because there was no black out-migration from suburbs to far outlying territory. The 'big surprise' for analysts at the Census Bureau, and others, was an absolute decline in the black population of four central cities with some of the largest black communities in the nation, Washington, Philadelphia, Cleveland and St. Louis, as well as a very severe constriction of black central city population growth across all metropolitan areas.[10]

Analysts were surprised because they had not expected metropolitan blacks to abandon the preference for central cities they exhibited so strongly in the 1960s. Those who had attributed the lack of black suburbanisation to white suburban racial exclusion found it difficult to believe large-scale black settlement of the suburbs could come about without vigorous governmental intervention. The failure of the suburban integration efforts we discussed in Chapter 6 had led them to expect minimal black suburban growth in the 1970s. Analysts who took the more optimistic view that statistics for the 1960s illustrated a middle-class black preference for central city living were the most surprised of all by the figures for the 1970s. The 1980 Census figures strongly supported sociologist William Wilson's controversial proposal that the black middle class should be expected to behave more like the white middle class than like blacks below them in class and status.[11]

Several aspects of the diffuse economy have been characteristic of central city blacks since the 1950s or earlier. Where turn-of-the-century immigrants could intensify family structure to support the husband and father's struggle for better industrial wages and working conditions, blacks had to develop a broad and varied resourcefulness for coping with the big city environment. Strengthening the family and sending forth a willing force of male factory workers in the 1950s would have been useless, for monopoly corporations had already forged the productivity bargain with the white industrial working class that made it unnecessary to increase the size of the factory workforce in order to expand manufacturing output.

In the face of corporate indifference, union discrimination and white working-class racism, blacks gained a sizeable number of manufacturing jobs through stubborn persistence. Before the industrial unions reached full strength in the late 1940s, accepting employment as strikebreakers provided black workers with a foothold and helped them pressure unions to abandon their white exclusiveness. Working in the dirty jobs in factories, cleaning, sweeping and oiling, offered slow access to higher wages and some opportunity to move into production or skilled work. Following the successes of the civil rights movement and the passage of the 1964 Civil Rights Act, direct integration of factories became possible. After a few brave souls had tested the hiring procedures at a plant and were taken in, word would spread through the black community and considerable numbers of people would apply for work. Factory integration often resembled typical patterns of school integration: after the initial testing, factories close to black neighbourhoods would rapidly become almost entirely black as white workers left or received transfers to other plants. The Chrysler corporation was noted for creating white-black segregation between city and suburban plants in and around Detroit.

Those blacks who gained and held on to manufacturing jobs were able to evolve a family life style grounded on secure wages and fringe benefits, similar to that of white industrial workers. But industrial work was not available to the mass of young central city blacks coming of age in the 1960s and 1970s, even if they were willing to submit to its hardships. Instead many developed a haphazard existence combining part-time and short-term employment, military service, welfare, or enrolment in poverty, job training and other social programmes with assorted deviant behaviours: burglary, robbery, street crime, drug trafficking, pimping and prostitution, gambling, trading in stolen goods. The riots were very important in loosening white official control and cultural dominance over the black community. Central city blacks enjoyed more freedom in their day-to-day lives, if not more reason for optimism.

Since the riots, a stalemate has prevailed between young blacks and those who might employ them: both capital and government. School enrolment and unemployment statistics clearly document an increasing desire for worthwhile full-time work and an ongoing failure of capital and government to provide it. Dropping out of school was an ever worsening problem during the 1970s primarily because the proportion of all black young people enrolling in high school and college was constantly increasing. Of blacks 16–19 years old, 56 per cent were in school in May 1983, when the comparable proportion for whites aged 16–19 was only 39 per cent.

Unemployment statistics for black youth tell a story of frustrated expectations that is difficult to believe. Contrary to popular conception, federal unemployment rates are not a measure of the proportion of people who do not have jobs, nor do they have any direct relation to the number of people collecting unemployment insurance. In order to be tallied at all in the unemployment count, you must either have a job, in which case you are considered 'employed', or have been 'actively' looking for work in the week preceding the monthly survey date. Anyone not working, but also not actively looking, is considered to be out of the labour force and is not included in the total count upon which the unemployment percentage is based.

The consequence of these counting methods is that the 'unemployment rate' for a group such as black teenagers represents not the percentage of *all* blacks aged 16–19 who do not have jobs, but only the percentage of those at work and *actively looking for work* who have not found jobs. For teenagers, a high federal 'unemployment rate' is much more a function of the number of young people who decide to look for jobs than of employers' disinclination to hire them. The situation black teenagers have experienced increasingly since the 1950s is that they have been looking for work more and more aggressively, but the number of jobs made available to them has increased extremely slowly. Hence, more than any other factors, it is increasing desire to find work that has driven up the black teenage unemployment rate. There is even reason to believe that when employers *do* increase hiring of black teenagers, it intensifies their efforts to find work by a greater amount and actually *raises* the measured unemployment rate rather than lowering it.

The long-term trend in federally measured black teenage unemployment shows young blacks intensifying their desire to work throughout the 1960s and 1970s and getting little satisfaction. In the 1950s, unemployment of blacks under 25 had been approximately the same as that among young white workers: about twice the rate for workers over 25. But as the first generation of post-war central city black children reached working age, just after 1960, black unemployment took off on its own trajectory. By the mid 1960s black teenage unemployment had risen to 26 per cent, twice the rate for white teenagers, and by 1976 it had continued to rise to 40 per cent. White teenage unemployment in 1976 was 16 per cent.

The standoff between black youth and capital and government intensified in the early 1980s. In May 1983, when overall unemployment was 9.8 per cent, white teenage unemployment was 19.8 per cent and black teenage unemployment had risen to 46.9 per cent. Workers between 20 and 25 fared slightly better but the unemployment rate for all blacks under 25 in May 1983 was 37.3 per cent. These almost unbelievable figures represent young black workers anxiously seeking jobs that did not exist. The height of the unemployment rate for young blacks, and its continual increase for more than twenty years, indicates a persistence in the face of frustration that social policy has distorted and misinterpreted. The economy has been enduring severe problems but black youth unemployment is not a function of temporary economic distress. It derives from the refusal of capital and government to grant the urban generation of blacks anything more than marginal admission to the employment system.[12]

If the diffuse economy becomes the new basis for coordination between capital and labour, the pattern of post-industrial work, production and life styles, what can black people expect? Central to the diffuse economy concept is the tendency for jobs to open up to workers of all kinds: male or female; married, single, or separated; with children or without; and for workers to become interchangeable and homogeneous, overcoming gender and other divisions among themselves. Whether employers will also become colour-blind and workers will overcome racial distinctions can be forecast only from hints at the moment.

Cessation of black migration to central cities, declining black birth rates within the cities, and the high rate of black suburbanisation are all indications of efforts to coordinate and merge with white settlement forces and social development. Blacks are abandoning their previous strategy of unifying and defending themselves by concentrating in central cities. Back-commuting, an important facet of this strategy, is declining; blacks with suburban jobs are tending to move to the suburbs rather than remaining in the city and commuting against the predominantly white suburb-to-city flow.

Perhaps the most telling clue in the 1980 Census concerning race and our urban future is the so-called feminisation of poverty. Contrary to expectations that an almost exclusively black and minority 'underclass' was evolving as the repository of most unemployment, dependency and misery in the social system, 1980 data revealed considerable increases in the proportion of white women living with children in their own households on incomes near or below poverty level. In crude jargon, white women have been taking on the role of 'welfare mother' long considered primarily a black cultural phenomenon resulting from weakening of the black family by three centuries of slavery and racial oppression.

The 'cause' of poverty for these white women and their children in the first instance is the absence of a male breadwinner from the household. The secondary cause is inability to work at full capacity due to childcare demands, and a third factor is economy-wide differentials in pay between men and women. To accept these factors as explanations, however, would be to cast the women entirely as victims and fail to recognise their aspirations to be independent and self-supporting. In fact, single parent families headed by mothers represented virtually the entire increase in families with children during the 1970s. The number of two parent white families with children decreased from 23.3 million in 1970 to 22.3 million in 1981, while the number of white families with children headed by the mother alone doubled from 2.0 million to 3.9 million. The same was true for black families: two parent families declined from 2.0 million to 1.9 million, while families headed by the mother alone increased from 0.9 million to 1.9 million. Mother-headed single parent black families have been prominent for several decades. What is remarkable about the 1970s is the rise to prominence of the same family type among white families.[13]

The many white single women with children who end up having to survive on poverty incomes have not come into their poverty status because the 'white family' is disintegrating, but as a result of their own struggles to escape dependence on marriage for economic support. The rapid increase in woman-headed one parent families as a white family type tends to discredit racially grounded explanations for the prominence of such families among blacks. New analyses are required that apply regardless of race. It is far more appropriate to consider these white women, together with black and other minority women supporting their children on their own, as a potential labour force with tremendous energy and determination. If capital and government can coordinate institutional arrangements making it possible and worthwhile for single women with children to work to the full extent of their capabilities, their racial and ethnic unity will appear as a new phenomenon among workers, rather than a new style of poverty.

'FORD TO CITY: DROP DEAD'

Policy's response to the onset of metropolitan deconcentration in the 1970s has been to abandon the metropolitan community as the object of policy and programme initiatives. The first sign of an inclination to shift the focus of policy to other community types was Nixon's proposal in 1973 to combine HUD, the Department of Transportation, the Department of Agriculture and some small agencies into a 'Department of Community Development'. The purpose was to downgrade metropolitan community development from its unique cabinet status and merge it with the other federal activities affecting settlement patterns and community types. The Department of Community Development would have considered policies and programmes for all sorts of communities on common terms, without special attention to metropolitan communities. Nixon's practical intent was to shift spending in the direction of small cities and towns outside the metropolitan sector.[14]

The big policy change did not involve shifting attention from metropolitan areas to non-metropolitan towns however, but creating a direct relationship between the federal government and the large central cities. In the mid 1970s, federal policy began confronting the problems of the big cities as if they were free standing, without metropolitan community functions or interactions. The change occurred precipitously, due to the urgent need for federal intervention in New York City's bankruptcy crisis of 1974–5. As with housing and redevelopment policy throughout the metropolitan era, the new federal–city relationship had a great deal to do with banking and finance.

The debate about suburban exploitation theories of central city crisis that we discussed in Chapter 6 set the stage for direct federal–city relations. Because exploitation theory proponents were not able to demonstrate suburban responsibility for central city fiscal problems, no grounds were available to justify making the suburbs pay when the problems worsened to the point of bankruptcy. As hypothetical questions turned into real financial disasters, it became clear that only two kinds of responses to the fiscal collapse of a metropolitan central city were possible: state government assumption of the city's financial responsibilities or emergency federal rescue.

If the first major central city bankruptcy had struck a city other than New York, federal urban policy might have reoriented more slowly. The outcome, however, undoubtedly would have been the same. New York was a good test case because its problems were so patently a result of metropolitan deconcentration and not such other factors as insufficient revenue sources or lack of political sophistication. New York's problems were worsening in the late 1960s, but Mayor John Lindsay believed he saw a way of turning crisis to advantage. Lindsay had been an outspoken member of the Kerner Commission on the riots, and he wanted very much to show that the Commission had been correct in arguing that white society could bring something good out of the riot experience by admitting its culpability and deciding to take appropriate action. He hoped to win the trust and cooperation of blacks, Hispanics and other minorities on the one hand, and the city's industry, business and finance interests on the other, in an economic and social revitalisation of New York City.

New York City was enduring all the hardships of metropolitan deconcentration and urban crisis. Several hundred thousand manufacturing jobs were lost in the 1960s and early 1970s. There was a massive white middle-class exodus. Considerable numbers of multinational corporations moved their headquarters to the suburbs. The New York Stock Exchange threatened to move to the suburbs when a city stock transfer tax was suggested to help alleviate revenue problems. New York City was not by any means poor, however. The danger threatened by metropolitan deconcentration was that the tax structure would have to be revamped so that banks, real estate investors and businesses paid for a much larger proportion of city expenditures. The best way to avoid this eventuality was to organise an economic renaissance that would create new jobs and expand the city's productive sector. The national economy was booming and federal programmes were available to provide money and assistance for the city. Credit markets were favourable. Lindsay began expanding city government programmes and encouraging expansion of state and federal programmes, hoping the private sector would take up the initiative and carry it forward. Between 1967–8 and 1974–5 governmental expenditures of all kinds in New York City increased from $644 a person to $1,574. Long-term debt for capital expenditures increased from $992 per capita to $1,485.

Unfortunately, international economic instability beginning in 1969 progressively worsened. As the world capital of capitalist finance, New York City sufferd more immediately than other US cities. To keep the governmental expansion going in hopes of weathering the crisis, Lindsay, and then his successor as mayor, Abraham Beame, borrowed short-term against expected revenues in increasingly dangerous amounts. Short-term debt per capita in 1967–8 was $109. By 1974–5, it had jumped to $639 for every city resident. The gamble might have paid off if the international economy had begun to improve in 1973. Instead, the OPEC oil crisis struck, followed by the worst world-wide recession since the late 1930s. By late 1974, the bond rating services were convinced that New York City would default on a bond repayment in the very near future. Chase Manhattan (the Rockefellers' bank) and other large banks dumped more than $2 billion in bonds, triggering a general panic and making the predicted default inevitable.[15]

The unexpected severity of the international crisis made it impossible for the banks to control the situation. The New York State legislature readily turned over control of the city's finances to an Emergency Financial Control Board (EFCB) headed by the Governor and dominated by representatives of the major banks. Bankers and city corporate capitalists were also granted control of a special state Municipal Assistance Corporation (affectionately referred to as 'Big MAC' after a popular fast-food chain's brand name for its hamburger sandwich) empowered to accept city bonds and replace them with its own bonds in an effort to restore faith in the creditworthiness of city debt. Big MAC bond prices plummeted to $600 for a bond of $1,000 face value, indicating lack of faith in the EFCB's ability to prevent calamity. By the autumn of 1975, no alternative remained but to beg for a federal rescue.

Gerald Ford, appointed by Nixon to replace Vice-President Spiro Agnew when he was forced to resign, and who then became President when Nixon resigned, was personally inclined to refuse the entreaties and let default and bankruptcy purge New York City of its evils. The New York *Daily News* captured the spirit perfectly in its banner headline: 'FORD TO CITY: DROP DEAD'. But the bankers soon persuaded Congress and Secretary of the Treasury William Simon that a New York City default would trigger a national banking crisis too dangerous to risk. Eventually Ford came around to this view as well, and federal loans and guarantees were arranged to aid the EFCB and the MAC in preventing disaster.[16]

LENDER OF LAST RESORT

The federal 'bail-out' of New York City set a pattern for direct federal–city relations that placed long-term responsibility in the hands of the banks, real estate investors and corporations with interests in large cities. Congress, President Ford and Treasury Secretary William Simon emphasised that New York City was receiving assistance on an emergency basis only because its problems threatened banking and credit nationally. To other cities in danger of default, their message was: the federal government may or may not step in as your lender of last resort also, for banking and credit reasons, but under no circumstances will cities be rescued from social or political crises. They directed the message at mayors on behalf of banks, corporations and investors, warning them not to try Lindsay's strategy of smothering social and political crisis with massive city government expansion.

Mayors who refused to cooperate with their city's bankers risked having default forced upon them. Dennis Kucinich, the radical white working-class mayor of Cleveland, had a confrontation of this kind with Cleveland's major banks when he refused to let the regional private electric power company take over 'Muny Light', the city's publicly owned electricity company founded during the public ownership movement at the turn of the century. Cleveland Trust, Ohio's largest bank, did actually put the city government in a technical state of default in December 1978, but Kucinich was able to expose the bankers' manipulations with the aid of sympathetic TV and radio news reporters. Later, some bankers and corporate leaders were even willing to reveal their true objective. One told a radio interviewer:

> The bond rating of the city of Cleveland will be restored when there's honest, efficient and competent management of the city's affairs in the City Hall. And when the people are together, and there is that kind of management in City Hall, it's my belief that it won't be too long before the city's bond rating will be restored. But without it I don't think the bond ratings will be restored. . . . The first step is to eliminate Mr. Weissman [former United Automobile Workers official serving as city personnel director] and his boy Kucinich from the City Hall.[17]

Proposals for large-scale federal–city cooperation to promote big city economic revitalisation made little headway in Washington. Felix Rohatyn, a prominent banker from the international investment firm Lazard, Frères who was participating in the New York City rescue as chairperson of the Municipal Assistance Corporation and a member of the Emergency Financial Control Board, proposed reviving the Reconstruction Finance Corporation concept from the Depression of the 1930s to channel capital to older, declining large cities. A specially chartered federal development bank would raise and invest funds in economic reconstruction projects in New York, Cleveland or St. Louis. 'Renaissance Center' in Detroit, a fantastically extravagant hotel, convention, office and retail complex privately financed and developed by Henry Ford II and associates in the late 1960s and early 1970s, provided a favourite prototype of what might be attempted.

Rohatyn received much praise for his ingenuity but failed to persuade anyone in the federal government to champion his strategy. More appealing to President Ford and many others was New York City Housing and Development Administrator Roger Starr's suggestion that the city systematically plan to make itself smaller and less expensive to run. 'Planned shrinkage', as this strategy came to be known, gained considerable popularity even among urban economics experts.[18]

THE DETERIORATION OF URBAN LIFE: CARTER'S POLICY FOR CITIES

Any hope that the Democrats might junk new federalism, revenue sharing, community development and housing allowances when they regained control of the White House vanished in the first year of the Carter administration. Some Democrats in Congress may not have given up on trying to save the central cities from urban crisis, but the President offered them no encouragement. Carter's advisers became so unhappy with his callous disinterest in urban problems that they deliberately leaked damaging inside information to the media. Carter appointed Patricia Harris, a black woman, as HUD Secretary and formed an urban and regional policy group under her direction, but he was not prepared to listen to the group's recommendations nine months later when urban items for the January 1978 budget had to be finalised. Reliable sources revealed that Carter was displeased with Secretary Harris. The *New York Times* learned that Carter had 'angrily' rejected the Harris group's programme proposals 'out of hand' and demanded they be reformulated. In March the Associated Press reported that Carter was planning to recommend a mere $2.6 billion in new spending. Before last-minute persuasion by close advisers, the AP was told, he had approved a package 'substantially less' than $2.6 billion.[19]

Finally, on 27 March 1978, Carter presented his urban programmes to Congress in a message billed as 'proposals for a comprehensive national urban policy'. Later in the year, he used the HUD authorisation act requirement that the President make biennial national urban policy reports to Congress as the pretext for a major statement justifying his approach to urban issues. The urban problem, the President proclaimed in introducing his 27 March message, was no less than 'the deterioration of urban life in the United States'. The press release quoted from a June 1976 campaign speech to the US Conference of Mayors:

I think we stand at a turning point in history. If, a hundred years from now, this nation's experiment in democracy has failed, I suspect that historians will trace that failure to our own era, when a process of decay began in our inner cities and was allowed to spread unchecked throughout our society.[20]

What the deterioration of urban life was supposed to mean as an approach to federal policy was explicated in the policy report. Emphasising deconcentration and the reversal in the direction of settlement forces during the 1970s, the report argued that the nation was entering a 'post-industrial' stage of its development in which central cities, 'perhaps economically restructured and less populous than in the past', would play a new and different role. Through a series of convoluted euphemisms the report explained that even a post-industrial economy needed 'nodes' connecting its economic, transportation and communications systems. The Carter administration therefore presumed that existing central cities would retain their nodal functions, in part because it would be expensive and wasteful to have to duplicate them entirely at new locations.

In short, 'deterioration of urban life' should be interpreted as the natural transformation of metropolitan central cities to post-industrial roles. Rather than vainly attempting to reverse central city decay, the report concluded, federal urban policy should strive to ease the transition process, intervening only to ensure that deterioration did not get out of control. 'Future urban policies', the report explained, 'have to be predicated upon what new patterns of urban settlement and living are becoming and what the country wants them to become; not what they used to be or even are today.' The 'limited federal resources' available to implement urban policy must be reserved to alleviate the distress of post-industrial transition and prevent 'disintegration and decay' from spreading to 'communities that are not yet distressed'.[21]

The Carter administration's choice of terms and phrases won few friends among big-city mayors or victims of urban decay, but the gloomy provisos were all necessary consequences of their assumption that policy could not attempt to alter the direction of settlement forces. Highlighting the deterioration of urban life was intended as a declaration and an admission that central cities as they had flourished in the metropolitan era were now receding into the past. Post-industrial urbanism was going to be different and policy should not define change as a crisis that must be confronted by preserving older cities according to models conceived twenty, or sixty, years ago. Many aspects of post-industrial settlement were not going to be 'urban' at all, in the customary sense of that term. The report anticipated national growth 'balanced' among all regions of the country and among all types of communities. There were numerous hints that 'urban' and 'rural', 'city' and 'country', 'metropolitan' and 'non-metropolitan' would lose their significance as distinctions between regions and communities.[22]

GOODBYE TO METROPOLIS

The Carter administration's urban policy followed the lead of settlement forces and felt perfectly justified in doing so. Settlement trends had turned away from metropolitan development, according to their interpretation of the mid-decade estimates, and a policy that continued to promote metropolitan patterns would be futile and wasteful. Concern with the deterioration of central cities represented the new administration's version of the direct federal–central city relations initiated under Ford. Committing himself to softening the hardships of decline and decay, instead of mobilising to combat them, highlighted Carter's unwillingness to aid or encourage central city revitalisation with federal resources. The farthest he was willing to go in this direction was to propose that Congress create an urban development bank of the type suggested by Felix Rohatyn. He gave the proposal little support however and no bank was established.

After almost forty years of metropolitan emphasis, the metropolitan community was no longer to be the focus of policy. Rather than protesting, urban analysts accepted the end of the metropolitan era with a shrug. Urban economist Wilbur Thompson, probably the most imaginative proponent of metropolitan development strategies in the 1960s, bluntly advised older central cities to gird themselves for 'depopulation'. Thompson offered no theoretical explanations for why metropolitan growth had stopped, he simply warned planners and politicians not to let the declining trend catch them unprepared. Some experts pointed to Mumford's critiques of industrialism, the automobile and megalopolitan sprawl, and suggested that decline might provide the ideal opportunity to restore the city's civilising powers. Most analysts were willing to agree that decline represented the 'maturity' of central cities and metropolitan communities. Few remembered that the urban experts of the late 1930s believed the American city had achieved its mature form at that time.[23]

History's principal analytic contribution to policy is always its delineation of temporal trends, identifying when distinct eras began and ended and how they should be characterised. Designating 1980 the end of a four-decade metropolitan era of US urban settlement and policy represents one interpretation of events and intentions. Other interpretations might differ not just over the significance of policy decisions or population changes, but about when policy and settlement underwent major transitions. Not every urban historian or policy analyst considers the late 1970s the end of an era, or the 1930s the years of transition from a previous era.

Policy, by definition, concerns change and forces that generate change. When analysts explain that the metropolitan community has entered its maturity, they validate and justify policy's abandonment of concern. Condensed to its skeletal elements, the policy history of the metropolitan era suggests monumental efforts that failed disastrously. Policy took up the goal of saving the central cities in the 1940s because they seemed incapable of renewing their aging urban designs, land uses and structures through their own efforts. Twenty-five years later, in the early 1970s, policy abandoned the saving the central cities objective on grounds that urban renewal had fulfilled its purposes. Yet at the moment this judgment was being made, and acted upon, crisis threatened to overwhelm the city government of almost every large, older central city. By 1978, the Carter administration could confidently, indeed optimistically, ground its policy on an evaluation that central city deterioration had become irreversible and should be left to follow its own natural course, as if decline and decay were preconditions for future improvement. Superficially, it would appear that central cities were no better off in 1980 than if policy had completely ignored them for thirty years, possibly worse off.

The cessation of metropolitan concentration means that if urban policy continues to emphasise the metropolitan community it will be ignoring the nation's prevailing migration trends and settlement preferences. Policy could confront the forces of settlement with the objective of preserving a desirable settlement type, such as the metropolitan community. The costs of trying to alter behaviour, however, can be enormous. Transportation was a severe problem for the metropolitan central city. In the late 1960s and early 1970s, the federal government committed itself to aiding the first of a new generation of metropolitan mass transit systems. Two multi-billion dollar subway systems were completed: the Metro in Washington, DC, and BART (Bay Area Rapid Transit) in the San Francisco–

Oakland area. The shift in settlement forces during the 1970s raised serious doubts about the wisdom of this course.

1980 Census figures on commuting revealed that the proportion of workers using public transportation had declined from 9 per cent in 1970 to 6 per cent. In particular, commuting by mass transit declined in metropolitan areas with extensive subway and trolley systems: New York from 52 to 45 per cent, Philadelphia from 21 to 14 per cent, Chicago from 23 to 18 per cent. Most astonishing were the figures for San Francisco–Oakland, where mass transit commuting increased by less than one percentage point from 15.5 per cent in 1970 to 16.4 per cent in 1980, and Washington, DC, where mass transit commuting actually declined slightly from 16.3 to 15.5 per cent despite the glamorous new subway system.[24]

Should urban policy ignore the declines in this form of travel and persist in encouraging metropolitan commuting, location and land use patterns typical of the 1960s? Those who believe that policy ought to reflect good social values may argue that the mass transit monies were well spent. They will also have to assume the burden of explaining why the metropolitan community pattern of central city workplaces and suburban residences is socially preferable to the deconcentrating trends of the 1970s. This is the dilemma perpetually confronting city planners, whose entire function is to design projects that successfully coordinate policy and social values with settlement and migration trends. At least one progressive planner who fought for the BART system in San Francisco–Oakland, Melvin Webber, now believes it should not have been built.[25]

In so far as this history of the metropolitan era contains a lesson for the new urban era now beginning, it lies in the importance of how settlement patterns and migration trends are officially defined, described and measured. If policy experts, federal urban bureaucrats, Congress, mayors, central city migrants to suburbs, Southern black migrants to Northern central cities, suburban shopping centre developers and many, many others had not been willing to accept the basic premise that all metropolitan areas from the very largest to the very smallest were socially, politically and culturally equivalent, the interaction between policy and settlement forces we have followed through four decades could not have taken the course it did. Without broad consensus about the similarity among metropolitan areas, residents of metropolitan fringes would never have acknowledged themselves as a suburban constituency of millions, and blacks in small cities would not have responded to rioting in Watts, Newark and Detroit as a national rebellion that they must join and intensify. The years from 1940 to 1980 deserve to be remembered as the metropolitan era because the vast majority of people played out their parts in American development as metropolitan community members. This could not have happened if people in Atlanta had insisted they had nothing in common with people in Seattle because of regional differences, if people in Phoenix had denied their similarities with people in Pittsburgh because of industrial and economic differences, or if people in Los Angeles' outlying valleys had insisted on being recognised as something other than 'suburban' because their urban area was a structurally different community type from New York or Chicago.

Before urban policy can complete its transition out of the metropolitan era, a new consensus about prevailing community types and structures must emerge. Despite strong popular agreement in the 1950s and 1960s that metropolitan areas were true communities, attempts to create unified metropolitan government were miserably unsuccessful. The metropolitan government question later entered policy debate as an aspect of the suburban exploitation controversy we considered in Chapter 6. Without a groundswell of local enthusiasm for metropolitan consolidation however, it was impractical to propose such solutions for policy problems. Eventually, even policy writers strongly sympathetic to unified metropolitan area government conceded that the prevailing fragmented structure had important functional advantages. If this experience is an appropriate guide, the new community types adopted for policy debate in the 1980s need not be existing or potential governmental units. Jean Gottman did not imagine that Megalopolis would ever acquire unified government, but neither did he consider the impracticality of political organisation a negation of the possibility that 50 million people occupying 40,000 square miles of territory could constitute a single local community.[26]

Another lesson from the metropolitan era derives from the way suburbanites of various ethnicities, religions and occupations united within their communities to create and validate their middle-class social standing. We should prepare to see race, ethnicity, occupation, class and community function less and less as independent axes of social orientation. Instead, we should expect the social structure to be transformed by dynamic multi-faceted groups analogous to the aspiring working-class and white-collar families of the 1940s who populated suburbia and forged the new middle class. More than ever, economic change will wait to take its cues from social developments: workers' willingness to tolerate productive rhythms, intensity and technology, and consumer preferences for life styles and family types.

The academic and policy worlds from which the analysis in this book comes, and in which it will find most of its readers, are under obligation to take the initiative as one era concludes and a new one opens. We cannot throw up our hands, as the Carter administration did, and proclaim the immutable inevitability of settlement forces. Patterns of migration and community formation require imaginative conceptualisation and description. The American city of tomorrow is rapidly taking shape. Before policy can proceed, we need to assess the metropolitan era in its entirety and then approach the future with optimism about the new urbanism that is in the making.

Notes

INTRODUCTION

1. Lee Rainwater and William Y. Yancey, *The Moynihan Report and the Politics of Controversy* (Cambridge, MIT Press, 1967), p. 193.

2. Martin Meyerson, 'Urban Policy: Reforming Reform', *Daedalus*, LXXXXVII, No. 4 (Autumn 1968); issue on 'The Conscience of the City', 1410–30; 1420.

3. Edward Banfield, *The Unheavenly City Revisited, A Revision of The Unheavenly City* (Boston, Little, Brown, 1974); (*The Unheavenly City* originally published in 1968), p. 279.

4. Robert Wood, *The Necessary Majority: Middle America and the Urban Crisis* (New York, Columbia University Press, 1972).

5. Banfield, *Unheavenly City Revisited*, p. 1.

6. The complete phrase was: 'the deterioration of urban life in the United States', and it was used in the press release accompanying the policy report; see *Congressional Quarterly, Urban America, Policies and Problems* (Washington, DC, Congressional Quarterly, August 1978) p. 1.

7. US Department of Housing and Urban Development, *The President's 1978 National Urban Policy Report* (Washington, DC, August 1978) pp. 8–15; quotations from p. 14.

8. *President's 1978 Urban Policy Report*, p. 14.

9. The controversy over comparing the New York Metropolitan District with Greater London, as well as other aspects of the introduction of metropolitan concepts and statistics, are discussed in Kenneth Fox, *Better City Government, Innovation in American Urban Politics, 1850–1937* (Philadelphia, Temple University Press, 1977), Chapter 7. For the New York–Greater London controversy, see pp. 145–6.

10. I owe a great debt to two people for forcing me to appreciate the mutual determination of social class and community: Peter Meyer, who refused to give up in numerous arguments, and Charles Levenstein, who has written an excellent article, 'The Political Economy of Suburbanization: In Pursuit of a Class Analysis', *Review of Radical Political Economics*, XIII, No. 2 (Summer 1981), 23–31.

11. These trends in geography and sociology in the United States began with the pioneering work of Robert Park, Ernest Burgess, Louis Wirth and their associates and students at the University of Chicago in the 1920s and 1930s. The best one-volume introduction to this tradition is Paul Hatt and Albert Reiss, Jr (eds), *Cities and Society, The Revised Reader in Urban Sociology* (New York, Free Press, 1957). Recently efforts have been under way to integrate the space and human ecology traditions with modern Marxist theory and analysis. Manuel Castells has been the leader in this enterprise; see his *The Urban Question, A Marxist Approach* (London, Edward Arnold, 1977); originally published in French in 1972. Chapter 5, pp. 75–85, is a discussion of Park and Wirth and the Chicago tradition.

12. Thomas Dye, *Understanding Public Policy*, 3rd edition (Englewood Cliffs, NJ,

Prentice-Hall, 1978), p. 3. Dye adds that almost all other definitions of policy boil down to no more than his one straightforward assertion.

1   SETTLING METROPOLITAN AMERICA

1. James Bryce, *The American Commonwealth* (London, Macmillan, 1888, 1889); 1st edition, two vols, I, p. 618.

2. For an extended discussion of Bryce and the national municipal reform movement, see Kenneth Fox, *Better City Government, Innovation in American Urban Politics, 1850–1937* (Philadelphia, Temple University Press, 1977), pp. 34–62.

3. The Bureau went so far as to become involved in running national municipal reform conferences. At a 1908 conference the Bureau chief for municipal statistics spoke on the Bureau's role 'as an agent of municipal reform'. See *Better City Government*, pp. 63–80.

4. Bureau of the Census, *Bulletin 101, Industrial Districts: 1905, Manufactures and Population* (Washington, DC, GPO, 1909); S.N.D. North, Letter of Transmittal, 15 May 1909, p. 7.

5. 'Population of Metropolitan Districts', *Abstract of the Census, Thirteenth Census of the United States: 1910* (Washington, DC, GPO, 1913), pp. 61–2; see also discussion of preliminary drafts of the metropolitan district report in *Better City Government*, pp. 146–7.

6. Robert C. Brooks, 'Metropolitan Free Cities', *Political Science Quarterly*, xxx, no. 2 (June 1915), 222–34.

7. The criteria defining metropolitan status have changed several times between 1910 and the present. Unless otherwise indicated, all comparisons from decade to decade here and throughout our discussions will be based on the criteria in use in the most recent year. Thus the figure '58' for the number of metropolitan areas in 1910 is derived from 1940 criteria. By 1910 metropolitan district definitions there were only 44 metropolitan areas in 1910.

8. For the states constituting each region see Table I, on p. 35.

9. The Census Bureau standardised its metropolitan criteria in the Census of 1930. To qualify as metropolitan, an area had to have a central city with a population of 50,000 and a total area population of 100,000. Previously the Bureau had required a central city population of 100,000. Numerous minor changes have been introduced since the 1930 Census but only for the purpose of maintaining conceptual consistency in the face of changing settlement patterns *within* metropolitan areas. For example, the requirement that an area should have a clearly identifiable *central city* was dropped in preparing for the Census of 1980.

10. For a detailed discussion of the spread of metropolitan development to all regions of the US, see Kenneth Fox, 'Uneven Regional Development in the United States', *Review of Radical Political Economics*, x, No. 3 (Autumn 1978), 68–86. Illustrative of the international basis of wealth and power in Denver is the importance in the plot of the TV melodrama *Dynasty* of manipulations over oil in the seas of Java. The coal and oil shale mining native to Colorado receive little attention.

11. Peter O. Muller provides a good historical survey of changes in suburban styles of development during this period in his *Contemporary Suburban America* (Englewood Cliffs, NJ, Prentice-Hall, 1981), Chapter 2. Muller's treatment places excessive emphasis on changing transportation technology. He does not even discuss the possibility that regional differences might have evolved and become permanent.

12. Sam Bass Warner, Jr, *Streetcar Suburbs, The Process of Growth in Boston, 1870–1900*

(New York, Atheneum, 1973); originally published in 1962, is an excellent study of three pre-metropolitan suburbs.

13. Mario Manieri-Elia provides an interesting critical perspective in 'Toward an "Imperial City": Daniel H. Burnham and the City Beautiful Movement', in Giorgio Ciucci, Fancesco Dal Co, Mario Manieri-Elia and Manfredo Tafuri, *The American City, From the Civil War to the New Deal* (London, Granada, 1980), originally published in Italian in 1973, pp. 1–142.

14. Willard L. Thorp, *The Integration of Industrial Operation* (Washington, DC, Bureau of the Census, 1924), p. 145.

15. Roderick D. McKenzie, *The Metropolitan Community* (New York, Russell and Russell, 1967), originally published in 1933, pp. 317–18.

16. Warren S. Thompson, *Population, The Growth of Metropolitan Districts in the United States: 1900–1940* (Washington, DC, Bureau of the Census, 1947), p. 5.

17. John Maynard Keynes, *The General Theory of Employment, Interest and Money* (New York, Harcourt, Brace and World, 1936). The two earliest prominent American Keynesians, Guy Greer and Alvin Hansen, presented a metropolitan redevelopment and housing strategy in their 1941 pamphlet: *Urban Redevelopment and Housing: A Plan for Post-War* (Washington, DC, National Planning Association, 1941). We will examine Keynesian policy making and Keynesian metropolitan strategies in more detail in Chapter 3.

18. C. Wright Mills, *White Collar, The American Middle Classes* (New York, Oxford University Press, 1951), p. ix.

2 SUBURBAN DEVELOPMENT AND THE MIDDLE CLASS

1. The survey data are summarised and discussed in Leonard Beeghley's *Social Stratification in America: A Critical Analysis of Theory and Research* (Santa Monica, Goodyear Publishing, 1978), pp. 111–20, and also E. M. Schreiber and G. T. Nygreen, 'Subjective Social Class in America: 1945–1968', *Social Forces*, XLVIII, No. 3 (March 1970), 348–56. No more than 2 per cent of respondents in any of the surveys rejected the idea of class, but also no more than 2 per cent identified themselves as 'lower' class. 1 per cent responded 'upper' class in 1952, less than 1 per cent in 1956, 1960, 1964 and 1968, and 3 per cent in 1975. Working-class percentages were 1952: 61%; 1956: 58%; 1960: 65%; 1964: 53%; 1968: 52%; and 1975: 46%. The 1963 study was by Charles Tucker, 'A Comparative Analysis of Subjective Social Class: 1945–1963', *Social Forces*, XLVI, No. 4 (June 1968), 508–14. Tucker found 31 per cent responding 'working class'. Schreiber and Nygreen felt Tucker's data differed at least in part because of methodological differences. Beeghley apparently had even stronger reservations; he entirely ignored Tucker and his findings. Finally, mention should be made of a 1945 study by Richard Centers that revealed 3 per cent upper class, 43 per cent middle class, 51 per cent working class and 1 per cent lower class. Centers' study is discussed in all the above writings. I have not included it in my discussion because I feel it reflects dislocations and complexities associated with military service and wartime economic necessities.

Class in metropolitan areas presents complexities all its own. Two sources that provide a good introduction to the issues are: William M. Dobriner, *Class in Suburbia* (Englewood Cliffs, NJ, Prentice-Hall, 1963); and Leo F. Schnore, *Class and Race in Cities and Suburbs* (Chicago, Rand McNally/Markham, 1972).

2. C. Wright Mills, *White Collar, The American Middle Classes* (New York, Oxford University Press, 1951), p. 65.

3. Mills, *White Collar*, pp. 239–40.

4. Mills, *White Collar*, Chapter 11, 'The Status Panic', and Chapter 12, 'Success'.

5. William H. Whyte, Jr, *The Organization Man* (New York, Simon and Schuster/Touchstone, 1956).

6. Whyte, *Organization Man*, p. 129. More important than evolving an ideal organisational psychology was being able to appear ideal when tested. Whyte included an appendix on how to avoid errors and pitfalls called 'How to cheat on personality tests'.

7. Martin Glaberman, *Wartime Strikes* (Bewick/ed, Detroit, 1980).

8. Ned Eichler, whose father was one of the leading builders of the post-war period, provides an intricately detailed account of the suburban building business in *The Merchant Builders* (Cambridge, MIT Press, 1982). Part One describes the 1945–59 period.

9. Herbert Gans, *The Levittowners* (New York, Vintage/Random House, 1967), p. 22.

10. Sociologist Talcott Parsons was one of the few analysts to recognise the importance of isolation to post-war suburban families; he elaborated his concept of the 'isolated conjugal family' in T. Parsons and R. F. Bales, *Family, Socialization and Interaction Process* (Glencoe, Free Press, 1955).

11. Benjamin Spock, *Baby and Child Care* (New York, Pocket Books, 1957), first published in 1945.

12. Erik Erikson, *Childhood and Society* (New York, W.W. Norton, 1950).

13. Spock, *Baby and Child Care*, p. 358.

14. Bureau of the Census, *1960 Census of Population and Housing*. Figures on other relatives living with families must be approximate because the Census publicises only the total number of other relatives, not the number of families with other relatives present. For Park Forest, for example, one-ninth of families, or 11 per cent, was the largest possible proportion of families with other relatives present. The actual percentage was somewhat lower than 11 per cent because some families included two or more other relatives.

15. Whyte, *Organization Man*, p. 281.

16. Whyte, *Organization Man*, p. 283.

17. Vance Packard, *The Hidden Persuaders* (New York, D. McKay, 1957); Marshall McLuhan, *Understanding Media, The Extensions of Man* (New York, McGraw-Hill, 1964).

18. Rolf Meyersohn, 'Social Research in Television', in Bernard Rosenberg and David White (eds), *Mass Culture* (Glencoe, Free Press and Falcon's Wing Press, 1957), pp. 345–57, esp. 345.

19. Several economists and political scientists have demonstrated that improved community appearance, and higher expenditures on community services, can increase the resale prices of houses relative to comparable houses in less ambitious communities. Economist Wallace Oates was able to measure significant price differences among New Jersey communities; see his 'The effects of property taxes and local spending on property values: an empirical study of tax capitalization and the Tiebout hypothesis', *Journal of Political Economy*, LXXVII (1969), 957–71. Political scientists Oliver Williams, Harold Herman, Charles Liebman and Thomas Dye demonstrated similar variations among Philadelphia suburbs in *Suburban Differences and Metropolitan Policies, A Philadelphia Story* (Philadelphia, University of Pennsylvania Press, 1965).

20. Robert Lynd and Helen Lynd, *Middletown, A Study in Modern American Culture* (New York, Harcourt, Brace and World, 1956; originally published in 1929), pp. 153–87, 211–22.

21. Bennett Berger provided a detailed description of the high-wage, working-class suburb of Milpitas in the San Jose, California, suburban fringe in his *Working Class Suburb, A Study of Auto Workers in Suburbia* (Berkeley, University of California Press, 1960). Milpitas grew up to house workers relocated to a new Ford Motor Company plant when the company closed their old factory in the city of Richmond, California. For most, it was their first experience of suburban living. Berger concluded from his

analysis of various social, cultural and psychological factors that they retained their working-class consciousness. However, the contradictions they experienced between their occupational status and their suburban circumstances were considerable.

22. A. C. Spectorsky, *The Exurbanites* (Philadelphia, J. B. Lippincott, 1955).

3 SAVING THE CENTRAL CITY

1. Mark Gelfand, *A Nation of Cities, The Federal Government and Urban America, 1933–1965* (New York, Oxford University Press, 1975), pp. 96–7.

2. Eric Foner, *Free Soil, Free Labor, Free Men, The Ideology of the Republican Party* (New York, Oxford University Press, 1970).

3. John Reps, *The Making of Urban America* (Princeton, Princeton University Press, 1965), pp. 386–8.

4. Fox, *Better City Government*, pp. 124–8.

5. Fox, *Better City Government*, Chapters 3 and 6.

6. John Mollenkopf argues that political factors were the primary determinants of urban policy at each stage of its evolution, and particularly at its origin in the New Deal. See his *The Contested City* (Princeton, Princeton University Press, 1983), Chapter 2.

7. Mark Gelfand, *A Nation of Cities, The Federal Government and Urban America, 1933–1965* (New York, Oxford University Press, 1975), pp. 24–6, 68.

8. Fox, *Better City Government*, p. 163.

9. Gelfand, *Nation of Cities*, p. 89.

10. Urbanism Committee, National Resources Committee, *Our Cities, Their Role in the National Economy* (Washington, DC, 1937), p. 4; the report was reprinted in: Ad Hoc Subcommittee on Urban Growth, Committee on Banking and Currency, House of Representative, *Hearings: The Quality of Urban Life*, Part 2 (Washington, DC, 1970).

11. *Our Cities*, pp. 52–3.

12. Henry Aaron, *Shelter and Subsidies* (Washington, DC, Brookings, 1972), pp. 110, 120; Subcommittee on Housing and Community Development, Committee on Banking, Currency and Housing, House of Representatives, *Evolution of the Role of the Federal Government in Housing and Community Development, A Chronology of Legislative and Selected Executive Actions, 1892–1974* (Washington, DC, 1975), p. 234.

13. *Housing and Community Development Chronology*, pp. 2–3.

14. Lloyd Rodwin, *Nations and Cities* (Boston, Houghton Mifflin, 1970), pp. 235–6.

15. Aaron, *Shelter and Subsidies*, pp. 54–5.

16. Gelfand, *Nation of Cities*, pp. 118–20; Rodwin, *Nations and Cities*, p. 237.

17. Stephen Bailey, *Congress Makes a Law* (New York, Columbia University Press, 1950; Vintage Paperback, 1964, p. 228); for a discussion of the impact of Keynes' ideas on US policy of all kinds, see Lawrence Klein, *The Keynesian Revolution* (New York, Macmillan, 1947).

18. Gelfand, *Nation of Cities*, pp. 112–28.

19. *Housing and Community Development Chronology*, p. 25; Gelfand, *Nation of Cities*, pp. 154–6; Rodwin, *Nations and Cities*, pp. 242–3. City planners borrowed the word 'blight', a term for diseases of plants and trees in which the leaves become spotted and darken, leading eventually to death, to describe deterioration of the physical appearance of neighbourhoods. The implication was that the urban blight was also a disease and that if blighted neighbourhoods went untreated they could become slums.

20. Gelfand, *Nation of Cities*, p. 170.

21. Phillip Singerman, *Politics, Bureaucracy and Public Policy: The Case of Urban Renewal in New Haven*, Yale University doctoral dissertation, 1980, pp. 96–7.

22. Singerman, *Urban Renewal in New Haven*, pp. 92–7.

23. John Mollenkopf provides excellent case-studies of the coalition strategies in Boston and San Francisco in *The Contested City*, Chapter 4. Mollenkopf reports that Boston activists copied Lawrence's strategy deliberately; see pp. 158–9. San Francisco's experience differed in that the mayors were not the primary organisers of the coalition.

24. Alan Altschuler has provided one of the best descriptions of comprehensive planning in his political case-study of Minneapolis and St. Paul: *The City Planning Process* (Ithaca, Cornell University Press, 1965).

25. Edgar Hoover and Raymond Vernon, *Anatomy of a Metropolis* (Harvard University Press, 1959; New York, Doubleday-Anchor, 1962); Raymond Vernon, *The Myth and Reality of Our Urban Problems* (Cambridge, Harvard University Press, 1966; originally published in 1962).

26. William Stull, 'From Urban Renewal to CDBG: Community Development in Nine American Cities', Community Development Strategies Evaluation Project, US Department of Housing and Urban Development, September 1979, Part 1 Urban Renewal, p. 21. The nine cities were New Haven, Pittsburgh, Birmingham, Memphis, Corpus Christi (Texas), Wichita (Kansas), St. Paul (Minnesota), Denver, and San Francisco.

27. Gelfand, *Nation of Cities*, pp. 222–30.

28. Chief among the enemies of the automobile has been Lewis Mumford; see *The City in History* (New York, Harcourt, Brace and World, 1961).

29. Manuel Castells, *The Urban Question* (London, Edward Arnold, 1977), p. 302.

4   CITY LIFE IN METROPOLITAN AREAS

1. David Riesman, *The Lonely Crowd* (New Haven, Yale University Press, 1950; 1961 abridged edition).

2. Clarence Stein, *Toward New Towns for America*, originally published in 1950 (Cambridge, MIT Press, 1966), p. 37.

3. Jane Jacobs, *The Death and Life of Great American Cities* (New York, Vintage/Random House, 1961), p. 15; see also her four principles of diversity planning, pp. 150–1.

4. Herbert Gans, *The Urban Villagers* (New York, Free Press, 1962).

5. Jacobs, *Death and Life of American Cities*, p. 221.

6. Jacobs, *Death and Life of American Cities*, p. 138.

7. Gunnar Myrdal, *An American Dilemma, The Negro Problem and Modern Democracy* (New York, Harper and Brothers, 1944), pp. 695–700.

8. Myrdal, *American Dilemma*, p. 183; and Bureau of the Census, *Historical Statistics of the United States, Colonial Times to 1957*.

9. Martin Glaberman, *Wartime Strikes, The Struggle Against the No-Strike Pledge in the UAW During World War II* (Detroit, Bewick/ed, 1980), p. 31.

10. Will Herberg, *Protestant – Catholic – Jew*, originally published in 1955, revised edition (Garden City, Anchor/Doubleday, 1960).

11. Nathan Glazer and Daniel Patrick Moynihan, *Beyond the Melting Pot, The Negroes, Puerto Ricans, Jews, Italians and Irish of New York City* (Cambridge, MIT Press, 1963), p. 17.

12. Ira Katznelson, *City Trenches, Urban Politics and the Patterning of Class in the United States* (New York, Pantheon, 1981), p. 132.

13. Gerald Suttles, *The Social Order of the Slum, Ethnicity and Territory in the Inner City* (Chicago, University of Chicago Press, 1968).

14. Laurence Lynn, 'A Decade of Policy Developments in the Income-Maintenance

System', in Robert Haveman (ed.), *A Decade of Federal Antipoverty Programs* (New York, Academic Press, 1977), pp. 55–117, esp. p. 67.

15. The report is available in its original form in Lee Rainwater and William Yancey, *The Moynihan Report and the Politics of Controversy* (Cambridge, MIT Press, 1967).

16. Moynihan, *The Negro Family*, p. 5.

17. Farmer's comments appeared on 18 December 1965; the article has been reprinted in Rainwater and Yancey, *Moynihan Report*, pp. 409–11.

18. Glazer and Moynihan, *Beyond the Melting Pot*, p. 16.

19. Lloyd Goodrich, *Edward Hopper* (New York, Harry N. Abrams, 1971), p. 139.

20. Goodrich, *Hopper*, p. 280.

21. Goodrich, *Hopper*, p. 106.

22. C. Wright Mills, *White Collar, The American Middle Classes* (New York, Oxford University Press, 1951), p. 184.

23. Langston Hughes, 'A Toast to Harlem', reprinted in *Simple Speaks His Mind* (New York, Simon and Schuster, original copyrights 1943–50), pp. 31–3.

24. Elliot Liebow, *Tally's Corner* (Boston, Little, Brown, 1967).

5. THE RIOTS OF THE 1960s

1. *New York Times, Report of the National Advisory Commission on Civil Disorders* (New York, New York Times Company, 1968), p. 36; hereafter cited as 'Kerner Commission, *Report*'.

2. Allan Spear, *Black Chicago, The Making of a Negro Ghetto, 1890–1920* (Chicago, University of Chicago Press, 1967), pp. 208–12.

3. Spear, *Black Chicago*, pp. 212–22.

4. Peter Rossi and Robert Dentler, *The Politics of Urban Renewal* (New York, Free Press, 1961), pp. 14, 19.

5. Harold Mayer and Richard Wade, *Chicago, Growth of a Metropolis* (Chicago, University of Chicago Press, 1969), pp. 284, 390.

6. Rossi and Dentler, *Politics of Urban Renewal*, pp. 21, 22, 26.

7. Rossi and Dentler, *Politics of Urban Renewal*, pp. 150–2.

8. Roger Lane, *Policing the City: Boston 1822–1885*, originally published in 1967 (New York, Atheneum, 1971), pp. 20–38.

9. Bruce Laurie, *Working People of Philadelphia, 1800–1850* (Philadelphia, Temple University Press, 1980), pp. 62–6; Michael Feldberg, 'Urbanization as a Cause of Violence: Philadelphia as a Test Case', in Allen Davis and Mark Haller (eds), *The Peoples of Philadelphia, A History of Ethnic Groups and Lower-Class Life, 1790–1940* (Philadelphia, Temple University Press, 1973), pp. 53–69; Bruce Laurie, 'Fire Companies and Gangs in Southwark: The 1840s', also in Davis and Haller, *Peoples of Philadelphia*, pp. 71–87.

10. James Richardson, *The New York Police, Colonial Times to 1901* (New York, Oxford University Press, 1970), Chapters 4 and 5.

11. Joel Tyler Headly, *The Great Riots of New York, 1712–1873*, first published in 1873 (New York, Dover Publications, 1971).

12. Charles Glaab and Theodore Brown, *A History of Urban America*, 2nd edition (New York, Macmillan, 1975), pp. 260–1.

13. August Meier and Elliot Rudwick, *From Plantation to Ghetto* (New York, Hill and Wang, 1966), p. 247.

14. Robert Fogelson, 'Violence as Protest', in Robert Connery (ed.), *Urban Riots* (New York, Vintage, Random House, 1968), pp. 27–44.

15. Robert Fogelson and Robert Hill, 'Who Riots? A Study of Participation in the 1967 Riots', in National Advisory Commission on Civil Disorders (Kerner Commission), *Supplemental Studies* (Washington, DC, Government Printing Office, 1968), pp. 217–48, esp. p. 243; Kerner Commission, *Report*, p. 128.

16. Kerner Commission, *Report*, pp. 37–8.

17. Fogelson and Hill, 'Who Riots?', p. 234; Kerner Commission, *Report*, pp. 56–69.

18. Fred Powledge, *Model City* (New York, Simon and Schuster, 1970), pp. 91–3, 110–14.

19. Fogelson and Hill, 'Who Riots?', p. 231; Powledge, *Model City*, pp. 110–11.

20. Kerner Commission, *Report*, pp. 95–7.

21. Kerner Commission, *Report*, pp. 129, 172, 107.

22. Kerner Commission, *Report*, p. 92.

23. Kerner Commission, *Report*, pp. 97–105.

24. Kerner Commission, *Report*, pp. 112–13.

25. Robert Fogelson, 'Violence as Protest'.

26. Kerner Commission, *Report*, pp. 1–2.

27. Michael Lipsky and David Olson, 'Riot Commission Politics', *Transaction* (later *Society*) (July/August 1969), 9–21.

28. Kerner Commission, *Report*, pp. 253, 413–24.

29. Governor's Commission on the Los Angeles Riots, *Violence in the City – An End and a Beginning* (Los Angeles, 1965), pp. 23, 27, 28. John McCone, the Commission's chairperson, had previously been head of the Central Intelligence Agency.

30. Angus Campbell and Howard Schuman, 'Racial Attitudes in Fifteen American Cities', in National Advisory Commission on Civil Disorders (Kerner Commission), *Supplemental Studies* (Washington, DC, Government Printing Office, 1968), pp. 1–67, esp. p. 48; Allan Silver, 'Official Interpretations of Racial Riots', in Robert Connery (ed.), *Urban Riots* (New York, Vintage, Random House, 1968, 1969), pp. 151–63.

31. Kerner Commission, *Report*, pp. 22–3.

6 URBAN CRISIS

1. Edward Banfield, *The Unheavenly City* (Boston, Little, Brown, 1970), and *The Unheavenly City Revisited* (Boston, Little, Brown, 1974).

2. Richard Wertheimer, *The Monetary Rewards of Migration within the United States* (Washington, DC, Urban Institute, 1970), pp. 57, 59, 76; Henry Aaron, *Shelter and Subsidies* (Washington, DC, Brookings, 1972), p. 30.

3. Charles Schultze, Alice Rivlin *et al.*, 'Fiscal Problems of Cities', in Roger Alcaly and David Mermelstein (eds), *The Fiscal Crisis of American Cities* (New York, Random House, Vintage, 1976), pp. 188–212, p. 207.

4. Interestingly enough, Hawley's study showed that each additional central city resident increased city government expenditures by only $1.30. Although the underlying reasons for these results are methodologically extremely complex, their initial conceptual implication is substantially accurate. Amos Hawley, 'Metropolitan Population and Municipal Government Expenditures in Central Cities', in Paul Hatt and Albert Reiss (eds), *Cities and Society*, revised edition (New York, Free Press, 1957), pp. 773–82, esp. p. 782.

5. William Neenan, 'Suburban-Central City Exploitation Thesis: One City's Tale', *National Tax Journal*, XXIII, No. 2 (June 1970), 117–39.

6. Julius Margolis, 'Metropolitan Finance Problems: Territories, Functions and Growth', in National Bureau of Economic Research, *Public Finances: Needs, Sources and Utilization* (Princeton, Princeton University Press, 1961), pp. 229–93.

7. Julius Margolis, 'The Demand for Urban Public Services', in Harvey Perloff and Lowdon Wingo (eds), *Issues in Urban Economics* (Baltimore, Johns Hopkins Press for Resources for the Future, 1968), pp. 527–64.

8. John Kain and Joe Persky, 'Alternatives to the Gilded Ghetto', *Public Interest*, No. 14 (Winter, 1969), 35–50; Anthony Downs, *Opening up the Suburbs: An Urban Strategy for America* (New Haven, Yale University Press, 1973).

9. Michael Danielson, *The Politics of Exclusion* (New York, Columbia University Press, 1976), p. 3.

10. Charlotte Fremon, 'The Occupational Patterns in Urban Employment Change, 1965–1967', Urban Institute Working Paper 113–32 (Washington, DC, 1970).

11. National Committee Against Discrimination in Housing, *Jobs and Housing* (New York, 1970).

12. Bennett Harrison, *Urban Economic Development: Suburbanization, Minority Opportunity and the Condition of the Central City* (Washington, DC, The Urban Institute, 1975), p. 100.

13. Danielson, *Politics of Exclusion*, p. 6.

14. Thomas Clark, *Blacks in Suburbs* (New Brunswick, Center for Urban Policy Research, Rutgers University, 1979).

15. Gary Orfield, *Must We Bus? Segregated Schools and National Policy* (Washington, DC, Brookings, 1978), pp. 15–27.

16. Roger Abrams, 'Not One Judge's Opinion: Morgan v. Hennigan and the Boston Schools', *Harvard Educational Review*, xxxxv, No. 1 (February 1975), 5–16.

17. Orfield, *Must We Bus?*, pp. 30–9.

18. *New York Times*, Friday, 16 April 1976, 'Supreme Court Rulings Awaited On Obligation of Suburbs in Solving Problems of Cities', and Wednesday, 21 April 1976, 'Justices Uphold Minority Housing in White Suburbs'; Irving Welfeld, 'The courts and desegregated housing: the meaning (if any) of the Gautreaux case', *Public Interest*, No. 44 (Summer 1976), 123–35.

19. Frederick Lazin, 'Federal Low-Income Housing Assistance Programs and Racial Segregation: Leased Public Housing', *Public Policy*, xxiv, No. 3 (Summer 1976), 337–60, esp. 358.

20. Irving Welfeld, a HUD official, called the Gautreaux remedy 'administrative and political insanity', but his predictions that it would clash with the objectives of the Section 8 programme proved incorrect; see Welfeld, 'The courts and desegregated housing: the meaning (if any) of the Gautreaux case', p. 132. For a description of the life of new Section 8 Chicago suburbanites two years later, see 'U.S.-Backed Chicago Test Offers Suburban Life to Ghetto Blacks', *New York Times*, Monday, 22 May 1978.

21. *New York Times*, 'Supreme Court Rulings Awaited on Obligation of Suburbs in Solving Problems of Cities', Friday, 16 April 1976.

22. Danielson, *Politics of Exclusion*, pp. 179, 351. The Hartford case is *City of Hartford v. Hills*, 1976.

23. Danielson, *Politics of Exclusion*, pp. 250–8.

24. Danielson, *Politics of Exclusion*, pp. 306–22, 325.

25. James Coleman, 'Response to Professors Pettigrew and Green', *Harvard Educational Review*, xxxxvi, No. 2 (May 1976), 217–24; esp. 224.

26. Thomas Pettigrew and Robert Green, 'School Desegregation in Large Cities: A Critique of the Coleman "White Flight" Thesis', *Harvard Educational Review*, xxxxvi, No. 1 (February 1976), 1–53; esp. 40–1.

27. Pettigrew and Green, 'Critique of Coleman', pp. 45–6.

28. Richard P. Burton, 'The Suburban Crisis and Industrial Manpower Communities: A Social Planning Proposal', Urban Institute Working Paper 86–116–54 (Washington, DC, 1971).

7   NEW FEDERALISM: FROM URBAN RENEWAL TO COMMUNITY DEVELOPMENT

1. Paul Peterson and J. David Greenstone, 'Racial Change and Citizen Participation: The Mobilization of Low-Income Communities through Community Action', in Robert Haveman (ed.), *A Decade of Federal Anti-Poverty Programs* (New York, Academic Press, 1977), pp. 241–78, esp. p. 242.

2. For the definitive description of the incorporation of blacks into city politics up to the New Deal era, studied in comparison with similar processes in British city politics since the Second World War, see Ira Katznelson, *Black Men, White Cities; Race, Politics and Migration in the United States 1900–1930 and Britain 1948–1968* (London, Institute of Race Relations; London and New York, Oxford University Press, 1973).

3. Frances Piven and Richard Cloward, *Regulating the Poor* (New York, Pantheon, 1971).

4. Peterson and Greenstone, 'Racial Change and Citizen Participation', pp. 242–56.

5. Peterson and Greenstone, 'Racial Change and Citizen Participation', pp. 257–76; John Donovan, *The Politics of Poverty*, 2nd edition (Indianapolis, Pegasus, 1973); Daniel Moynihan, *Maximum Feasible Misunderstanding* (New York, Free Press, 1969).

6. See Chapter 3 on the *Our Cities* report.

7. Mark Gelfand, *A Nation of Cities, The Federal Government and Urban America* (New York, Oxford University Press, 1975), pp. 246–63.

8. Gelfand, *Nation of Cities*, pp. 321–35.

9. Congressional Research Service, Library of Congress, for the Subcommittee on Housing and Urban Affairs of the Senate Committee on Banking, Housing and Urban Affairs, *The Central City Problem and Urban Renewal Policy* (Washington, DC, 1973), pp. 171–2. On the Wood task force, see Bernard Frieden and Marshall Kaplan, *The Politics of Neglect: Urban Aid from Model Cities to Revenue Sharing* (Cambridge, MIT Press, 1975), pp. 36–49. My treatment of Model Cities in this section is based in considerable part on an interview with Robert Wood, currently Henry Luce Professor of Government at Wesleyan University, conducted 3 April 1984. His candour, assistance and encouragement are gratefully acknowledged.

10. Subcommittee on Housing and Community Development, Committee on Banking, Currency and Housing, US House of Representatives, *Evolution of Role of the Federal Government in Housing and Community Development, A Chronology of Legislative and Selected Executive Actions, 1892–1974* (Washington, DC, 1975), p. 115.

11. Congressional Research Service, *Central City Problem and Urban Renewal*, p. 174. Details about the HUD task force and Johnson's intentions are from the Wood interview, 3 April 1984.

12. Congressional Research Service, *Central City Problem and Urban Renewal*, p. 175.

13. Frieden and Kaplan, *Politics of Neglect*, p. 73.

14. Congressional Research Service, *Central City Problem and Urban Renewal*, p. 173. For the classic exposition of the reform dilemma, described through a case-study of the War on Poverty community action programme, see Peter Marris and Martin Rein, *Dilemmas of Social Reform, Poverty and Community Action in the United States* (New York, Atherton, 1967).

15. Congressional Research Service, *Central City Problem and Urban Renewal*, pp. 197–207.

16. Wood interview, 3 April 1984; Royce Hanson, 'The Evolution of National Urban Policy, 1970–1980: Lessons from the Past', Background Paper for the Committee on National Urban Policy, National Research Council (Washington, DC, National Academy Press, 1982), pp. 4–5.

17. Alan Altschuler, *The City Planning Process, A Political Analysis* (Ithaca, Cornell University Press, 1965); Paul Davidoff, 'Advocacy and Pluralism in Planning', *Journal of the American Institute of Planners*, xxxi, No. 4 (November 1965), 331–8.

18. Wood interview, 3 April 1984; Frieden and Kaplan, *Politics of Neglect*, pp. 40–1.

19. Laurence Lynn, 'A Decade of Policy Developments in the Income-Maintenance System', in Haveman (ed.), *A Decade of Federal Antipoverty Programs*, pp. 55–117, esp. pp. 107–9.

20. Laurence Lynn, 'Policy Developments in Income Maintenance', pp. 108–9.

21. Henry Aaron, *Shelter and Subsidies*, pp. 30, 53–73.

22. *Housing and Community Development Chronology*, p. 145; Congressional Research Service, *Central City Problem and Urban Renewal*, pp. 251–2.

23. Laurence Lynn, 'Policy Developments in Income Maintenance', pp. 109–11; Henry Aaron, *Shelter and Subsidies*, pp. 167–73.

24. Congressional Research Service, *Central City Problem and Urban Renewal*, p. 253.

25. *Housing and Community Development Chronology*, pp. 183–4.

26. Laurence Lynn, 'Policy Developments in the Income Maintenance System', pp. 109–10; *Housing and Community Development Chronology*, pp. 190–1.

27. *Housing and Community Development Chronology*, pp. 201–4; Congressional Quarterly, *Urban America, Policies and Problems* (Washington, DC, Congressional Quarterly, 1978), appendix pp. 8–13; CDBG Training Advisory Committee, 'An Advocacy Guide to the Community Development Block Grant Program', *Clearinghouse Review*, National Clearinghouse for Legal Services, xii, No. 10 (January Supplement 1979), which is the best available history and discussion of community development.

28. Congressional Quarterly, *Urban America*, appendix pp. 8, 12–13.

29. Participants in the 1974 evaluation of federal poverty programmes after ten years in operation generally agreed that because of advances in participation by blacks and other low income groups, the War on Poverty should be considered a success. See Robert Haveman (ed.), *A Decade of Federal Antipoverty Programs* (New York, Academic Press, 1977).

30. 'Detroiters Confronting a Choice: New Jobs or Old Neighbourhoods', *New York Times*, Monday, 15 September 1980; 'Huge New G.M. Plant, Like Many, to Get Subsidies', *New York Times*, Wednesday, 25 February 1981; 'Detroit, G.M. and Court Act to Doom Neighborhood', *New York Times*, Sunday, 15 March 1981.

31. Norman Krumholz, Janice Cogger and John Linner, 'The Cleveland Policy Planning Report', *Journal of the American Institute of Planners*, xxxxi, No. 5 (September 1975), 298–304; and by the same authors: 'Make No Big Plans . . . Planning in Cleveland in the 1970s', in Robert Burchell and George Sternlieb (eds), *Planning Theory in the 1980s* (New Brunswick, Center for Urban Policy Research, 1978), pp. 29–40, esp. p. 36.

32. Ira Lowry, 'The Dismal Future of Central Cities', in Arthur Solomon (ed.), *The Prospective City* (Cambridge, MIT Press, 1980), pp. 161–203.

33. Royce Hanson, 'Evolution of National Urban Policy', p. 70.

8 GOODBYE TO METROPOLIS

1. Calvin Beale, 'Rural and Small Town Population Change, 1970–80', Economics and Statistics Service, US Department of Agriculture, Washington, DC, February, 1981; and a newspaper article on Beale's report: 'Rural Areas End Trend, Surpass Cities in Growth', *New York Times*, Tuesday, 3 March 1981. Beale reported on preliminary rather than final figures so his US total is slightly lower than the official figure eventually announced.

2. '36 New Metropolitan Regions Are Designated', *New York Times*, Monday, 30 November 1981; 1970 figures from Beale, 'Rural and Small Town Population Change, 1970–80' and from the 1970 Census. Beale's method differs from the official Census method in that he compared 1970 and 1980 population of metropolitan and

non-metropolitan counties based on designations of metropolitan or non-metropolitan status as of 1974. The Census method compares 1970 population of metropolitan and non-metropolitan counties according to 1970 designations with 1980 populations according to 1980 designations. See US Census Bureau, *1980 Census of Population, Supplementary Reports*, 'Standard Metropolitan Statistical Areas and Standard Consolidated Statistical Areas: 1980', October 1981. Puerto Rico's population is not included in any metropolitan, non-metropolitan or national totals.

3. Brian Berry, *Metropolitan Area Definition: A Re-evaluation of Concept and Statistical Practice*, Bureau of the Census Working Paper No. 28 (Washington, DC, 1968).

4. Jean Gottman, *Megalopolis, The Urbanized Northeastern Seaboard of the United States* (Cambridge, MIT Press, 1961), pp. 26–7.

5. Lewis Mumford, *The City in History* (New York, Harcourt, Brace and World, 1961), pp. 205–4, 525–8.

6. Among the more contrived attempts to explain the cessation of metropolitan concentration was Brian Berry's concept of 'counter-urbanization'; see his 'The Urban Problem', in American Assembly, *The Farm and the City: Rivals or Allies* (Englewood Cliffs, NJ, Prentice-Hall, 1980), pp. 36–59.

7. Berry, *Metropolitan Area Definition*, p. 19.

8. Harry Braverman, *Labor and Monopoly Capital, The Degradation of Work in the Twentieth Century* (New York, Monthly Review Press, 1975). I am grateful to Battista Borio and Evan Stark for much of the formative thinking about the diffuse economy. Battista Borio provided the current name for the new concept.

9. 'Census Finds More Blacks Living In Suburbs of Nation's Large Cities', *New York Times*, Sunday, 31 May 1981; 'Blacks Moving to Suburbs, But Significance Is Disputed', *New York Times*, Sunday, 15 August 1982.

10. 'Blacks Moving to Suburbs, But Significance Is Disputed', *New York Times*, Sunday, 15 August 1982.

11. William Wilson, *The Declining Significance of Race* (Chicago, University of Chicago Press, 1978).

12. 'Black Teen-agers' Jobless Rate Constant Despite U.S. Recovery', *New York Times*, Sunday, 11 July 1976; US Department of Labor, *Employment and Earnings*, xxx, No. 6 (June 1983), 25–7.

13. US Census Bureau, *Household and Family Characteristics: March 1981*, Current Population Reports, Series P-20, No. 371 (May 1982), p. 7.

14. *Housing and Community Development Chronology*, p. 185.

15. Kenneth Fox, 'Cities and City Governments in the Current Crisis', in Economics Education Project, *U.S. Capitalism in Crisis* (New York, Union for Radical Political Economics, 1978), pp. 174–81, esp. pp. 176–9; William Tabb, *The Long Default* (New York, Monthly Review Press, 1982), pp. 66–75. For a broad historical analysis of the crisis and the city's future prospects, see Matthew Edel, 'The New York City Crisis as Economic History', in Roger Alcaly and David Mermelstein (eds), *The Fiscal Crisis of American Cities* (New York, Random House, 1976), pp. 228–45.

16. New York *Daily News*, 30 October 1975.

17. Andrew Winnick, Judith Gregory and Jerry Mandina, 'The Financial Crisis in Cleveland', in Kenneth Fox, Mary Jo Hetzel, Thomas Riddell, Nancy Rose and Jerry Sazama (eds), *Crisis in the Public Sector* (New York, Monthly Review Press/Union for Radical Political Economics, 1981), pp. 112–33, esp. p. 119.

18. Kenneth Fox, 'Cities and City Governments in the Current Crisis', pp. 178–9; Roger Starr, 'Making New York Smaller', *New York Times*, magazine section, Sunday, 14 November 1976. An excellent case-study of the effects of the crisis on a working-class New York City neighbourhood is Ida Susser, *Norman Street, Poverty and Politics in an Urban Neighbourhood* (New York, Oxford University Press, 1982).

19. Congressional Quarterly, *Urban America, Policies and Problems* (Washington, DC,

Congressional Quarterly, 1978), pp. 19–22; 'Carter Urban Policy Seems Snarled in Political and Economic Demands', *New York Times*, Wednesday, 1 February 1978; 'Carter Is Reported to Approve a $2.6 Billion National Urban Policy', *New York Times*, Saturday, 25 March 1978.

20. Congressional Quarterly, *Urban America, Policies and Problems*, p. 1.

21. Department of Housing and Urban Development, *The President's 1978 National Urban Policy Report* (August 1978), pp. 11, 14.

22. *President's 1978 Urban Policy Report*, pp. 14–15, 29–31.

23. Wilbur Thompson, 'Toward a Strategy for Central City Depopulation', pp. 142–53; and F. Stevens Redburn and David Stephens, 'Choices for Older Metropolitan Regions', pp. 154–69; in Edward Hanten, Mark Kasoff and F. Stevens Redburn (eds.), *New Directions for the Mature Metropolis* (Cambridge, Mass., Schenkman, 1980).

24. 'New Mass Transit Data Rekindle Urban Issue', *New York Times*, Thursday, 31 March 1983.

25. Melvin M. Webber, 'The BART experience – what have we learned?', *Public Interest*, No. 45 (Autumn 1976), 79–108.

26. It is extremely instructive to observe how Robert Wood inverted his opinions about suburban political fragmentation between writing his first study, *Suburbia, Its People and their Politics* (Boston, Houghton Mifflin, 1958), and his contribution to the New York Metropolitan Region Study, *1400 Governments* (Cambridge, Mass., Harvard University Press, 1961). Also, Royce Hanson has drawn a conclusion similar to mine from his analysis of urban policy in the 1970s. Hanson confirms that consensus about metropolitan settlement has dissipated, but fails to emphasise that *policy* has the primary responsibility for debating and building a new consensus about community types and national settlement patterns; Royce Hanson, 'The Evolution of National Urban Policy 1970–1980: Lessons from the Past', Background Paper for the Committee on National Urban Policy, National Research Council (Washington, DC, National Academy Press, 1982), p. 75.

Suggestions for Further Reading

The urban affairs of the metropolitan era are no longer current, but they are too recent to be history. Historians are still determining which topics require intensive investigation. My emphasis on metropolitan settlement, and on the metropolitan orientation of policy, has been selective; it neglects a good deal that others would include, or even emphasise. I offer here a selection of materials that helped me shape my interpretation. It follows the order of the chapters, pointing out avenues for further exploration. I have also indicated topics for research. These reflect my own interests, but I encourage those who sympathise with the argument of the book to join in the search.

INTRODUCTION

Readers interested in theories and conceptualisations of population settlement should begin with three sources: the sociological tradition founded by the 'Chicago School' of Robert Park, Louis Wirth and Ernest Burgess in the 1920s, best introduced by Paul Hatt and Albert Reiss, Jr (eds), *Cities and Society, The Revised Reader in Urban Sociology* (New York, Free Press, 1957); the ecological approach, imaginatively presented in Leo Schnore's collection of his own essays, *The Urban Scene* (New York, Free Press, 1965); and a Marxist/Althusserian critique of both these approaches, Manuel Castells, *The Urban Question, A Marxist Approach* (London, Edward Arnold, 1977). On policy, in addition to Thomas Dye, *Understanding Public Policy*, third edition (Englewood Cliffs, NJ, Prentice-Hall, 1978), discussed in the text, I have relied on political economist Charles Lindblom's ideas concerning the use of social science analysis in policy controversy; see his *The Policy-Making Process*, second edition (Englewood Cliffs, NJ, Prentice-Hall, 1980). Lindblom has offered a new, extremely imaginative, proposal concerning the future of policy-making and policy's ability to shape the world in *Politics and Markets* (New York, Basic Books, 1977). Issues in need of further theorising and conceptualisation include the cultural origins of preferences among types of settlements, and concepts of policy and policy-making that stand apart from electoral, partisan and interest group politics.

1   SETTLING METROPOLITAN AMERICA

The origins of my emphasis on the metropolitan pattern of national population settlement in the 1940–80 period lie with the 'system of cities' approach to spatial organisation of population and economic activities. Two volumes of collected articles can provide an introduction: John Friedmann and William Alonso (eds), *Regional*

Development and Planning, A Reader (Cambridge, Mass., MIT Press, 1964), and Harvey Perloff and Lowdon Wingo, Jr (eds), *Issues in Urban Economics* (Baltimore, Johns Hopkins Press for Resources for the Future, 1968). Particularly useful are two articles by Brian J. L. Berry in the Friedmann and Alonso collection, 'Cities as Systems Within Systems of Cities' and 'City Size Distributions and Economic Development'; and two articles by Eric Lampard, 'The History of Cities in the Economically Advanced Areas', in the Friedmann and Alonso collection, and 'The Evolving System of Cities in the United States: Urbanization and Economic Development' in the Perloff and Wingo collection. The most pressing topic for research is the detailed processes by which industrial corporations made locational decisions about expanding existing facilities and building new ones. How did companies rationalise their decisions to shift to the suburbs beginning around 1900, and to emerging metropolitan areas outside the North-East–Great Lakes industrial heartland of the late nineteenth century?

2 SUBURBAN DEVELOPMENT AND THE MIDDLE CLASS

The germ of the argument about the suburbs and the middle class comes from Charles Levenstein, 'The Political Economy of Suburbanization: In Pursuit of a Class Analysis', *Review of Radical Political Economics*, XIII, No. 2 (Summer 1981), 23–31. As Levenstein's title suggests, a class analysis of suburbanisation does not exist yet; much research and analysis are needed. Ira Katznelson's *City Trenches, Urban Politics and the Patterning of Class in the United States* (New York, Pantheon, 1981), was important to the argument's elaboration. *City Trenches* is not about suburbs, but it is one of the few studies daring to contemplate that classes could form in communities rather than in workplaces. The portrayal of television as a medium of communication between suburban families and monopoly manufacturers in the development of a suburban, middle-class culture derives in considerable measure from pioneering work in advertising, media, culture and class consciousness by Stuart Ewen and Elizabeth Ewen: Stuart Ewen, *Captains of Consciousness, Advertising and the Social Roots of the Consumer Culture* (New York, McGraw-Hill, 1976), and Stuart Ewen and Elizabeth Ewen, *Channels of Desire, Mass Images and the Shaping of American Consciousness* (New York, McGraw-Hill, 1982).

Detailed analysis of suburban life is in abeyance at the moment. The sociologists have moved on to other interests and the historians are still pondering the questions they want to answer. The first histories of Levittown or Park Forest should appear within the next ten years. An interesting national study of suburbs that is primarily historical in method is Peter O. Muller, *Contemporary Suburban America* (Englewood Cliffs, NJ, Prentice-Hall, 1981).

3 SAVING THE CENTRAL CITY

The assertion that saving the central city was the objective defined for urban policy in the 1940s originates with Lloyd Rodwin's excellent comparative study of urban development and policy in five countries: *Nations and Cities, A Comparison of Strategies for Urban Growth* (Boston, Houghton Mifflin, 1970). The best history of federal policy up to the establishment of HUD in 1965 is Mark Gelfand, *A Nation of Cities, The Federal Government and Urban America, 1933–1965* (New York, Oxford University Press, 1975). John Mollenkopf presents an interesting 'politics of policy-making' analysis of urban policy from the New Deal to the community development era in *The Contested City* (Princeton, Princeton University Press, 1983). The most thought-provoking case-study of the beginnings of urban renewal in a city remains Robert Dahl's *Who Governs? Democracy and Power in American City* (New Haven, Yale University Press, 1961). The city is New Haven in the era of Mayor Richard Lee.

From the mid 1960s to the late 1970s it was fashionable to treat urban renewal as a crude programme that failed, doing much damage to blacks and poor people in the process. This is not likely to be the judgment of history. Central city redevelopment could probably have been done better, but the federal urban renewal programme should not be blamed for the shortfall. We need to know much more about the origins of the save the central city policy, about policy controversy in the 1940s, and about why Congress became so interested in large cities after slighting them during the Depression. The Keynesian revolution in economic policy-making is part of the answer, but we need a better understanding of Keynesian interest in cities.

4 CITY LIFE IN METROPOLITAN AREAS

The tone of the discussion of city life in the 1950s derives from my own memories, especially of New York City. After the riots, pessimistic accounts of the 1950s, such as Mills' *White Collar*, remained popular, but little survived to convey the serenity and comfort of city life. An interesting impressionistic comparison of city and suburban life in metropolitan New York around 1960 is Louis Schlivek, *Man in Metropolis* (Garden City, Doubleday, 1965), illustrated with hundreds of the author's excellent photographs.

One very important controversy about city life in the 1950s and early 1960s centred around Lewis Mumford's *The City in History, Its Origins, Its Transformations, and Its Prospects* (New York, Harcourt, Brace and World, 1961). This was Mumford's masterpiece, crowning a career that spanned forty years at that time. Mumford mobilised fifty centuries of history toward a condemnation of American metropolitan life. He crucified nineteenth-century industry and railroads, and twentieth-century automobiles, for destroying the city's ability to contain and nurture an urban culture. Mumford saw no practical course that could repair the damage. He offered planners no guidance and no basis for optimism. The end of the book left the reader staring over a precipice at the imminent demise of modern urbanism.

I have not discussed this aspect of Mumford's writings, or the controversy it aroused, in the text. Stimulating as the arguments were at the time, they had little lasting effect on planning and urban policy. Critics castigated Mumford's distaste for the automobile as a form of snobbery; he had failed to appreciate the freedom and pleasure cars brought to working-class life. The riots and the urban crisis displaced the automobile, and related physical planning questions such as placement of highways, traffic congestion, and containment of suburban sprawl, as central concerns. Jane Jacobs and Herbert Gans, the planning critics I have spotlighted, emerged as more relevant commentators than Mumford.

The problems of researching the pre-riot, pre-crisis city are enormous. No pre-conditions of turmoil and conflict were apparent in day-to-day city life in the 1950s, yet post-riot readers, knowing what followed, expect researchers to dig deep and unearth them. An excellent case-study of Washington Heights–Inwood in northern Manhattan, New York City, is contained within Ira Katznelson's *City Trenches, Urban Politics and the Patterning of Class in the United States* (New York, Pantheon, 1981). Katznelson's analysis of social and political change in the neighbourhood from the 1950s to the 1970s is rich, complex and thoughtful. Because he conceptualises the social and political arena in terms of New York City, and not the entire metropolitan area, city and suburbs together, however, suburban migration, the dynamism of suburban growth in contrast to the city's stagnation and decline in the 1950s and 1960s, and the aspects of black demands and violence that were reactions to suburban development, do not enter into the discussion.

I have argued that the riots and the urban crisis cannot be properly understood as national phenomena apart from the suburban, middle-class revolution that preceded them. I feel the same applies to studies of individual cities and I hope researchers will begin to include the suburbs in more prominent ways, on the assumption that the metropolitan area is the 'true' city, not just the territory within the central city's political boundaries.

5   THE RIOTS OF THE 1960s

Twenty years later, the riots are still too hot to handle. Consider recent writing on Detroit. Two major books appeared in the 1970s on 'revolutionary' trends and events in Detroit, yet neither was about the 1967 riot. Rather they concerned a radical black movement arising in the auto factories in the early 1970s, involving in one stage an organisation called the League of Revolutionary Black Workers. While both books, *Detroit: I Do Mind Dying, A Study in Urban Revolution*, by Dan Georgakas and Marvin Surkin (New York, St. Martin's Press, 1975), and *Class, Race, and Worker Insurgency, The League of Revolutionary Black Workers*, by James Geschwender (Cambridge, Cambridge University Press, 1977), credit the 1967 riot for making the struggle of the early 1970s possible, they leave readers with the impression that the movement culminating in the formation of the League was more significant for the future of Detroit than the 'insurrection' (Geschwender's term) or 'Great Rebellion' (Georgakas and Surkin's term) of 1967.

Another example is William Wilson's *The Declining Significance of Race, Blacks and Changing American Institutions* (Chicago, University of Chicago Press, 1978), one of the most intelligent analyses of the changing status of black people in the post-war period. Wilson devotes only two pages to the riots, explaining them primarily as an effort by poor, central city 'ghetto' blacks to gain more attention from the leaders of the civil rights movement and their middle-class black and white supporters. 'If nothing else,' Wilson comments, 'the ghetto revolts of the late 1960s helped to shift the philosophy of the black protest movement' (p. 138), and he cites Martin Luther King's heightened concern for the 'human rights' of 'the black underclass' along with the civil rights of all black people. It is doubtful that this is Wilson's primary assessment of the riots and their significance; rather, as with the studies of Detroit, he has sidestepped the issue.

Perhaps future research and writing on the riots will conclude that they were not of major significance for long-term social development. I have argued above that migration out of the rural South and central city rioting are the most important forms of black participation in post-war politics and social change. We know a great deal about the leaders of the civil rights movement and the movement's achievements. We need to learn much, much more about migration in the 1940s and 1950s, and about the rioting in the 1960s, in terms of their meaning for people who participated and their impact on central cities and metropolitan areas.

6   URBAN CRISIS

As the early 1970s recede into the past, the urban crisis will remain of interest only as an incident in the history of federal policy-making. In this guise, it is well worth studying. I have provided only the outlines and prominent features of the urban crisis controversy. Particularly deserving of detailed investigation is the role of Representative Henry Reuss of Wisconsin and other members of the Subcommittee on Urban Affairs of the

Joint Economic Committee of Congress. Reuss and his colleagues fashioned the subcommittee's hearings into a forum where social researchers and influential policy participants could express their views and findings. Published volumes of the subcommittee's hearings were essential reading for everyone involved in debating the urban crisis.

The urban crisis controversy was the first major social policy debate in which 'think tanks', policy research institutes, played a major role: the Urban Institute of Washington, DC, founded by HUD and funded primarily by HUD and the Ford Foundation; the Brookings Institution, also of Washington, DC, founded independently in the 1920s but heavily supported by federal agencies in the 1970s; the RAND Corporation of Santa Monica, California and New York, originally founded by the US Air Force to do military research, and others. Harold Orlans, *The Nonprofit Research Institute, Its Origin, Operation, Problems, and Prospects* (New York, McGraw-Hill, 1972), is an excellent general introduction to think tanks. Studies of their participation in urban policy are much needed.

7   NEW FEDERALISM: FROM URBAN RENEWAL TO COMMUNITY DEVELOPMENT

Analysis of the Nixon administration and the Republican philosophy of new federalism lingers under the cloud of partisan warfare. Social scientists and historians of a liberal or Democratic persuasion are reluctant to credit Nixon and the new federalists; they fear their comrades will banish them from the liberal Democratic fold. Equally undesirable has been the behaviour of those who personally favour the new philosophy, for they have attempted to make it the foundation of a 'new conservatism' and to construct a conservative research and policy establishment to rival the older liberal Democratic institutes and journals. Most prominent among the new conservative efforts have been the journal *The Public Interest*, and the American Enterprise Institute, a conservative think tank.

A possible harbinger of better times is Royce Hanson's 'The Evolution of National Urban Policy, 1970–1980: Lessons from the Past', Background Paper for the Committee on National Urban Policy, National Research Council (Washington, National Academy Press, 1982). Unfortunately the committee's formal statement on future policy, Royce Hanson (ed.), *Rethinking Urban Policy, Urban Development in an Advanced Economy* (Washington, National Academy Press, 1983), makes little use of Hanson's insights about Nixon and about the achievements of the 1970s. Instead the committee sketches an unimaginative strategy for linking national urban policy to anticipated industrial development and job expansion. They apparently rejected at a preliminary stage policies based on the new federalist, community development orientation initiated by Nixon, or perhaps never seriously contemplated them at all. The Committee's proposed programmes are unmistakably Democratic in character and do nothing to raise policy debate in the mid 1980s above the level of partisan wrangling.

An interesting collection of articles on policy in the Johnson–Nixon–Ford–Carter period is Dale R. Marshall, (ed.), *Urban Policy-Making* (Beverly Hills, Sage, 1979). An excellent place to begin contemplating the efforts of planners to respond to the changes of the 1970s is Robert Burchell and George Sternlieb (eds), *Planning Theory in the 1980s, A Search for Future Directions* (New Brunswick, Center for Urban Policy Research, 1978). No author in this collection espouses a clearly delineated new theory, but most of them agree that urban planning underwent a theoretical crisis in the late 1960s and early 1970s and therefore cannot simply resuscitate its old values and theories. As with the liberal policy analysts, no contributor credits Nixon, new federalism and community development revenue sharing (block grants) for abetting progress.

8   GOODBYE TO METROPOLIS

As yet no one has presented a 'post-metropolitan' conceptualisation of the national settlement pattern. It is too soon to perceive the type of community that will supplant the metropolis as the focus of settlement, migration and economic and social structure. Two books that make painfully clear the stagnation of metropolitan settlement are Arthur Solomon (ed.), *The Prospective City, Economic, Population, Energy, and Environmental Developments* (Cambridge, Mass., MIT Press, 1980), and Edward Hanten, Mark Kasoff, and F. Stevens Redburn (eds), *New Directions for the Mature Metropolis, Policies and Strategies for Change* (Cambridge, Mass., Schenkman Publishing Co., 1980). Of all the authors in the two collections, only Wilbur Thompson, the leading expert on metropolitan economics in the 1960s, even begins to suggest that the metropolitan area is in process of being supplanted by some other type of urban community. Thompson's wry title, 'Toward a Strategy for Central City Depopulation' (in Hanten *et al.*, *New Directions*), implies that he did not think his readers were in the proper frame of mind to contemplate a non-metropolitan future.

The most pressing research need is for cultural analysis of the origins of community forms. The lack is most apparent in the Solomon collection, *The Prospective City*, where almost all the authors are economists. None of them seems able to imagine that anything other than microeconomic opportunities and costs might shape communities and the national settlement pattern. Although they discuss the possibility that federal policy and expenditures might alter settlement, no author concludes that a strong federal initiative is likely in the near future. Most of the discussion in the volume suggests that federal settlement initiatives are a mistake because the cost effectiveness per dollar of federal expenditure is far too small. The massed microforces of a 2 trillion dollar economy are too immense to be affected by a few billion federal dollars, however imaginatively inserted.

The idea that cultural change can level microeconomic mountains in one place, and raise up new ones in another, is not unacceptable to economists, but they do not consider cultural analysis their responsibility. Yet anthropologists and historians, the social scientists concerned with culture, are rarely invited to testify before Congressional committees or to sit on prestigious urban policy councils.

Many historians believe direct involvement in policy controversy compromises one's professional objectivity. This view recklessly disregards the indispensable role historians play in foreign policy. Without historians to investigate what was actually done and said by nations, leaders and diplomats in the past, no secretary of state, foreign minister or international expert would fear any risk in deceiving the media and the public in the present. More importantly, understanding other nations today depends in very large part on understanding their history. Historians participate in foreign policy by writing books and articles, but they know their writing will be read. 'Domestic' historians, for the most part, have not thought of themselves as participants in policy-making. If urban policy suffers from insufficient historical analysis, it is historians who are partly to blame. This deficiency can be remedied, however. For a discussion of the current status of urban historiography that emphasises the need for more interest in policy, see Michael Ebner, 'Urban History: Retrospect and Prospect', *Journal of American History*, LXVIII, No. 1 (June 1981), 69–84.

Index